EXPERIENTIAL PSYCHOTHERAPY WITHIN FAMILIES

Experiential Psychotherapy Within Families

by
WALTER KEMPLER, M.D.

BRUNNER/MAZEL, *Publishers* • New York

Library of Congress Cataloging in Publication Data

Kempler, Walter.
    Experiential psychotherapy within families.

    Bibliography: p.
    1. Family psychotherapy.   I. Title.
[DNLM: 1. Family therapy. WM 430.5.F2 K32e]
RC488.5.K45   616.89'156   81-7664
ISBN 0-87630-267-3   AACR2

Published by
BRUNNER/MAZEL, INC.
19 Union Square West
New York, New York 10003

MANUFACTURED IN THE UNITED STATES OF AMERICA

To all of the families I've been a part of:
patient and personal; past and present.
And especially to my personal here
and now family who provided
the fertile soil in which this
volume grew.

Contents

Acknowledgments

Although countless people have contributed and assisted in the production of this work, all of whose efforts I deeply value, I wish particularly to express my appreciation to Sister Mary Magdalen Wieck, for her gentle yet persistent press to produce and her capable, practical assistance, and to Janet Tricamo, for her sincere and sensible efforts to see that the manuscript reached fruition: Mary and Janet, I thank you.

EXPERIENTIAL PSYCHOTHERAPY
WITHIN FAMILIES

SECTION I

1

An Overview

What is Psychotherapy Within Families?

Psychotherapy within the family is a plenary psychotherapeutic approach for distressed individuals which takes place in the framework of their existing family. The family approach is appreciated by most individuals who are committed to family, whether by dependency, such as children, or by inclination, such as adults who identify their distress as rooted in the intimate family relationship. For therapists who have tried family therapy and felt its success, it becomes a preferred mode, broadly applicable.

Therapy with couples has frequently been explored separately from family therapy in which children are included. This reflects the therapist's preference for treating either couples or entire families rather than the need for a significant modification of the treatment model per se. The presence of children may modify the language used on occasion, but then, so does the presence of some adults. Expectations from children are adapted, hopefully with some accuracy, to their capabilities. But again, expectations vary also with adults. This treatment approach operates equally well with couples or with families including children, and can work equally well with those labeled schizophrenic, neurotic, character

5

disorders, employers, employees, foreign born, natives and therapists. In other words, any group of people—familial, social, industrial—dedicated to a common endeavor, can be considered suitable subjects for experiential psychotherapy within their "family."

→ This approach considers the family scene as a most valuable and appropriate site for therapeutic interaction. The entire family is brought in and worked with in the same room at the same time. The potentials of each member are seen and utilized to assist in the modification and/or understanding of every other member's behavior in the family. More ← specifically, when one child is named the problem, all the children are brought in. When one child is identified as a problem in a family, it is unlikely that the other children are not in some way caught up in the web of interaction that painfully laces the identified problem child. If there are two parents in the home, they too must be brought in. The grandmother and uncle or anyone living in the household and functioning as a part of it might also be included. All this is predicated on the "problem" being identified in one or more children.

When parents or couples conceive of their difficulty as lying between themselves only, children are excluded. However, should the children, if there are any, become the center of discussion, their presence is preferred. A colleague recently consulted me about a depressed, martyred mother who was seen in individual therapy with little success. Her husband drank, two children were in speech therapy clinics with lisps, another child was failing school, and a fourth son was in individual therapy elsewhere for hyperactive-destructive behavior. Dramatic and gratifying results were evidenced in a few months when members of the family were treated together. Such experiences are commonplace in psychotherapy within the family.

→ In the setting of the family, the greatest personal impacts occur. From infancy it is our intimates, our loved ones, who have the greatest influence on our lives. The utilization of a patient's current intimates then, coupled with an intimate commitment of the therapist, can and does have a powerful influence towards altering behavior. The family frame is utilized also in the recognition that the emotional atmosphere in which any individual lives, that is, the effect on him of the behavior of the intimates around him, is crucial to the maintenance and/or alteration of an individual's own behavior. Donne's famous line "No man is an island" can find no more dramatic proof than in the field of human behavior. For those with families, individual therapy is an unnecessarily difficult task for both the therapist and the individual. Family members can be the most powerful allies we can find. Often they are unwitting enemies to the further growth of a loved one. Yet, their inclusion in the treatment program is alone frequently sufficient to change this status, while their exclusion from it offers them, too often, an opportunity to distance themselves from their loved ones and, even worse, to create unnecessary frictions and suspicions.

In families, one particular member may fail to fit into an established pattern and object to it. He is, in essence, saying "ouch." If all the other members agree, this first member may be labeled as sick and the objection labeled as symptom. A boy raised in such a family may never have learned how to express his objections or, if he does, he may be unwittingly ignored. In family therapy it becomes possible to change dramatically even significantly disturbed behavior merely by encouraging or offering family members the opportunity for a different perspective or awareness. In individual therapy the tendency is to work with the individual identified as the patient, to assist the individual, in effect, to adapt to what may well be a most noxious environment. By insisting that the entire family come in, it is implied that the prior labeling of the problem by the patient or the family will be scrutinized. This can be, and often is, in itself therapeutic.

In this process of reorienting ourselves regarding the nature of human problems as they are shaped within the frameworks of families, it is important that we do not fall into the common error of blaming a new monster. By this I mean the tendency to exonerate the children and consider the parents malevolent. In this family approach, no one individual is to blame. It is the patterns of behavior that must be altered in order to transform the family environment from one in which one or more persons suffer to the emotional sanctuary and resource that the family should be.

What is Experiential Psychotherapy Within Families?

Experiences are the essential phenomena of existence. Experiences in which we interact with other people, called encounters, are the most powerful of all experiences for the development of skills which we can use to cope with future experiences. The encounters which we have within our families, past and current, are the most significant in generating and influencing our capabilities. The development of properly functioning individuals is the goal of experiential psychotherapy within the family. The term experiential is used to describe this approach wherein the working session itself is used as a laboratory in which we have new experiences. It is not a "talking about" therapy but rather an action therapy. By working within the framework of the current family, by examining the nature of new encounters during the therapy session, and with the full participation of the therapist as a person within the group, we shape the essential forces for attaining the goal.

Beyond these principles, the therapy is shaped by the myriad nuances of each personality, including that of the therapist, impinging on each moment of the encounters in the session. For these moments there are no principles or theories; there are only people. The important things are who we are to each other and what we do with each other. The chief complaints of those being treated are all essentially the same: "Ouch, I am not getting what I want and it hurts." Beyond this, however, every pattern of painful interlocking behavior is unique. How people fail to say, search and strive effectively for what they want, how they find and collaborate with others in this failure, is the unique challenge of each therapeutic hour, during which the therapist, by example, also strives to get what he or she wants from these people—their individual and familial effective, integrated behavior.

Experiential psychotherapy is an ahistoric approach. It is predicated on the assumption that in this moment of existence each individual is a unique composite of his entire past and that the aspect or facet which is most pertinent to the current moment will emerge, and, as when looking into a diamond, the person's entire past history will gleam through. Fundamental to this approach is a belief in the vital importance of the immediate, the present, not in order to exclude a larger perspective but to establish a central point to which a larger perspective can be readily related.

This approach is an experiential or phenomenological one, characterized by exploration, experiment and spontaneity. By spontaneity, I mean allowing subsurface material to emerge whenever possible from myself and the people I sit with. It means encouraging an atmosphere in which the underlying flow of affect towards or away from each other is welcomed as a part of our verbal exchange. I encourage this atmosphere by doing it, being it, and sometimes by exploring verbally my difficulty in doing it—not by talking about (broadcasting or announcing) this desired atmosphere. In exploring and experimenting, no topic is tabu; we can toy with it, tease it apart, or "try it on for size." However, spontaneity is not a license for irrelevant or abstract discussion, no matter how tempting. In the experiential approach such behavior on the part of the therapist or the patient would be considered encounter-diminishing. The approach is predicated on the assumption that, in this room, within the accepted setting, the family members and the therapist have needs which will emerge. These needs may emerge as thoughts fully or partially expressed, feelings subtly indicated or vehemently vented, changes of posture, gesticulations, or perhaps even as fantasies which develop in the mind of the individual and which may or may not be shared with the group.

To the expression of these needs, adequate, or more likely, halting reactions occur: comfort, antagonism, worry, detachment, horror, disgust, resentment, indifference, pleasure, and so on. Sensitivity to these evidences of human interaction is encouraged, and attention is directed to the use to which awareness of them is put. This applies to the therapist and patient alike.

This approach, then, involves a vitally experienced exposition of ourselves in relation to others: how we experience them, what we want from them, how we go about getting what we want from them, and finally, what we do as a result of succeeding or failing in our efforts.

Being and doing are focal points; talking about behavior and exploring the "why" of behavior are usually obstacles to growth. I say "usually" since sometimes I find it necessary to "talk about," which I consider a "leavening agent" or a preamble, not to be confused with or mistaken for the therapeutic impact. In the past, some of us thought of the "talking about" as the therapy and the "working through," that is, the adaptive behavior changes, as something to be left for the patient to work out on his or her own. Not so in experiential family therapy; here the office is the laboratory in which the work is done. The learning is in the experience the family and the therapist have together.

My aim is to utilize family sessions as a meaningful experience and to encourage the participants to engage themselves likewise, not as spectators or aloof commentators, but as vitally concerned combatants. The process still involves pointing out and ferreting out resistances, as traditionally formulated; however, the orientation here considers the patients as resisting awareness of themselves and involvement in *the current moment.*

I am interested primarily in the what and how of behavior; my concern with the verbal content is almost exclusively in this perspective. The actual verbal content or subject matter of a group session may be compared to the launching rocket: something to be jettisoned as soon as possible in favor of the free flight of self-awareness and self-expression, the direct expression of one's self in the atmosphere of another. Such experience is generally intense, something not all people can readily accept. Sometimes it becomes necessary to dilute the intensity by temporarily returning our attention to verbalizations, or better still, if possible, to explore the pain of such an experience. An exploration of our differences, our differences in perceptions of others, then takes place not in introspective isolation but rather in an atmosphere of human, familial and immediate concern, which makes a crucial contribution to progress in therapy.

In terms of the familiar concept of transference, experiential psychotherapy within the family does not foster regressive phenomena in relation to the therapist, only to have the patient be confronted at some later "suitable" time with the reality of who and what the therapist is as distinguished from the images projected upon him/her. Experiential psychotherapy presents a constant exposure of the transference phenomenon whenever experienced in the fabrication of a stylized or stereotypic image labeled "therapist." "I am whatever I happen to be" is, of course, an oversimplification, but it suggests a rough approximation with a status I think essential to this therapy. The family group not only has the opportunity to know this, but should any of them at any point confuse my identity with, for instance, a projection of a parent as that parent occurred to them earlier in life, this would become the focus of my attention. Members of the group have the same privilege of offering, or insisting upon, what they feel is a more accurate personal image. In this atmosphere the therapist often feels most keenly the therapeutic aspects of the experience. By being as nearly as possible a total person, rather than playing the role of therapist, I help create an atmosphere which encourages all members to participate more fully as total personalities.

In this therapy, as the therapist I laugh and cry, I rage and sometimes even outrage. I sometimes do things usually assigned to those called patients. In an initial demonstration session, for example, I said vehemently to a wife who droned on morosely about her 20 years with ulcerative colitis, "You make me sick. I feel that I'll vomit if you continue. Be quiet! I don't want to hear any more of this. I hate the way you use your colon to destroy yourself and everyone around you. I refuse to let you do this to me. Be quiet, if that is all you can say." I actually felt disgusted, I looked disgusted. I couldn't stomach this woman, and I told her so. I didn't want to drive her away, and I told her so. However, I felt overwhelmed by her colonic expression and had to fight this. When I discussed this session afterwards with colleagues who had witnessed the session, they assumed that this woman would not return. She not only returned, but she had dramatically improved. She took heart from my expression. I had dared to challenge the power of this vengeful colon. Gradually she took back the power she had relinquished to her colon. At the moment I'd reacted in that initial session, I wasn't thinking that I was speaking to her colon. I was aware. I acted.

With another family, I had just completed an exciting and moving exchange with the wife. My attention then turned to her husband. I wanted him with us. The ensuing dialogue went as follows:

Therapist: Where are you?

He: I don't know (*pause*) I was thinking of something else (*pause*) I don't understand what is going on. I guess that's it (*pause*) partly thinking what I had to do today.

He was always inarticulate, always speaking haltingly and tentatively. His eyes blinked nervously as if he were being buffeted. I had mentioned this before. On past occasions I had confronted him with his inarticulateness and his blinking, but we had made no progress with it. It seemed that I had tried everything I knew to no avail.

Th: Damn that makes me angry. You're a clod. That's the word I want to buffet you with. Damn you. So insensitive. No wonder you've got problems in your marriage. (*then, cooling down enough to make an "I" statement instead of the "you" accusations, I continued*) I want you to hear; I want you to join in; I want you to at least acknowledge our presence some way other than leaving. At best, I'd want you to appreciate us in what happened, at worst, to tell us you don't like us for being inane; but not just to abandon us.

He: (*thoughtful*) Earlier I was aware of something like envy (*pause*) resentment (*pause*) I don't know.

Th: (*Still angry*) You never know. That's your standard answer. Now *I* don't know. I don't know what the hell to do with you to get in touch with you.

He: I'm sorry. (*pause*) I always say I'm sorry. I guess I'm sorry. I was envious. (*pause*) I felt angry 'cause I was envious.

He was trying to be with me now, and I wanted to try harder myself. I decided to try clarifying and/or intensifying his statement:

Th: Try on: "I long to be close to both of you but I never learned how."

I felt my own sadness when I said that and knew I was on target— or else I would not have been so angry with him. His tears were confirmation as he choked up trying to say the sentence.

Th: You don't have to, but I wish you could talk to us now.
He: I can't. It's too sad.
Th: It?
He: I'm too sad every time I think of it.
Th: It?
He: The sentence . . .
Th: Then try to include all the words "I'm so sad when I think of how I long to be close and can't because I never learned."

I kept wanting to return to this key phrase and yet I did not want my urging to become more central for him than his experiencing his longing. He sat thoughtfully, still tearing and saying nothing. Several minutes passed.

Th: I'm suddenly aware of my own difficulty in speaking about longing. I could debate with you more easily than I can speak of feeling the longing to be close. I realize I still haven't spoken of mine and can only hesitantly speak about yours. (*I began to cry. He was now trying harder to look at me through his tears. I found myself smiling through my tears.*) This feels better than debating or idly chatting but it sure is sad. (*"It," I thought. How clever.*) I feel closer to you in our sadness. (*He nodded, still unable to speak.*)
He: (*Finally*) I can do it with my car—feeling close by racing people. . . . I'm so safe that way. I can't just be close.
Th: (*I seemed finished with me for the moment and was free to turn*

once again to him. I offered the sentence again—modified.) "I long to be close but never learned how, but now I'm learning finally."

He began to cry more heavily as he nodded his head and turned inward again, looking down. His wife reached out warmly, "This reminds me of the time that you . . ." I interrupted her, "Leave him alone now. You can talk to him later." She grasped, or at least readily accepted, my command. I wanted him to be wherever he was with his feelings, not diverted to some other time and place. Her comment sounded like an "aha" announcement and I felt no compunction to honor it. She could keep it to and for herself.

I left them and was visiting my father, fluttering through historical scenes like a hummingbird. His lovingly tousling my hair—the only times he ever touched me that I could recall. His angrily shouting at me. His intellectual lectures to teach me something. I became painfully aware of his absent touch and never being spoken to affectionately by him. He never told me he loved me or even that he liked me. I recalled the surprise I once felt when I overheard him admiring me to one of his friends. I am sad. Of course I long.

I came back to our session and was aware of this couple once again. They were both looking at me. I shared my thoughts. Then he related clearly, articulately his own longings, recalling, smiling through his fresh tears, his father teaching him to drive, the only closeness he knew with his father. To intensify his experience, I suggested that he envision his father. He couldn't. He just cried. "Tell him," I suggested, "how you longed to be close to him but just didn't know how because you never learned." After long pause, he replied: "I used to feel angry and frustrated. I realize now he never learned either."

He was integrating and I was pleased. I became vacant and we all sat silently, alone and close.

Action is an essential characteristic of this approach. Expanding awareness is a small, necessary, nuclear action, but without further development treatment becomes a hollow social game. Awareness is not enough. Words are not enough. If an inefficient behavior is exposed and acknowledged, then failure to utilize this awareness may become the focus of attention. Excuses, explanations, understanding and analysis are sops which are no substitute for altering unsatisfactory behavior. Sarcasm, crying, helplessness, etc., ad infinitum are still not substitutes for modifying behavior. Debating about whether action should be conscious, willful and effortful versus a "natural" free-flowing effortless modification of behavior is also no substitute. At every moment we are obliged to accept responsibility for our non-behavior as well as our behavior.

"I want to change but I can't" is a frequent response I hear in therapy—as though the patient were identifying with the first "I" and denying any alliance with the second. It is essential in the integrating process that the individual identify with each aspect of his person. One way of doing this is for the individual to change this sentence to "I (one part of me) want to change but I (another part of me) won't." Once we have established an identity with the second part, the person can now in various ways attempt to identify with this "I won't" part of himself. It is necessary to accept responsibility for all parts of our person and not to pretend to be victimized by some vague, all powerful monster within us. Psychodrama techniques, or projection techniques if you will, are helpful means for assisting a person in identifying with such parts of himself. Suggestions by the therapist who can recognize and restructure these statements in this manner serve as powerful tools in assisting the patient to acknowledge these detached parts of self. Part of the task is meeting with vigor the person's objections to acknowledging detached parts of his own being as really belonging to himself.

I am paid to manipulate. I am commissioned to relieve my client of his inquisitors. I am grateful that I am not commanded to succeed. I am not even required to give a guarantee. This permits me to work more effectively. Sometimes I think to myself that all that is required of me in therapy is to be whoever I happen to be at the moment. In a sense I believe this to be true. Sometimes I say to myself that all I am trying to do in therapy is to expand awareness—to improve awareness of who we are to each other, or perhaps expand awareness of one's self. At the moment that I think this, or perhaps say it in therapy, I mean it. I believe at that moment that all I can hope to achieve is perhaps an awareness of our differences—at that moment. But somehow, underlying this I must acknowledge that my goal, never to be abandoned, is to fulfill my manipulating commission. To do this, I must be effective. To be effective, I must have an impact. For this, I must be heard emotionally, not merely audibly. To work with the entire family whenever possible, to focus my attention on the behavior shown in our encounter, and to respond as richly and fully as I can as a participant—this is how I conduct experiential psychotherapy in families to achieve the therapeutic goal.

The Special Values and Advantages of Experiential Psychotherapy Within Families

The advantages of psychotherapy in the family frame accrue to both patient and therapist. For patient-families, the briefer course of therapy, compared to other modes, and the durability of improvements are the most obvious benefits. For the therapist, family therapy is exciting, interesting, and with this experiential approach, particularly fulfilling.

The family approach shortens the course in many ways. First of all, the ever-present sources of intrafamily irritations serve as a constant stimulus to work. The atmosphere is less conducive to dawdling or ruminating vaguely about inconsequential and nonrelevant material. Secondly, it precipitates active therapy from the very first moment of the interview. In individual and group therapy, a period of getting acquainted is required, during which time the social facades are gradually let down— always of course by the patient first. In family therapy, there is far less need to get acquainted with the therapist before beginning the real work of therapy. The presence of family members with whom one is in open conflict and from whom one has needs that must be fulfilled provides a more natural and less circuitous avenue for fruitful engagement. Artificial social behavior is impeded from the outset by the structure of therapy itself. Usually the children are the first to make good use of this atmosphere, the parents are next, and all too often, unfortunately, the therapist is last. The experiential approach encourages the therapist to compete for first place.

It is with one's own intimates that people must ultimately learn to cope —or refuse to cope. Why, then, should patients spend years examining their responses to and with an alien therapist on his emotionally foreign soil? Why not keep the meaningful emotional experiments as close at hand as possible? Why not make the office appointment a working laboratory rather than a dispassionate, often indifferent, classroom? The task of psychotherapy is simplified if all benevolently and malevolently clinging hands are available at once. Aid may then come from many quarters—a spouse, a child, a parent. The power of each family member becomes available to help the therapist alter behavior.

On one occasion, a mother called for assistance, identifying her 14-year-old daughter as the problem. There were two younger sisters, ages 12 and 10, in addition to a 3-year-old boy in the family. I invited the mother to bring her husband and all four children in for the initial evaluation. The mother reluctantly agreed to bring the other daughters and her husband, but desperately tried to exclude the 3-year-old son. I insisted and, short of an ultimatum from her, decided to hold my position. She finally consented. An attractive family of six came to the office, sat down, and looked at me uncertainly. This lasted only a brief moment as the 3-year-old boy got out of his chair and began wandering around the room, knocking down ashtrays and coffee tables. All eyes focused on him, but no one said a word. After a while the three older girls alternately tried whispering to the young lad to sit down. It was all to no avail. He finally moved to the doorway and kept opening and slamming the door. After what seemed like hours, but in reality was about 10 minutes, the 14-year-old, so-called problem child turned to me and, pointing to her parents, angrily burst out, "It's like this all the time at home. They never take over." The mother looked at us, smiling triumphantly, and said, "There is our problem, Doctor. She has such a low threshold." I looked at her in astonishment and replied, "It is higher than mine." Therapy had begun.

This approach identifies the patient as the family rather than any single member in it. Including the entire family in the sessions circumvents many objections by family members to my initiating a probing search into what seems to me to be the actual difficulty within the family. In one family, the father, a policeman, brought in his "delinquent" son, identifying the boy as the patient. The essence of the father's attitude toward his son was: "I don't want you to be a delinquent and I try to prevent it by showing you criminals so you can see what they are and how they have become so, and by insisting you do not break rules, but overlooking it when you do." When this attitude was examined in the family sessions, all family members assisted in deterring this delinquent-provoking behavior. Had I seen the boy alone, with the family continuing to identify the problem as solely that of the son's behavior, this hidden domestic pressure would have been a tremendous force in thwarting any efforts the boy and I could make by ourselves. Had the father been identified or confronted as the patient, I am certain he would have immediately discontinued treatment.

When one member of the family begins to modify self-defeating behavior, often another family member, fearful of change, automatically tends to resist the change. Should this happen during the course of our interviews, it immediately commands our attention. In individual therapy, such activities often go unnoticed by the patient and, consequently, also by the therapist.

Another way in which working with families favorably affects the course of psychotherapy is in the empathic response. To witness another member of the family exposing, for instance, some fear or anxiety, rather than exhibiting a defensive pose of bravado, usually elicits a new response from the observer. The others suddenly see through the defensiveness and respond with compassion and understanding as they feel less threatened. Another important contribution is the developing awareness by momentarily silent members that they are not the sole cause of each other's problems. As projections are lifted off spouses and children, all members have greater freedom to seek new ways of responding in order to resist and prevent entangling, interlocking psychopathological activity.

Family members have the effect of both serving as unique stimuli to each other and responding uniquely to each other. Ultimately, comprehension of themselves in relation to each other in their intimate lives is an essential part of the goal. It is indeed a short cut to delve into these relationships from the outset, rather than first exploring one's self in relation to a therapist, and then returning to the family later for the necessary critical confrontations.

Durability of improvements is insured as distressing family patterns are disrupted. Instead of one, there are now many pulling away from distressing patterns, making it difficult, if not impossible, for one member to bring the entire family back into an orbit of painful interaction. For instance, a mother, who constantly brought her family into a painful, passive submission with threats of suicide, could no longer use that mode of behavior once the entire family witnessed the therapist's active confrontation of this manipulative and self-defeating behavior. The husband in this case reflected the entire family's response: "What fools we have been; we thought feeling sorry for her was being loving, but I now realize our behavior played into it. What a relief." He followed this with an active tirade towards his wife that he had been accumulating for years, and the entire family felt better, including the wife. In a subsequent session, after finding out she really could not return successfully to that destructive behavior and, furthermore, didn't need to, she expressed her gratitude to all of us.

Advantages to patients from the experiential character of this particular approach extend well beyond the aforementioned practical considerations inherent in working with families. This approach is ahistoric in the broadest sense—infancy, childhood, yesterday and even this morning are all part of a patient's history. Excluding past and future expectations, attention must remain on how each of us functions right now. When this is done, action is inevitable and immediate. The work of therapy has begun. Never mind who we are or why we are—that is a dilatory diversion. The essence of these encounters is what we are and how we act with each other now. By encouraging family members to be accountable for present behavior, we circumvent idle speculation and the verification of conflicting stories. Useless hours of bickering and blaming are averted.

The therapist's rolled-up-sleeve attitude of wading into the discussion at will facilitates an active encounter and creates an atmosphere of intense involvement that cannot fail to encourage responsive behavior quickly. By abandoning encounter-diminishing social roles, postures and rules, we evoke productive confrontations that are difficult to escape.

For the therapist, the experiential approach offers the privilege, the right, the obligation to live emotionally through the working day as a whole person. Impatience is converted to interest, anxiety to action, and exhaustion to excitement. Instead of saying, "uh huh," the therapist can say, "I'm not interested in that." Instead of silence when he does not know what to make of something that has been said, he can say bluntly, "None of this makes sense to me. I don't know what you want from me now." Instead of patiently enduring hours of boredom, he can say, "I cannot listen to what you say. I am bored." For the therapist, it means coming home relaxed, or even exhilarated, after having finished his psychological business with each person he has met through the day. He is now able to attend and enjoy his own family, unencumbered. It even becomes possible to grow at any moment during the working day as the therapist abandons guilt-inducing and worthless premises that glorify a static posture of studied indifference.

The advantages to patients are increasingly evident. Patients frequently come to family therapy after years of individual therapy have failed them and report with astonishment, and sometimes chagrin, the speed with which their lives are altered. One family with two children was seen ostensibly because one child was having difficulty in school. On the second visit, the mother learned from her husband that he could no longer stand her and had been planning to leave her for several months but only now had the courage to confront her. She had just "completed" two years of individual therapy. By our seventh session, she was reconciled with her husband, and said she had received a report from the child's school which expressed surprise and lauded the child's remarkable improvement. She told us, "In spite of what has happened in the last couple of months, I must tell you I never once got so upset in the whole two years of individual therapy as I get each time I come here." I chuckled and suggested she try trading "involved" for "upset."

Symptom removal, improved family interaction, altered observable behavior in the sessions and subtle peripheral cues usually confirm the value of experiential psychotherapy within the family and point to other progress as well. After three sessions a wife reported, "I have been living with my husband 15 years and now he suddenly stopped biting his nails." He added, "Yes, and I didn't even notice I had quit." Nail biting had never been discussed. After five sessions with an abandoned mother and her four children, the mother revealed a teenage bed wetter had been dry for three weeks. This had never been mentioned in therapy before. The identified patient, who had precipitated the family seeking help, was a sister whose behavior had been labeled delinquent. She too had improved.

INDICATIONS FOR EXPERIENTIAL PSYCHOTHERAPY WITHIN FAMILIES

No psychodiagnostic category need be excluded from this type of treatment. Actually, standard diagnostic classifications for individuals seem obsolete when one begins to conceptualize in terms of family psychopathology. At best, an individual diagnosis is only a partial diagnosis. The whole person psychologically extends beyond what we can see physically. We are all of our current emotional attachments, both real and fantasized.

An obese, frequently unemployed male who constantly whines about his life circumstance was presented to me as a passive-dependent personality. On the second visit his wife came to the meeting, and suddenly he was transformed into a domineering, aggressive husband. A paranoid psychotic individual to one diagnostician is a weeping depressive to another, as a result of a different encounter. Even with the same therapist in the same hour, psychodiagnostic categories shift.

A husband and wife came into treatment with the wife babbling incoherently, her content containing accusations towards her husband and others. Before the interview ended, she was sobbing heavily, and out of her sadness came a tale of loneliness and inadequacy. A psychosis, paranoid type (295.3x), became a depressive neurosis (300.40). She seemed locked in a hopeless conflict with her rigid husband. In our encounter, my participation offered a ray of hope. After I interrupted their painful encounter, her diagnosis changed.

I do not deny the concept of individual intrapsychic conflict; however, people's distressed behavior is of necessity interlocked with the behavior of others as a condition of its existence. In families, the self-diminishing behavior of one member is either tolerated in the name of love or is used by others unknowingly. Not only in reality, but also in fantasy, every human being thinks, feels and lives in a sea of intimate others. Deprivation studies and reports of prolonged accidental isolation reveal how we are compelled to fantasize the presence of others in their prolonged absence. Hermits treat rocks and trees as humans and talk with animals. The individual can no longer be considered a patient in isolation. The patient is properly understood when viewed in the family matrix. The rules governing behavior, their accepted attitudes, their secret agreements —sometimes so secret that no one is even aware of them—their hierarchy of values all appear in proper perspective in the matrix.

Often I have concluded that the identified patient is the healthiest member of the family. The disturbed behavior frequently signals a grossly defective family milieu in which the identified patient could not or would not manage a suitable self-crippling behavior that would permit blending in.

Since we are individuals in appearance only, it is not unusual to find the symptom in one person and the motivation for change in another member of the family. Prior to the practice of family therapy, therapists operated on the premise that the patient was the one who came for treatment and it was to the patient alone that we owed our allegiance. We allied ourselves against unseen family members. We chose to ignore the frequent concern that this premise necessarily created in other family members, which, of course, intensified interpersonal conflict for our patient at home. When both complainer and complainee are seen by the therapist, the scene takes on a different complexion.

In one instance, a reluctant father, a cold, indifferent visitor in his own home, joined the treatment scene at my insistence, out of love for his 12-year-old son, the identified patient. The mother was in individual therapy elsewhere. She attended this session much like the father, to help the boy in his therapy. The boy was a nervous wreck, twitching and blinking constantly. He couldn't sit still. He had run away from home, and this precipitated our session. The mother was delighted to have the father join us, as she spent much of her time in her therapy complaining of the lack of a good relationship with her husband and the children. It can be said that the son had the symptom, mother had the motivation, father had the problem. Who, we might well ask, was the patient?

Family therapy obviates the need for such questions. What is pertinent is that the family is distressed, that all members have pain and are attempting to solve it in their own way: the son with symptoms of disturbed motor behavior; the mother by her relationship with her therapist; and the father by overworking and staying away from home. Each had found a "solution" outside of the home except the boy. He was still hopelessly trying to find a resource for comfort in his family.

A serious problem in treating offenders of the law is that the motivating person is often a probation officer instead of a family member. This seriously impairs the capacity for a sustained and substantial therapeutic impact. These offenders are notoriously poorly motivated for treatment. Many offenders whose treatment is made a condition of their probation attend until probation is completed and then abandon treatment, essentially unchanged. If family treatment is instituted early, the motivation can often be developed within the family. The evolution of the offender's family as a place for hope and growth can become a source of sustenance to the offender. Significantly, statistics show clearly that criminal recidivism is indirectly proportional to the presence of a concerned family in the offender's life.

A new diagnostic frame for the total individual, a person in an encounter, does not readily present itself as yet. It will come, I am certain, and when it does it will be based on the kinds of combinations that people create with others. It will properly evaluate each specific encountering combination and will be a time-limited classification, applicable only to a specific encounter. The idea that you always take your neurosis with you is obsolete. The potential for repetitive behavior is another matter, which usually requires, however, an interlocking counterpart from someone else. An inverse corollary is the obvious fact that person-to-person therapy could not otherwise be successful.

Initially, all patients who come to treatment, whether an individual or a family, have three characteristics in common. The first is some definable undesirability in some part of their world, usually identified as a part of themselves, someone else, or something else. The second is a criticism of that undesirable part. This is an essential and inherent part of that symptom. A behavior per se is not a symptom unless it is condemned by someone. The old story of the person who routinely vomited after breakfast comes to mind. When this was mentioned incidentally during a psychiatric interview, the therapist was astonished. The person responded with the question, "Doesn't everybody?" A symptom was then born. Normal behavior in one culture is sometimes labeled "pathology" when transposed into another culture. Psychoanthropological studies are full of such examples. Thus, the symptom only exists as the target of some objector.

The third characteristic is a willingness to present themselves for therapy. This is so whether their presence is voluntary or not, whether they are sent by a probation officer or brought by a spouse or parent. Some people must back into assistance, and one way to do this is to produce sufficient pain in someone else to induce them to become the motivating force.

Family therapy is seen by many therapists as a reasonable approach to problems identified as familial. Children's behavior is generally acknowledged as significantly influenced by the family life. That there is any doubt left seems incredible to me, yet in some professional quarters children face years of analysis without the presence of their families, for disturbed behavior that I am convinced could be rapidly resolved in family therapy. "We left our one-year-old boy with a friend and her small children for four days," one woman told me. "It took him seven days—a whole week—to return to his normal behavior. It was five days till he could sleep through the night again, and seven days before he smiled and reached out to us once more." Had they been impatient with their son's distressed behavior during those seven days, I am sure they could have extended the pattern into months and perhaps years.

In addition to children's behavior, some other complaints are also readily accepted as a basis for family therapy: conflicts over sexuality, money, a husband's ambition, mother's housekeeping, father's discipline with the children or involvement in the home, or in-laws, to mention but a few—in other words, conflicts which are clearly identified as interpersonal and family related. Such conflicts are the battlefields upon which intrapsychic struggle becomes manifest. The battlefields are interpersonal; the battle is intrapsychic. The most intimate interpersonal relationship—the family—is used as the site for therapeutic impingement, since here the greatest leverage can be applied for altering behavior. It is here that the omnipotence of the intrapsychic determinants can be successfully contested. Our loved ones move us; this is the reason therapy within families works.

But what of individual behavioral problems that everyone in the family agrees are individual: a gambling husband, a husband with homosexual tendencies, a wife with a compulsion to shoplift, a husband who drinks and beats his wife, a promiscuous housewife, a father of four who cannot hold a job? I have rarely seen what I would call a healthy mate to any of these people, even when such problems were brought to the marriage, such as in the case of the gambling husband or the uncertain husband who tasted homosexuality prior to and then, sneakily, during his marriage. Spouses often seem to have selected a mate through whom they could vicariously and safely live an antithetical life. Not that this is bad. My wife, for instance, carries the spirituality of my existence by proxy quite well, living largely by faith and spiritual conviction. But it is no accident; it is significant and had best not go unnoticed.

The homosexual or uncertain man's wife was so "cooperative and understanding," according to the husband, that she would gladly come to his treatment sessions although they both concurred in the viewpoint that his problem had nothing to do with her since it predated her. It took us about 20 minutes to expose the fact that she was "cooperative and under- standing" about everything except any masculine assertiveness in her husband. She was cooperative to the point that she wanted to speak for him, clarify for him, do for him, and of course, help him to understand the "ugliness" of any vigorous assertion or disagreement with her. She wanted him a heterosexual in fantasy alone. As a person, he was to function as a woman. When he became frustrated or angered with her, he would, in fact, serve her secret wish and become a woman by having an affair as the female counterpart to some man. Gradually, as he began to stand up to his wife, his homosexual interest diminished, and she became temporarily frigid.

And of course, the gambler's wife was diligently in full martyred garb, forever paying off debts incurred by her gambling husband, who she knew would never leave her as long as she put up with his undesirable personal defect. Where else could he find a better martyr? After all, doesn't she complain regularly as she obtusely ignores his obvious sneaking off and placing bets? She never asked who was calling if she suspected it was the bookmaker. "I couldn't embarrass him like that," she told me, adding wistfully, "I suppose I am wrong." They had an agreement that had never been discussed. One such wife finally decided not to buy her husband this way, and he promptly stopped gambling. To attempt treatment of the gambler alone would immeasurably compound the task of therapy, for such a wife's power is far greater than mine. With her as my ally, there is hope.

Psychotherapy within the family for families with a psychotic member, whether a parent or child, is most desirable. When the psychotic member is a child, treatment is more difficult as the parents are rather uniformly reluctant to share responsibility for the dilemma. Superficially, they seem most eager to "help," but only as long as there is no implication that they themselves might be contributing to the creation of the pathology. In addition, despite the presence of two parents, which is the norm in most families with a child exhibiting psychotic behavior, these families often act like single-parent homes. One parent rules and the other either collaborates cooperatively or is remarkably remote and uninvolved. Invariably, the ruling parent is the most difficult one with whom to negotiate. When interacting with such a parent, I generally feel more like the child than the spouse, but since I can behave neither remotely nor psychotically, I am left with little more than a strong combative attitude.

A teenage boy, recently discharged from a state hospital, was taken out of family therapy in search of an organic diagnosis when the father's child-crushing behavior was questioned. Until that moment, the father had been most cooperative and enthusiastic about the treatment program. We had, until then, been working with his wife, who was responsive and appreciative. However, when father responded with his ultimatum, his good wife merely shrugged, shed a few tears, and loyally defended her husband, saying, "It's possible that all the doctors are wrong. Doctors don't have all the answers. My neighbor said. . . ." This response is not inevitable in family therapy, just annoying. However, treating the child in an attempt to integrate him back into this family would be absurd, and successfully helping him out of this family when his age makes him a captive is impossible. I do not consider such failures to be due to the family approach, but rather to each therapist's individual inability to penetrate a particular family at a particular time in his or her professional career.

Are there any contraindications to psychotherapy within the framework of the family? To this I must answer that there are absolutely no contra-indications per se. Any two people, emotionally tied to each other and wishing to remain in contact with each other, can utilize this approach. Two homosexual women, living together, for example, asked for assist-ance, not to change their way of life, but rather to improve it. During the course of our time together, their emotional relationship was explored, and for each of them the treatment program was successful.

There are times when a family member refuses to participate and, under these circumstances, the remainder of the family need not be deprived of the opportunity to work together. However, this is actually quite rare, particularly when the entire family has been initially re-quested to participate, at least for the first session. During the opening interview, a reluctant and usually frightened member may be assisted to overcome this reluctance. This may be the goal of the first session.

I can only recall one situation in my experience in which it was the therapist who refused to continue working with the family. This involved a family of three members: mother, father and a 17¾-year-old daughter. The parents initially refused to come in, sent the daughter, and then in-formed me over the phone that she was incorrigible, was running around with the wrong crowd, lying, stealing, drinking, getting into night clubs by lying about her age, and coming home at impossible hours. The mother's closing statement was, "I hope you can do something with her—we can't."

I accepted the parents' ultimatum and saw the girl alone, planning to inveigle them into the treatment at a later date. The daughter came in, dressed in an outlandish costume and rather casually confirmed all of the mother's accusations and considerably more. The daughter and I worked well in therapy together, but I continued to feel that it would be helpful to invite her parents so that their life together could be more bearable. I also thought that if she could resolve some of her conflicts directly with them, she would be less burdened in her future associations. After several weeks, I approached the daughter with the request that she bring her parents in. Although she acknowledged some fear, she agreed to it. I next contacted the parents and they did agree to come for a single session. They were also motivated by curiosity about the treatment.

The hour began with the mother developing two themes. The first was directed toward me and essentially was, "What are you doing to my daughter and why isn't she better?" The second was directed toward the daughter and was a further barrage of, "How could you do this to me?" Mother's verbal push was incessant and could be interrupted only by the father's joining in to attack the daughter. The daughter fought back with her mother. The father's position was, "You can shout and holler at me all you want, but you can't talk that way to your mother." Within a matter of minutes, from the outset of the session, all three of them were shouting at the top of their voices at each other: mother accusing daughter, daughter attacking mother back, and father loudly and ineffectually defending mother.

I asked them to stop interrupting each other and no one heard me. I abandoned my composure and yelled at them to be quiet, still no one heard me. Finally, I stood up, slammed both hands on the desk as loud as I could, and yelled at the top of my voice, "Shut up!" You could have heard the proverbial pin drop. They were astonished that I had learned so quickly how to function in their family. I then proceeded to explain some of the rules: no interrupting, no shouting, each one will get a turn. I invited the father to start. Within five minutes, all three of them were yelling and shouting at each other again. Finally, I told them: "All of you are impossible. You do not hear each other; you do not listen to each other; you are only interested in seeing who can shout and attack the loudest. All three of you are involved in this equally, and I feel it's hopeless to attempt to have you communicate with each other."

The daughter looked at me and smiled and said, "I told you so." Father turned to the daughter and said, "What do you mean by that?" Mother turned angrily to the father and said, "You know what she meant by that. She probably told the doctor that it is all our fault and that we don't listen to her." And they were off again. When I stopped them this time, I had made my decision. The daughter would move out in two months, at the age of 18. I announced that I would not work with them under these circumstances as it was impossible for me to function in this atmosphere. I not only refused to work further with them, but told them how angry I was with them and explained what about them made me angry. I confronted the mother with her guilt-producing helpless behavior which thwarted any attempt on the part of her daughter to reach maturity; I attacked the father for his contribution towards her delinquency, citing the instance he had related in which he stood idly by while his daughter showed a false driver's license to obtain an alcoholic drink in a bar. He had complained to me about it, yet he had done nothing to stop it at the time. I told them both I thought they were making a mess of their daughter's life, and then I turned to the daughter and told her I thought that she was not doing much to help matters.

When I was through with my five-minute polemic, the mother looked at me and for the first time spoke calmly, sincerely and directly, "Thank you, Doctor. We have kind of suspected this all along, and it is something of a relief to have it said out loud. We have done the best we can, and it isn't very good, and we appreciate what you are doing." They rose and departed. They encouraged their daughter to remain in therapy. The daughter continued in therapy and continued to improve, moved away from home, and has, since moving, achieved an improved relationship with her parents, largely by phone and infrequent visits. For this therapist and family, then, family therapy was not indicated.

GOAL OF EXPERIENTIAL PSYCHOTHERAPY WITHIN FAMILIES

The goal of experiential psychotherapy within the family is the integration of each family member within him- or herself and within the family. Though not identical by any means, the achievement of these goals is often simultaneous. Sometimes individual integration means familial disintegration. I consider my primary responsibility to people—to each individual within the family—and only secondarily to the organization called family. I consider the family as a sound, valuable and profoundly important organization. Sufficient research and common sense tell us that, during infancy, a familial relationship with at least one person is synonymous with existence. At least initially, then, the family is as important as the individual. At no time subsequently do I consider the family of greater importance.

Integration of the individual within him- or herself means, at least, awareness of the conflicting components within and, at best, their partial resolution plus the attitudes necessary for a continuing development of integration. Integration means recognition, appreciation and expression of one's being. To appreciate and express one's being is not selfish, nor is it wanton disregard of others. Appreciation of one's own person inevitably leads to appreciation of others. It is impossible to give what you do not possess. Integration also means the recognition and appreciation of the individual's differences with others. It means togetherness through appreciation of individual uniqueness instead of through confluence (togetherness, not onegetherness). It means changing isolation and loneliness to separateness and aloneness with others. The development of one's person will be discussed more fully later as I share my ideas about the construct of personality as a struggle between one's selfness and one's socially inspired concept of what one should be—one's self-concept or self-image—and the emergence into more gratifying beingness when such aspects are integrated.

I want much for the individuals I treat in their family. I want them to become aware of what they want, when they want it. I want them to develop their social negotiating skills to full capacity. I want them to act, to act in their own behalf, to use their negotiating skills to get what they want. I want them to know when it is impossible to get what they want from the others and to learn how to finish each encounter, regardless of this. I want them to learn from their experience what is possible for them to achieve—and not from pronouncements, admonitions or fears expressed by others. I want each member to learn to use the family as a resource, a place for emotional development and refueling, and a sanctuary where each can safely be. Finally, I want everyone to take personal responsibility for this family to keep an atmosphere conducive to personal growth.

All of this is a rather high-flown, idealistic fantasy. In practice, the ultimate goal of therapy is partially established by the therapist. All members of the family have their own conceived goals for themselves as well as for their desired level of family interaction. This very subject often requires our mutual attention. Achieving the initial goal sought by the family, such as removal of symptoms manifested initially in one member, often signals the end of therapy. Other families become aware of many heretofore hidden discomforts they wish to alter, so therapy goes beyond resolving the immediate precipitating problem. Occasionally, one member wishes to continue, motivated by an internal unrest that is of no concern to the others. We discuss it, and on rare occasions, family therapy ends while one individual continues his or her personal internal search.

Each family is a unique composite of inimitable individuals, joined like a most fascinating three-dimensional picture puzzle. Each individual alteration affects the total configuration of the family. Each family has its own uniquely organized rules, standards and values—overt and covert—just as any social organization, be it gangland or fatherland. Since the family is generally the smallest social organization, and since it safeguards the emotional core of people, each member necessarily carries more influence over the others and, in turn, is more influenced by changes within its structure or function than in larger organizations. Although the broad goals prescribed here apply to all individuals of all ages and all families regardless of ethnic, geographic, religious or national considerations, the specifics cannot be detailed. Each family subscribes to and strives toward integrating into its own singular design.

The goals of therapy are negotiated by vigorous attention to, and manipulation of, our current encountering. The current encounter is the focal point. The therapist keeps the encounter vital by insisting that the members stick to the present moment, by insisting on the fullest measure of participation appropriate to the context of that moment, and by actively challenging any encounter-diminishing behavior.

2

The Encounter

Two or more people meet. Each comes for something. They try in both learned and spontaneous ways to extract what they need from the encounter. They part, fulfillment varied, each having experienced something that will become part of future encounters.

Existence is composed of experiences. In fact, experiences are the essence of, the proof of, one's existence. Encounters are peopled sequences, limited in time, bounded by other experiences. The sequence called life is a single continuum; encounters, an artificial division to permit closer scrutiny. To influence encounters so that each participant achieves greater, more consistent fulfillment is the task of therapy. The therapeutic interview is a special encounter through which this end is achieved. It is special in its attention to the encountering that occurs within the interview itself. In the therapeutic interview, the subject of this encounter is the very nature of this encounter. To become aware of the encounter itself should not be considered unusual. In all encounters, regardless of the subject matter (content), it is well to consider the encounter (process) also. Only the emphasis differs. A good encounter is a therapeutic encounter.

"GOOD" AND "BAD" ENCOUNTERS

Two people are bickering over some issue when one interrupts to say, "Our bickering doesn't seem to be getting us anywhere. I don't think we're listening to each other. Let's go for coffee and let it set awhile, then maybe we can start again from a different, more profitable vantage point." This expression—interruption, if you wish—is a therapeutic intervention which goes from content to process and includes a positive suggestion.

The old saying, "The product is no better than the man selling it," comes to mind. It describes experiential encounters. It means, "Pay attention to how and who is selling, not merely to what they are selling." Both the colloquialism and the theory of experiential encountering express the belief that the encounter itself is the critical phenomenon.

People in cars stop at a traffic signal and proceed, by prearrangement, when a signal changes. This is a simple, successful, albeit not intimate, encounter. All of those people at that corner at that time, thus encountered, and also by prearrangement, pass without recognition of each other, having agreed to attend only the traffic signal in order to avoid confusion and collision. This is a good encounter. A pair of lovers ecstatically embrace, climax simultaneously and drift off to sleep together. This is again a good encounter. Two strangers pass on the street, each glances at the other briefly and continues on his way. At the moment of eye contact one thinks, "He looks familiar," scours his memory, decides, "Ah yes, he reminds me of so and so, but obviously he isn't so and so," and concludes his experience. The other wonders, "What's he staring at?" Wondering if it is his appearance, he glances down, sees everything is in order, and dismisses the question. His attention moves on to a store window. A completed encounter has been achieved for each.

A good encounter is a completed encounter, one that leaves no residue of uneasiness.

The obscuring or diminishing of encounters prevents completion. Incomplete encounters—unfinished situations—are the source of psychological astigmata. Unfinished situations result in painful residues, carried like a large bundle of stones which burdens the individual with its weight and partially obscures or distorts perception.

As old situations are completed, the stones are dropped, and individuals feel a sense of lightheartedness and become more discerning—about themselves and the peopled world about them. As each new situation is finished, the person is permitted to continue life enlightened and undaunted, more knowing and less fearful of existence.

Thus far, this may sound remarkably similar to other historic-genetic based theories. The significant difference here lies in emphasis and centrality. By paying attention to the current encounter, old unfinished historical and/or genetic encounters can be more quickly discovered. Also, current encounter completion inevitably provides the necessary vehicle for completing ancient unfinished situations, frequently without recalling the memory or connecting associations to the present, although this often follows spontaneously in the wake of a completed current encounter.

In one instance the husband, rather tight lipped, neat, composed, always polite and excessively cooperative, began a session by speaking distantly to me:

Husband: Sometimes I feel put upon by people.
Therapist: By whom? (*to encourage him to sharpen his statement*)
H: (*Vaguely*) Numerous people.
Th: You find it important to tell me. (*again urging sharpness, now with a hint*)
H: I suppose you are one of them.
Th: You suppose?
H: I have thought on occasion that you ask too much of me. Even now, the way you talk to me, you seem to expect from me more than I can give you.
Th: (*Now that he has spoken to me, about us, in the here and now, he is negotiable. We can begin to explore our differing perceptions.*) At the moment, all I ask is that we be as clear with each other as possible about what it is we want from one another.
H: It feels like you're asking for so much more.
Th: (*I silently search myself for evidence that I may be asking for more and come up with nothing. Then suddenly I think of something.*) Try an experiment: Say it in reverse.
H: You mean, express the idea that I expect more from you than you can give?

He was sincerely trying to cooperate but he did not do what I suggested. Instead, he preambled with "Did you mean . . .?" and couched the expression in a question. I felt, however, that the question was truly for clarification, not merely an encounter-diminishing tactic, so I responded simply, "Yes."

He sat looking thoughtfully, directly at me for a working moment of silence and then said, "I want help from you. I want more from you than I'm getting. Yes, it's true (with mounting excitement). I don't think you will give me what I need." He fell silent, obviously touched.

"Repeat that last sentence," I suggested, wanting him to intensify his excitement which told me of its importance to him. But it had already worked and my comment was unnecessary. He said sadly, "I didn't hear you. I just had a flash of me sitting on the living room floor as a child. I must have been about 9 or 10, and my father is in his rocker, reading the paper." He fell silent again and I suggested, "Stay there, talk with him, tell him how he doesn't give you what you need." He began to weep as he said, "Please put down your paper and pay attention to me. . . ."

This affect-laden encounter with his father began his work towards completion. As was borne out subsequently, he became less inclined to see others as so imposing.

Suppose in the earlier example of the lovers, one had come to the encounter motivated by fear—fear of facing his or her loneliness—or possibly desiring to avenge a previous love loss. At the point of climax, instead of a calming completion, a wakefulness or a mounting tension more likely would have occurred. Suppose, in the instance of the passerby, that the one who wondered, "What's he staring at," could not let go of this thought but instead continued to mull it over; he suspected that perhaps the other man was sizing him up in order to do him harm. These are incomplete encounters for some participants, reflecting unfinished business brought from previous situations and compounding their disability by now adding another unfinished encounter.

Regardless of past defective encountering, if in a current encounter a person functions differently, the course of his or her life is altered. Thus, if the thwarted lover could become aware of what he or she needed, that encounter might be more fulfillingly spent. If the passerby in the street could speak to his would be assailant, useful clarification could result. Although they are oversimplified, these anecdotes suggest the pathways to be explored in this volume for altering behavior via attention to and enhancement of the encounter.

The point may be raised here that awareness alone will not permit this lover to function differently and that, if the passerby could have spoken to the other man, he would have. Granted. However, although simple awareness or simple suggestions do not always resolve or alter bad patterns of behavior, it is surprising how often they are helpful. Furthermore, even when they are not, a study of the encountering behavior within the therapy session is far more fruitful than historical surveys, which tend to match the duration of therapy with the duration of the previous bad encountering.

Each person in an encounter is responsible to himself for utilizing that encounter to obtain what he needs. A successful encounter is an individual matter, to be judged by each encountering person alone. A successful encounter for one very often coincides with a successful encounter for the other, but a double success need not occur. The encounter per se is the matrix for human behavior, but it is the individuals who compose the encounter, who command attention, and by whom results for each are judged.

Before embarking on a more detailed discussion of encountering, I wish to reveal explicitly some of my premises, or prejudices, if you wish: The responsibility for an encounter lies fully on the shoulders of each person in that encounter, man, woman and child alike. At the same time, however, no one can be held solely responsible for an encounter. Responsibility in an encounter always falls equally and fully on each participant. The above statements, contradictory as they may seem at first glance, reflect a fair appraisal.

Acts of ignorance are as powerful in an encounter as acts of will, since the consequences of behavior, and not the intent, are the criteria. Generally speaking, our social code is constructed on a premise that acts of commission are more reprehensible than acts of omission. We are not guilty if we watch a murder or if we allow ourselves to be murdered. A newspaper article reports the murder of a man at the hands of a 15-year-old boy who was presumably defending his mother's honor. The man, who had been dating the lad's mother, and the lad's mother had just broken up. The man returned, banged on the door threateningly, and insisted on seeing his erstwhile love. The mother cowered fearfully, and the boy leaped to her defense, killing the man. The murdered man was, of course, not considered the murderer, and the boy's mother was not held. The boy alone was apprehended. To me, all three should have been equally charged: The boy was responsible for his action; the murdered man for his inciting action; and the mother for her act of omission. She "did" nothing. Inaction, naivete, helplessness and fear are some of many forms of behavior that we use to surrender our responsibility in an encounter. Such behaviors do not diminish personal loss, but they often successfully, as intended, diminish criticism from others.

I am aware that initially I respond almost automatically in defense of an underdog in a controversy, before knowing anything of the circumstances. For you, perhaps this is different. It is valuable to know where each of us stands in relation to various kinds of behavioral tactics. In working with families, one generally learns painfully that the downed party is no less potent and often, because of support from other members of the family, may exercise a far greater influence than any other person in the group. The lives of all members within a family have often been directed, almost without opposition, when behavior such as a threat of suicide, fear or illness was permitted to go unchallenged.

In one family of four, the mother, who had been in individual therapy for 18 years, controlled every move within this family, of course, with their unwitting cooperation, by being afraid. When the family would go out, whether or not the family would go out, where the family would live, what schools the children should go to, almost any topic that you might select was decided upon by mother. After all, she was the sick one and "couldn't help herself." Therefore, it was agreed that whatever she expressed as a fearful need would come to pass. After 18 years of individual therapy, her retiring therapist referred her to me. I refused to see her unless she brought her entire family. "I'm afraid to ask them," she responded. To which I replied, "I'm not."

I spoke with her husband, who was most cooperative and who managed to get one of the two children to accompany him and his wife for the first session. In that session, the wife's use of her fear became the most obvious obstacle to any kind of constructive encountering and I tackled it vigorously from the outset. I decided that this woman, in effect, was saying, "I don't want or I don't like something," whenever she said, "I'm afraid." I offered this analysis to her and to her family. She, of course, promptly rejected it, and we had a terrible argument. The result of this was awareness by her husband that she was not the fragile creature he had assumed her to be all these years.

I refused to see the family unless the other son was also brought in. The mother, of course, promptly said that she was afraid to ask him as he might leave home. The father, a quiet man who had adjusted to his family by working 11 hours a day, six days a week, took heart after what he had seen this day and replied, "I'm not afraid. The worst that could happen is that he would leave home. He is 20 years old. It might do him some good. I don't think he will find so easily someone else like you who will bring him his food on command while he lies on the couch watching television." My paternally supported ultimatum was that, if the son were a part of the family, he was to participate in our work together as a family member. If not, he qualified as a boarder and was to be charged room and board, should they decide they wish to have a boarder in their house, otherwise, out!

The boy moved out and managed to stay out for three weeks. By the fourth week, he had moved back into the home. He attended our family interview, and the mother gleefully reported, "He complimented my cooking for the first time in his life." In this family as in all others, it required active cooperation by all members to permit encounter-diminishing behavior to exist.

Young children, since they are captive in the family and often without good parental examples, can be ineffective in treatment. However, their innocence is sometimes remarkably enlightening in exposing the dynamics of the family interaction. Their presence in treatment is also an extremely valuable learning experience for them.

As she neared the end of a first session with her mother and father, a girl of 22, who had just been released from a hospital after an acute psychotic episode, spoke for the first time, saying, "We should have had you when I was 10." This came after I had confronted her parents with some of their more gross encounter-diminishing behavior. I turned to her and responded, "But you're not 10 years old now." In encounters, there are no victims and victimizers bearing different responsibilities to the encounter. I must stress again that each individual in an encounter is fully responsible for him- or herself in the encounter. At the same time, no one individual can be held solely responsible for the encounter. Consequences ensue whether responsibility is acknowledged or not.

Blaming is a variation on the attempt to shed responsibility in encounters. It is an attempt to control by intimidation and simultaneously to deny responsibility for the sake of a cruel conscience. This phenomenon badly serves the blamer for, if it is successful, a manipulated situation exists where, by mutual agreement, one party controls and the other is controlled. Should the blaming ploy fail, it is still a waste of energy that might better have been spent attempting to extract what one needs from an encounter. People who blame others, of course, suffer the same fate and, at times, succumb to such influences whether they are blamed by someone else or by their own conscience. Results are the same regardless of the source.

Responsibility is often erroneously thought of as being accountable or answerable to another person. "You aren't assuming your responsibility . . ." can be said by one spouse to the other, parent to a child, employer to employee, or vice versa. In these instances people are usually referring to an expected commitment from another person. This expected commitment may be expressed as, "What I want you to do, what I assume you will do is based on statements made in the past or on your behavior in the past. It cannot be based on what you are now for I don't know what you are now unless it is demonstrated by your behavior now."

Personal responsibility—the ability to respond to a commitment—is essentially an internal phenomenon within each individual, based on his or her own internal psychic determinant at any given moment; it has little to do with others. The term responsibility has come to have social implications and is used as a social weapon with which to attack others when they do not fulfill our expectations of them. It is the responsibility of each of us to maximize our potential for knowing what to expect from others. It is perhaps wisdom to look to ourselves in search of our own blindness when our perception is erroneous, rather than to attack the other person with the label "irresponsible."

At this time I do not chose to consider a broader application of this principle to our entire social fabric, but I do feel that in the therapeutic encounter it is both crucial and valid. However, one might well wonder if each social organization established to enforce expected commitments and punish failures does not at the same time discourage a sense of personal responsibility.

I can only be responsible to and for myself and there it ends. This thought frightens many people and the word "anarchy" comes to mind. Responsibility to and for oneself, on the contrary, produces greater commitment for others. We cannot give what we do not have. Anarchy actually results from excessive and enforced commitments. It is only when I am being responsible for myself that I can make commitments with others and fulfill them. My sense of personal responsibility must not be extended as some kind of privilege or weapon to others for use against me, for then it is corrupted into a despicable social weed whose fruit is poisonous for blamer and blamed alike. Consequences are no one's fault yet everyone's responsibility.

OBJECTIVES OF ENCOUNTERS

There are essentially four requirements for having a successful encounter, which are, correspondingly, the sites of defective encountering:

1) *A clear knowledge of "who I am" at any given moment. This requires a dynamic awareness of what I need from moment to moment.*
2) *A sensitive cognition or appraisal of the people I am with and the context of our encounter.*
3) *The development and utilization of my manipulating skills to extract, as effectively as I am capable, what I need from the encounter. This aspect is expressive.*
4) *The capability of finishing an encounter. This is possibly the most significant aspect. It means completing any unfinished feeling which may represent the gap between the original goal of the encounter and the actual results. A common error is to consider unfinished encounters as synonymous with unachieved goals. The goal of an encounter is to finish our psychological business with the other person, not necessarily to achieve fulfillment of the original need brought to this encounter.*

In the earlier models for psychotherapy, the essential assumption implied that the pathology was exclusively in the first category mentioned above, in the clouding of the "I am." Patients, therefore, were those who asked for help. Why waste our time on those who do not know enough to ask?

Persons diagnosed as character disorders, those who did not suffer, for instance, with anxiety or depression and, therefore, did not come to the psychiatrist asking for help, were considered largely untreatable and thought of merely as provocative agents inducing pathology in others. They were diagnosed, labeled and dismissed. Their problem was that they had no outspoken doubts about who they were. They were not susceptible to reason. They felt no pain and were therefore unmotivated to ask for what we wanted to give them. The kindest among us considered them in severe pain—so severe as to cause us to imply charitably that they had become immutable, unreachable, stone.

This earlier model also said, in essence, that disturbances in the second and third categories were matters for social workers, since they merely required the offering of sound advice and suggestions for modifying the environment. The fourth category, completion of unfinished feelings, was given some consideration. However, to be eligible, the unfinished feeling had to be derived from childhood and was viewed skeptically if it was born of recent experiences.

The attitude toward so-called character disorders represented a glaring projection: It was not that we were unskillful, but rather that they were unreachable. In family therapy we are faced with many people who would be labeled character disorders. True, they frame problems outside of themselves. True, they don't respond to commonly taught psychotherapeutic "techniques," but they are not stones; they do respond. When the therapeutic model is modified and the therapist less of a stone, these people come to therapy, they work in therapy, and they change during the course of therapy.

Another unfortunate consequence of earlier psychotherapeutic models was that, once we accepted the premise that the difficulty lay exclusively in the area of who "I am," we limited ourselves to a scrutiny of who "I" was. And the next step: "In order to change, there is something that I must undo because of this past history." This is false. By considering the defect as existing in any one of the four areas required for successful encountering cited above, we see behavior as remarkably more flexible than was previously thought. Behavioral changes can often be seen as a result of a single exposure to a new, more effective mode.

People are like infinitely faceted gems, suspended and turning at random. To know "who I am" at every given moment is a most difficult task, requiring awareness of which facet or need is uppermost and most squarely presented in any encounter. One could well ask, "Am I my awareness at any given moment or am I my need at any given moment?" Further, "Am I what I am being at any given moment or what I am doing at any given moment?" One might ask as Pirandello's characters do, "Am I what I think I am or what someone else thinks I am at that instant?" Can I know what I am at any given moment or is it only afterwards in the wake of my experience that I can know?

The confusion as to one's identity encompasses far more than the issues surrounding the admittedly difficult task of identification and separation from parental figures. It involves learned patterns of what one should be aware of and what one should not be aware of, often unintentionally absorbed from the nature of family interacting. The thought process and the social organization through which the thought process is manifested are an ever-extending potential for confusion as regards a person's identity. Identity often becomes associated with what one thinks one is or what society says one should be, rather than an acknowledgment of what one is as determined by what is sensed and experienced. This will be discussed subsequently as we postulate an admittedly artificial division of human personality into the components of self, the self-image (social self or self-concept) and the beingness of a person.

As an immediate illustration, let us consider, "I want to tell him to go to hell but I should be more reasonable. I can't decide what to do." This statement manifests the three divided—unintegrated, if you will—facets of that person—the self, self-image and beingness, all expressed at that moment. First there is the "I" that wants—representing self. Then there is the "I" that should—the self-image or self-concept—representing the learned conception of what this person should be. Finally there is the indecisive "I"—representing the current state of being (or beingness). The state of being, in this instance the person's indecisiveness, is the summation of this person at this moment, regardless of the "I" with which he or she may identify. Example: "I'm not an indecisive person" (speaking generally). "I *really* want to tell him *off* but something tells me I better not" (still being indecisive).

The beingness is the significant representation. This does not mean we should ignore the other "I"s, but rather that we acknowledge that our beingness is our behavior, whether we admit it or not. It is here the consequences of our existence are born, whether we like it or not.

A goal of therapy is to unify the components so that behavior represents the total person—an "I am" that is fully represented in willful action. A therapeutic task is to assist the patient to confront each component by each other component until all three negotiate a mutually acceptable settlement. This does not mean an armed truce or an uneasy coexistence but rather an emotionally experienced integration.

This is sometimes accomplished by urging an active exploration of each facet of personality via serious identification and confrontation of each component with each other component, as in psychodrama, with a continuous interchange until resolutions occur. At the same time, by always holding the "I" component representing a person's state of being responsible at any given moment, the therapist can discourage sly maneuvers designed to defeat the integrating experiment. For example, should the patient be following the therapist's suggestion in order to please the therapist rather than to know him- or herself, it is incumbent upon the therapist to call attention to what the person is being at the moment—a performing monkey, perhaps, or a compliant child in search of favor. This confrontation should be as vigorous as needed to prevent further negating behavior, patients' protestations of "But, I am trying . . ." notwithstanding.

Beingness is always responsible and integration is always the goal. From personal experience, I suspect that complete integration has never occurred, just as attempts at such integration never cease—with or without benefit of therapy. This is probably the essence of the psychological life process.

All psychotherapy has, as a significant aspect of its functional goal, the objective of encouraging greater awareness of "who I am." This automatically includes helping patients to develop skills for continuing to achieve greater awareness. Failure to know what it is a person wants from an encounter portends failure in that encounter unless this deficit becomes an acknowledged part of the encounter. "I need to be with you and talk with you but I don't know what I want" is an honest and qualified starting point. It is often far superior to pretenses such as engaging others on areas of their interest, pretending none of one's own, and ending the encounter vaguely displeased. Because of constricting sexual mores, sexual gratification has often been falsely considered as "what I need" only to have the person involved experience anguish upon completion. A more pertinent need, such as "I am lonely" instead of "I am sexual," has not been more than momentarily fulfilled, if at all.

Our awareness and perception of circumstances result from a unique psychological astigmatism each of us has evolved. The "why" of this astigmatism is best left to psychophilosophers. Experiential psychotherapy urges, instead, the development of an awareness of one's psychological astigmata, thereby enhancing the potential for more successful encountering. This is encouraged by an exploration of the comparative differences in our perceptions of ourselves and each other during our time together. The exploration will be discussed further subsequently.

To watch a very young child at play is to see the epitome of the searching, explorative manipulation characteristic of the greatest learning period of our lives. Unfamiliar objects immediately invite attention, exploration and experimentation. Unfamiliar sounds are responded to quickly, and familiar objects are tested and manipulated over and over. Such behavior includes observing others and attempting imitations, though it is never limited to this. Experimentation with objects occurs with the exclusive goal of satisfying that inner tension we sometimes call curiosity or interest. The child's goal is the fullest possible experience with the object, and in the process, manipulating skills are developed.

These young humans also know about finishing a situation. A painful fall, for instance, produces immediate and total affect—motoric response and nearly equally immediate relief. Should they fall while climbing stairs, their behavior reverts instantly to crying and attending their wound, for this is the new business which commands their full attention and must be finished. When this is completed, the child then decides whether to continue up the stairway, move to something else or perhaps just to lie there and sleep.

To finish the feeling associated with the experience, for the child, is always paramount. The child knows the task is self-fulfillment, not other-inspired (self-image) achievement. Just as finishing an external task becomes unimportant in the face of a subjective internal need, manipulation of others beyond fulfillment of an extant need is also beyond the ken of the healthy child. Infants and young children complete each encounter. Completion may mean obtaining what I want; readjusting my goals; sitting down and crying; moving elsewhere for completion, having satisfied myself that I have thoroughly exhausted the possibilities for completion within this encounter; or any combination of the above components.

Common statements that evidence tolerance of incomplete encounters are such oft-heard bitter remarks as: "I don't *really* mind"; or "It doesn't bother me a bit," accompanied with a shoulder shrug motivated by the fact that it, of course, does bother; or the sneering smile accompanied with, "I couldn't care less"; or the ineffectual, "What good would crying do?"; or "So what?" Awareness of how we thwart our capacity for completion today and experiments which encourage recapturing our skills for completion, not discussions of why we lost them, are essential aspects of experiential psychotherapy. The goal is to finish encounters, not to win them.

A wife complains, "I spent all day shopping for special ingredients with which to bake his favorite cake, intending to surprise him. He came home from work irritable, and when I showed him the cake, he threw it on the floor. Naturally, I was furious. After all the trouble I had gone to just to give him something. . . ." There are, of course, many aspects of this encounter to be scrutinized, but I should like to limit my attention to this woman's statement at this time and her comment that she "gave." She did not give, she tried to bribe. Her hidden contract might read: "In exchange for my efforts you owe me one helluva appreciation. PS: I am so selfless I don't even ask that you appreciate me, just my production. I'll extrapolate from there." The husband clearly recognized the "hidden" contract and rejected it by throwing the cake on the floor.

This woman was not creating from a self-fulfilling level. She was creating through her self-image, an image which said that she should be a good housewife and prove this by "doing what a good housewife should do." Her behavior was designed to obtain an acknowledgment of "good wife" from her husband.

She was not really interested in him. The man that he was when he came home was an unhappy man who needed something she never bothered to discover. She was busy attempting to fulfill a need of her own. This is said not as a criticism but simply for clarification. The need that she had to fulfill, since it was in the service of her self-image or social self, she could not fulfill for herself, because social or self-image fulfillment must be acknowledged or paid off by others. Had she baked this cake in her own "self" interest, she would have completed her encounter with the cake when it was baked (or when she had eaten it) and felt fulfilled.

In the example cited, baking a cake fulfilled the wife's "self-image"; baking a cake was for the other person. Witness, by contrast, the creation of something self-fulfilling: A mother on giving birth feels either a calm, relaxed wakefulness, or is sound asleep. She needs no one to tell her she is fulfilled at that moment or that she has done well. Similarly, an artist, satisfied with a creation, moves on to further creativity. Witness further: a child who has exhausted himself at play; any game well played; any lovemaking that is completed. Fulfillment signals completion. Attention moves on. Interest changes. Involvement ends.

Completion is a rare phenomenon in adult human behavior. It is constantly hampered by cloudiness as to whether people are acting for themselves, in behalf of some socially desirable image, or self-image, implying what they are supposed to be, or whether they are in fact *being* (the integrated self/self-image). Such unclarity leads one astray, towards unintended goals, with resulting frustration and conflict.

This would not be so bad, for perfection cannot be. What may be considered bad is the compounding of such confusion by the inability to accept, appreciate and create caused by such conflicts. How can we enjoy and create through conflict? By sharing and expressing our more intimate concerns. Instead, expression becomes tabu and resolution comes to a halt. Completion becomes impossible.

It is in the struggle for clarification that resolution may emerge. So, one might ask the cake-baking wife, "What have you to say? Can you come closer to your own soul by being the cake that you nearly were at that moment of truth? Can you not speak to your husband? Are you saying, 'I come to you as best I can for your love and appreciation, fearful that you might turn away. I had to come disguised, for had I come as my open soul, and had you not accepted me, I would have died. I've learned to hide. Yet I still come for your love, to be taken for your very own, to be used for your fulfillment. Therein lies my need'?

"To which he might respond, 'So, you should be contented. You have filled my needs—my need to rage, my need to crush, my need to refuse, in short my need to deny my need for your love at this moment.' "

She: How could you?

He: It was easy.

She: You are cruel.

He: Have you no place in your love for my cruelty? Must you deny its existence in me? I question such love.

She: My love has bounds. Can you ask for my destruction as proof?

He: Yes.

She: (Reconsidering) Then I must be destroyed for I am truly yours.

He: Now you are the cruel one. How can I deny my need for love when such profound love is offered?

She: Then destroy me for I am admittedly cruel.

He: And your cruelty destroys my barrier; I can no longer support it. (tearfully) I must admit I need your devoted love.

She melts in silence. They embrace. Somewhere they both know this too shall pass, and again return, for change remains the only constant.

3

Theory: Me, Myself and I

Theorizing, if not theory, is treacherous. Woven initially out of our fantasies, theories can become powerful, dominant, controlling shackles. Like a child loved simply, theory can grow and enrich those around them; like a child loved with consuming adulation, theory can become a monstrosity that constricts and destroys. The influence of the theory/child will vary with the power the therapist/parents need to project onto the theory/child. Too often, motivated by a diminished self-worth, parents and therapists grant excessive and controlling power to children and theories. In the end such power hampers and hurts, curbs and crushes, as though it were a retaliation for the intemperate and inordinate loving.

All products of the thought process (i.e., thinking, planning, anticipating, recalling, memorizing, judging, etc.) I chose to call fantasies, not to diminish their value, but rather to keep my own head about them. For me it is hazardous to believe in others rather than in myself. Theories, especially those considered "scientific," are particularly alluring to me. "Good" theories tend to usurp or, at least, distort the place that rightfully belongs to my own experiences, derived from my sensate being.

I have, however, created some of my own theories, which I will now submit as the fantasies I need them to be. For those stalwarts not lured by theories, I suggest this chapter be bypassed in its entirety.

In my fantasy, we all begin life in a psychological state of *beingness*. That is, we function as a singly oriented, biologically rooted organism with no particular awareness of an insidedness versus an outsidedness. In the course of growth, beingness meets with environmental objects and the resulting behavior is called adaptation. There are two modes of psychological adaptation which can occur. The first can be called simply primary psychological adaptation. It consists of the engagement or envelopment of the environmental object in a primitive biological sense, much like digestion, where the object is decomposed, useful aspects are absorbed, becoming part of the organism, and the remainder is extruded. This is a painless procedure and results in continued adaptation of a now modified organism which still, however, functions as a single, integrated unit, psychologically known as the state of being. Both organism and environmental object have been altered.

We could describe the experience similarly from the viewpoint of the environmental object. The environmental object, a carrot for instance, invades the organism, uses what it can to alter the organism and, in its new adaptation as a part of the organism, can now extrude or discard its unneeded portions, such as its pulp, color and the title of carrot.

The secondary psychological adaptive process is the confrontation of the organism by an environmental object, and, instead of a digestive, integrative type of experience, the organism elects instead to accept the environmental object like a coat, superimposing it over some part of the organism's beingness. This underlying ("underwhelmed") part of the organism which has been "overwhelmed" by this covering coat—no longer a part of one's beingness—is now called the *self*. The environmental object, now glommed on to part of this organism, covering a part of the organism, is called the *self-concept, social self* or *self-image*. Prior to the first impacting experience there were no parts called self or self-image. In the secondary psychological adaptation process, an aspect of being is altered into two new parts: the self and the self-concept. Conceptually this transition may be likened to the development of a blister.

A small child playfully slaps a chair and is injured slightly. The child cries and, in the future, after a few more trials, is more careful. The demand of the environmental object, in this instance the chair, is exclusively for recognition. It does not ask the child for altered behavior, it does not try to teach the child the difference between good and bad; nor does it attempt to make the child feel guilty for what he or she has done. It does not ask the child for altered behavior regardless of what the child wishes. The child is free to experiment again and again with the chair and usually does, until he integrates or digests the experienced relationship with the chair. This is primary adaptation.

By contrast, consider the events that ensue when the same child playfully slaps the mother in the face, much as he might slap the chair. Now, though the child may be hurt slightly, mother is also slightly hurt and is likely to respond, "No, no, mustn't do that," or perhaps, "Naughty, naughty, you bad boy." Other responses of mother, either singly or in combination, may be withdrawal, misplaced irritability or inconsistently hitting back. The child is no longer free to experiment and integrate his experience at his own pace. Instead the mother attempts to jockey the child's behavior at her time and on her terms. The child now has no choice. Regardless of which behavior the mother uses and regardless of whether or not it is consistent, the child no longer learns experientially for himself. The child must adaptively learn that "No, no," for instance, is equivalent to the painful sting of the hard chair when experientially the child knows it is not. In fact, learning about "No, no" is often experienced by the young child as a game in which he and mother can become engaged.

In the name of love, mother imposes and demands how the child "should" respond regardless of what the child experiences, converting a possible primary adaptation into a secondary adaptational experience. Mother would do better to prevent the painful slap or to respond in her own behalf for recognition, rather than to preach, teach or screech. Mother is used as the prototype here, but father, grandmother or any other available parent figure is, of course, implicated. Secondary psychological adaptive process differs from primary in that stress is a part of the adaptive experience.

A further complication occurs when, as we commonly witness, a parent attempts to interrupt crying associated with an integrative experience by some verbal or behavioral variation of "You don't need to cry." Of course, the child does need to cry, just as adults need to cry. Crying in infancy, childhood and adulthood often accompanies integrative experiences and should be neither encouraged nor discouraged. In therapy with adults we often witness crying as an associated phenomenon of profound behavior-altering cognitions.

The secondary adaptive process, in my fancy, is "pathological," resulting in internal disharmony or nonintegration, which must inevitably diminish the richness of the individual's existence. The blister is localized to specific areas of encountering related to the original encountering experience. Such blisters are often lauded by others who themselves are blistered. "He is so nice and polite. He never says a harsh word to anyone." That he never speaks up in his own behalf or that he lives alone in a one-room flat utilizing a fraction of his capability and has not shed a tear since the age of two is not part of the admirers' awareness or concern. They are blinded by the beauty of the blistered adaptation.

This is reminiscent of the story about a man who purchased an ill-fitting suit of clothes. One of the coat sleeves was too long so the salesman suggested that he pull up the sleeve slightly and keep that arm bent at the elbow. He then complained that the trousers were too long and too loose at the waist so the salesman suggested he hike them up and keep one elbow pressed to the waistband. Finally, he complained that the coat was cut badly with one shoulder higher, and was advised merely to raise the opposite shoulder. He purchased the suit and struggled out of the store. As he passed two men on the street, one commented, "Did you see that poor fellow, all crippled up. Must have been in a bad accident." The other replied, "Yea, but he sure has a good tailor. Did you see how perfectly his suit fit?"

Whenever secondary adaptation occurs, it affects a segment of one's beingness, not one's total beingness. Susceptibility for this type of adaptation varies directly with the degree of insult. As life proceeds, susceptibility varies inversely with age. The reason for this is simple. Initially, all experiences are met by one's beingness. As blisters and calluses form (self-image), experiences are often met with this portion of the individual. Thus, the damage from an encounter and the attendant responsive behavior will vary. As we grow, each of us develops a unique variegated pattern of behavior and susceptibility that represents all three factions—beingness, self and self-concept. The infinite number of possible combinations is evident in the infinite variations in personalities.

During therapy, when either the self or the self-concept aspects of the person are confronted, the individual will identify himself as either the victimized self or the righteous self-image—never both at the same time, and never one without, at some later time, the other. People often say, "I wanted to tell him, but I just couldn't." If asked, "What or who stopped you?" the response will vary depending on how they have distanced themselves from the unacknowledged other parts of themselves. The unacknowledged part can be simply denied (rejected) or extruded (projected). "One doesn't do things like that," "I don't know what stopped me," "Something . . ." or "It was just something I felt" are all samples of denied responsibility for that portion of one's person. As in the last response, the person feels the impact of "it" but is clearly not identified as "it."

Projected responses can be heard in answers such as "I was never taught to speak up" (here mother and father are the culprits) or "He (the encountered one) wouldn't like it."

A common expression is "So I told myself . . ." to which I respond querulously, if not poetically, "Who told who and which one are you?" There are others: "*I* want to but *I* can't," "I shouldn't but *I* will," "*I* want to but *they* would feel bad if *I* did."

With such comments, four pathognomonic qualities of secondary adaptation become obvious. First of all, the individuals have aspects of their personality which are "dis-integrated." That is, they have two separate and opposing forces within themselves: I do–I don't; I want–I can't; I'm tired–I shouldn't be. Sometimes one of the parts is detached and an attempt is made to shift it outside of themselves; it is then called an *it* or *they*.

Next, whenever such separations are made, the individuals always see themselves as representing only one part in this internal struggle. It, God, People, They, You, My parents, My conscience, Time, Heredity, Circumstances—all are labels we often use to identify the other part of ourselves to which we prefer to lay no claim at this time. "I don't know what made me do it, it must have been. . . ." Fill in your favorite. The label with which the individual identifies determines the words and the offered personality, while the detached, denied aspect strongly influences the actual behavior. They are separate but not equal. The space or battleground between these opposing forces is filled with what we call "personality."

Not only are there two opposing forces, but criticism is always a part of the self-concept, just as submission and helplessness characterize the self. The last pathognomonic sign is the denial by (or innocence of) both components concerning responsibility for the conflict.

"Let me cite an example." This sentence is a demonstration of a burned out dis-integration. Of whom am I seeking permission: The reader? The publisher? Part of my own mental structure, of course. This represents a comma in the flow of thought, inspired by a piece of anciently formed self-image, no longer alive: an historical psychological scare in the sentence construction of today.

During a tirade against her husband, an enraged woman tells me, "I am going to tell him to stop nagging the children even if *it* kills me." Who is "it"? Her husband? Her conscience? Her mother? Obviously it wasn't her husband or she would have said so. No one, in fact, ever threatened her life for "telling" her husband anything. "Oh, it's just a figure of speech," she might answer. Perhaps, but it is undoubtedly a different statement without the phrase ". . . even if *it* kills me." Some energy within this individual threatens her at the thought of "telling" her husband and manifests in these words. The source of this energy is *in* this patient, yet she chooses to separate this threat by one part, the self-image, against another part, the self. She claims the identity of the threatened self. She disclaims the oppressor or "killer" self-image. She is also able to know "it" is not a person outside of herself, so this "killer" becomes a vague indefinite pronoun; she, then, is the striving but threatened self. Now what has happened to her behavior and her personality? Her behavior is angry, defiant, threatening and aggressive. She acts like the killer. She talks like the victim. With her husband she often reverses roles: meek and helpless in her behavior, murderous in her thoughts.

A bright young man reports, "I want to marry her, but I know it will interfere with my professional career if I marry now." As his story unfolds, he reveals a strong need to present his social "I" (self-concept) as intelligent, undemonstrative and socially achieving. The other, renounced "I" (self) is represented by a wish to "belong to someone," to "be loved," a wish to blossom—a feeling that buds when he is with his potential fiancée. Identified as the professional "I" (self-concept), he requests assistance to eliminate or at least tame his longing "I" (self). As the professional "I" moves seriously through books and courses, preoccupied with grade averages, his longing "I" sees a girl, dates her, feels pleasure and wants more. The presenting statement is "I want to be successful professionally, but I know that if I get serious with her and start giving in to *those feelings* I'll fail as a student and forfeit my career (self-image)." "Those feelings" representing self say, "I just want to feel good." Any move to get that feeling endangers the self-concept, who reasons, "She really isn't that pretty or interesting, so why don't you just date someone else so you won't feel lonely." The self takes the sop, saying, "OK for now, but I won't let you forget about her." He dates someone else and comes to therapy as the now victimized self-image, saying, "I can't get her out of my mind."

Behavior developed through identification can occur by either the primary or secondary adaptation process. When it is a part of the primary process, it is absorbed, and the resultant identity is fitted into the person's total being. The behavior is sufficiently synthesized to make its origin doubtful even when viewed in close proximity to the donor. By contrast, when the identification is a result of the secondary adaptive process, it is carried like a tool and retains its own boundaries. It is readily identified as imitative behavior and often noted to be incongruent with other aspects of the person's personality.

A part of my fantasy is that thinking represents an aspect of the secondary psychological adaptive process. During primary adaptation thinking is superfluous. The thinking process is dedicated to justifying and providing approval for the organismic division. Its goal is to create "meaning" and is inspired by the painful meaninglessness of the splitting experience. Example: A loved one dies. Who has not struggled to find "meaning" in this? Who, at some time, has not come up with an explanatory balm? How difficult it is simply to allow the experience. "It just plain hurts—no meaning—just pain and tears." It seems easier for us to try to explain or justify: "It's beyond me but God must have some meaning in mind." (Here, since no explanation could possibly be adequate, the mind, in order to continue its thinking operation, creates an outside object, in this instance a mysterious, silent "God" to carry the responsibility for the meaning.) If this doesn't satisfy, then we may "think" of another explanation, denial. "Nothing 'really' means anything so why should it hurt?" It seems so difficult to dismiss these two extremes with the simple truth of the experience, "It just plain hurts—no explanations —just pain."

No one comes to therapy concerned with the aspects of themselves that have remained integrated. Beingness is never a patient. We are confronted only with the derivatives of the secondary psychological adaptive process, the self and the self-concept, and their intolerance with one another. The treatment is the reintegration of self and self-concept into aspects of beingness.

What are the causes of these two types of adaptations? This is a "think" question requesting an explanation. No one "knows" the answer but everyone may speculate about it. We each have our fantasies.

From somewhere, I hope more from my experiences than from my thoughts, a fantasy emerges that perhaps the secondary process occurs when there is neither the time nor the capacity to leisurely and genuinely digest, when perhaps something in the organism decides it would be better to sacrifice a part for the sake of the whole, like a lizard that abandons its tail in order to preserve its life. The remaining unscathed beingness offers the hope, if not the promise, of possible reintegration someday.

At the site where self and self-concept are created there is an arrest of development of that aspect of beingness. Any further changes at that locale are reflected in the development of the self-image. Associated with this change is a diminution of the organism's energy for adaptation, a part of which is now in the service of supporting the split. Another aspect of the change in energy is the substitution of chronic tension in place of relaxed energy potential. This tension is felt as a tonic muscular tension associated with anxiety or may be experienced in a clonic form such as tics. It can also occur internally. This is the nature of psychosomatic (and perhaps all) physical disorders.

As a result of this split, the phenomenon called hostility is born. This is not to be confused with organismic aggressiveness, which is a healthy, normal aspect of any organism's beingness. Hostility is a distorted, attenuated, ineffectual behavior that is often mistaken for aggressiveness. Aggressiveness is in the service of being, while hostility is in the service of either the self or self-concept, whichever part we are not identifying with at any given moment. Aggressiveness seeks to wrest from the environment whatever the organism needs. Hostility barks ineffectually, too involved with the internal struggle between self and self-concept to be competent.

Self and self-concept are opposing polarities like the two sides of a balanced scale; they cannot exist apart from each other. Any modification of self or self-image inevitably affects the other. When integrated, both disappear and an aspect of beingness is reborn. In treatment, supporting one against the other is tactical only and is for the purpose of setting the scene for reintegration. Reintegration occurs when the sides become evenly matched and there is no alternative to confrontation. Integration occurs spontaneously as each side simultaneously wins by submission.

In my experience, the creation of self and self-concept during the course of secondary process adaptation is relatively silent and without direct gross visible evidence. Indirect evidence is the birth of resentment. In the reversal process during therapy, reintegration is often associated with spontaneous laughter or crying, sometimes both simultaneously, followed by a diminution or complete loss of resentment or hostility in the involved area. Appreciation of others can also be observed in the involved area, where resentment previously prevailed.

One characteristic, a law of nature, is shared by all three components of personality: Everything functions to fulfill its own destiny. The essence of beingness is the need to fulfill itself. Self-concept comes into being, or—perhaps better said—"onto" being, as an imposition, that is, it is imposed on some part of a person "for its own good," so to speak. This is part of the nature, then, of self-image: to impose. To impose becomes one of its fundamental traits. Similarly, the self, that portion of beingness which was oppressed or depressed in the process of the imposition, must fulfill its destiny and continue to be thwarted. Thus, the self-image and the self collaborate with each other in their fulfillment. The pain and joys, the highs and lows, the polarities of feelings must all be experienced by both of these aspects of the person. In one way or another this has been noticed and expressed by many alluding to man's apparent need for trouble and pain. "I wonder why he does that when he knows that the consequences will be. . . ." "He" has a dozen "explanations" and keeps doing it.

Encourage a patient to do something he has a great desire to do but has not allowed his self (s.c. doesn't allow s.) and, should he do it despite the reluctant s.c., just stand back and watch s.c. go to work and retaliate. A new car is purchased impulsively by the self of a man over the objections of his self-concept. When he promptly goes out and injures his car or himself, many will say, while shaking their heads in amazement, "He wanted it so desperately" (desperation speaks of their recognition of the self's struggle to emerge from under s.c.) "I can't believe what happened," or "What a pity this happened to him" (fate is credited with the disaster, not s.c.).

Thinking and emotional feelings are the expressions of the stress-type of adaptation. These are the labels given to the expression of self (i.e., feeling) and self-concept (i.e., thinking) respectively. A mother in her fifth month of pregnancy said, "I'm ashamed to admit it, but I had the thought that I am missing something in pregnancy. I don't feel it." As she continued to explore this idea, associating it to her recent study of natural childbirth, she exposed her ideas: "I thought pregnancy was associated with physical discomfort, culminating in a painful labor and rewarded with a feeling of joy and pleasure with the baby. Without discomfort, how do I experience the pregnancy—by buying maternity clothes, with baby showers, by deference of others in elevators because I'm pregnant? I want to feel it."

She wanted to feel it with her brain. If she turned off that desire she would be able constantly to experience her pregnancy. She was caught up in the stress type of adaptation in which experiencing her pregnancy meant either feeling it as joy or pain or thinking about it. To experience the pregnancy as an aspect of the integrated or primary psychological adaptation she would "feel" it by awareness of her own bodily changes, "feel" her own circulatory changes, "feel" the uterine growth and the baby's viability and vitality. This is the "feeling" of an integrated primary psychologically adapted pregnancy.

In the state of being, feeling is organic; in the world of self vs. self-concept, feeling is emotional. In the state of being, feeling is sensing and experiencing sensations; in the world of self vs. self-concept, feeling is a midbrain irritation.

I had been working with one couple and their daughter for about six months. He was a prizefighter turned professor. She worked in the field of communications. They had always struggled sincerely and diligently in therapy and they were thoroughly honest. I had long since become very fond of both of them. On this occasion they came in and she began. She innocently and naively told him, "I can't understand what makes you so cold to me since my return." (She had been on a week-long business trip.) He angrily and disdainfully accused her of distorting the facts.

The "facts," as he saw them, were as follows: She did not immediately come downstairs when he came home from the office and shouted "hello"; when she did descend, she merely said "hello" in a cool manner and quickly retreated to the kitchen. As further proof of her indifference, the husband reported he had had time to put the flowers he had bought her in a vase before she deigned to come downstairs and greet him. Furthermore, she dismissed them (also) with a casual "How nice." They both sat silently through dinner. He didn't eat and afterwards sat down in the livingroom to read a paper. She followed, sat at his feet, put her head on his knee and asked what was the matter. "You know damn well what the matter is—and you always come over when *you* are ready, after you've made me mad, and then you give me that innocent act." She responded innocently, "I don't understand what you mean."

These were the "facts" which they both agreed upon, with the exception that she did in fact call him at work but his secretary failed to notify him. But it was not "promptly on her return," for he had called home about the time she was expected and learned from the housekeeper that his wife had already arrived and, after a cup of coffee with a neighbor, had departed to pick up their son at school—all this before placing the call to him as she had promised. Oh yes, and he had on previous occasions advised her to speak directly to him at work, and on this occasion she had not insisted on being put through to him.

She now was still, if not more so, innocently aloof and ostensibly understanding, while he was still, if not more so, disdainful and angry. Such postures! Each is the posture of a self-image. They are learned social poses that are painful, lonely and require considerable energy to maintain. Neither could move in this encounter to alter the situation.

I told them of my anguish, sadness and feeling of helplessness. I told them what I saw: two people who needed and wanted each other, yet each similarly hiding the needs and wants, although in slightly different ways; both suffering from the same inability to express their remarkably parallel responses to the separation. They both felt the natural (self) fantasies of concern, such as, "Will this separation change our love? Will we feel the same about each other afterwards? Will he or she become interested in someone else? Is my place in his or her life altered or threatened?" All doubts stemmed from the same source—doubts about their own lovableness. And all went uncorrected because of the same obstacle, the self-image of each that said that each self dare not express fears or concern; the self-image that said that the self dare not admit anguished feelings, especially to a loved one, since there was some doubt of the other's love (their own lovableness). It pained me to see how they needed to hide from each other. For me these were the "facts" as I both experienced and expressed them. The expression of my "self" to them became the spokesman for each of theirs. My expression became new added "facts." Sharing my anguish with them altered their responses to each other.

Interventions will be discussed more thoroughly in a later chapter, but for the present I wish to translate this encounter in terms of self, self-concept and beingness. Our individual needs are more than individual; they are universal. What is individual is merely the degree to which we recognize them and the highly unique way in which each of us strives to fulfill them—both factors learned in preceding experiences.

Disdain, anger, innocence, aloofness are all expressions of self-concept or self-image. They are social responses, not biological responses. They are learned poses. I am not interested in *why* these are used; I am only interested in whether they are used. I prefer that they not be used, for I have tried them and found them lacking. They are used to save "face." This is the goal of the imposed self-image or self-concept and the face that it saves is only its own. But the face on the self-image is not enough for me when it means sacrificing other parts. Some of us think that saving face is necessary. Thinking is another tool that the self-image uses to achieve its ends. When our entire being has an experience, we become acutely aware of how limited and hollow thinking can be.

As the husband and wife began to absorb what I said, they changed. As they began to admit into their own awareness the other parts of themselves which had been excluded, his anger turned to tears and his disdain to affection. Her innocence changed to an embarrassed confession of knowing, and then her aloofness became a smiling, relaxed reaching to him and holding his hand. I had attenuated their images, allowing each "self" to emerge. This followed from what I was, not merely what I said. Had I only "interpreted" their behavior I would have gained only "understanding." Their work was not done. It had just begun. With this new awareness, the work of integrating these divided aspects of self and self-concept into the re-creation of being, into the restoration of the fully acceptable "I am," began.

In their initial statements each of them was saying, "I (self) feel fearful and unlovable but I (self-concept) must not admit this into my (and your) awareness." The righteous anger or the aloofness was the expression of the self-image as it struggled to obscure the self. I, the therapist, responded in part with my more reintegrated self and spoke to their self portions. My previous experiences with them told me that I could ignore their self-concept; in revealing my pain, helplessness and perceptions as I did, I was "being" with them.

I revealed my awareness of me. I continued to do this. As long as I am able to do this, progress in therapy is possible. As long as any one of us in an encounter is able to do this there is hope of progress. It need not always be the therapist. It is never *only* the therapist.

With another couple, the husband continually pushed people away by endless interrogations and accusations reminiscent of the cartoon depicting the patient saying to the therapist, "I don't know why all the stupes in the world can't get along with me. Can you help or are you a fathead like all the rest?" Each of the husband's sentences began with either "What do you mean by . . ." or "You are . . ." followed by either a one-word label such as "stupid" or a phrase label such as ". . . trying to tell me what to do." He never started a sentence with the word "I." After I pointed this out to him during repeated encounters with his wife, he began doing it with me. I pointed out both the behavior and its continuation in relation to me, and he continued with his same kind of response. Finally I became exasperated, then furious. I angrily pointed out his game of coming here and telling me that I am an authority and that I should help him and then dismissing anything that I might say. He did this with his wife and I am sure elsewhere also. As he astutely labeled me—"you're angry"—I became even more angry and found myself shouting at him from my very core. I stopped because our time was up and I dismissed them. His parting comment was, "I want you to know that I am as upset about our communication problem as you are." He remained impassive, and I was silent; we parted.

As this engineer came in with his wife on the next visit, he sat down and asked my permission to respond to our encounter of the previous week. He pulled out a booklet and began to read his response to that session. His wife said, "Why in hell don't you just talk to him and stop reciting?" He responded solemnly, if not admirably, "This is the way I choose to do it." I appreciated this as it represented an "I" statement. He continued reading to me. The essence of what he read was that he concluded that I must have been playing a game with him by becoming so angry, and the object of my game was either to make him angry or to force him out of the office. I interrupted him at this point to say that my anger, on the contrary, was an expression of me which permitted me to remain with him and that it was in no way artificial. He told me his response to me now was the same as last week, "My feeling right now is that I am perplexed. I may also be scared."

I pointed out to him that I knew we lived in different worlds and that perhaps just exploring our differences might be our starting point now. He appeared grateful and we continued to work. I told him I could appreciate his perplexity as well as his fear, but I could not appreciate his accusations. I told him of the impossible bind I felt I was in when he asked for help and then accused me of trying to tell him what to do with any suggestion I made. He replied by telling me that he had no intention of doing something just because I said so and that he intended to take it under advisement. I told him I thought that was a rather stupid comment for such an intelligent individual as he appeared to be, since it seemed to me an obvious assumption for all encounters. He agreed, adding affectlessly, "But I don't like what you said." This was a tremendous improvement for him. It was as though he suddenly learned that he could not like something though it was logical. He did not accuse.

An essential consideration in any encounter is the difference in the way people respond depending on whether they are in the self/self-concept world or in the world of beingness. In the world of beingness anger can be understood as a reaching towards, while in the world of self-image and self such behavior is seen as manipulative. The essential differences in these two worlds is that, in the world of beingness, behavior is directed towards the fullest possible expression of one's total person in the context of others; in the world of self and self-concept, attention goes exclusively to "the other" and behavior is seen in relation to and in response to "the other." This behavior of the world of self and self-concept can be either intellectual, as we saw in this encounter, or emotional. There is, for example, crying because one is sad as well as crying to achieve mastery of someone else. To me it is unimportant whether self/self-concept behavior is conscious or unconscious, witting or unwitting; such knowledge may modify my way of responding to it, but it would not stop me from combating it.

With this couple it might be easy to say that what he does intellectually, his wife does emotionally. That is, he attempts to manipulate with logic and she with affect. Both function in the world of self and self-concept. Both function to manipulate the other. She can no more cry for herself ("What good would it do?") than he can be logical exclusively for himself. For instance, he could never come to a concluding statement such as, "I don't care whether I have convinced you or not, but I sure feel good having made all those logical sequences."

THEORETICAL CONSIDERATIONS OF REALITY

Definitions and arguments concerning reality are endless and for the most part futile, and that is as it should be. We are an intimate part of reality and for reality to define reality with one of its working tools—

words and ideas—is quite impossible. The tools are far too limited to cope with the concept, and the subject is much too much a part of the object. Yet it is sometimes fun to wile away moments of our "real" existence speculating. (Really, it is.) Besides it is "really" helpful to be conversant with some "real" ideas about reality that could possibly lend "real" substance to discussions about reality, especially since reality can be looked at in so many ways and there are so many different kinds of reality.

Psychological reality is the unique composite of awareness and experience in the evanescent moment.

Awareness is the lens through which we perceive ourselves and the world around us. It may or may not accurately describe our experience. Accuracy is validated by others whom we select to be our validators.

At birth, awareness does not differentiate self from others, thus the internal signal of hunger and the external absence of mother's breast are felt as one pain. As we develop, we are taught not only to differentiate, but what we should or should not differentiate; we are taught what we should be aware of. "Be aware of my sadness when I cry" one mother teaches. "Ignore my sadness when I cry" another mother decrees. "Finish the food on your plate" means "Awareness of the emptiness of your plate should determine your gastric satiety, not the awareness of signals from nerve endings in your stomach wall."

Tattoos, I was taught, were not to be a part of my image. I learned that they were unattractive, "low-class," indicative of self-mutilation and to be stricken from my awareness. Some 30 years later, I spent many hours with a most likable patient, observing many nonverbal aspects of his behavior such as grimaces, postures and gestures. Such awareness of behavior I have been encouraged to develop. It was not until someone else inquired about this man's tattoos, which were in plain sight, covering both arms, that I became aware of them. Had I not liked this man, his tattoos would have immediately drawn my attention. Thus, the lens of awareness for each of us develops a unique, though often not singular, astigmatic composition through which we perceive our world. Astigmatism is not necessarily good or bad, healthy or pathological. It is simply inevitable.

At any given moment our awareness may or may not be different from the awareness of another person, though different is more likely. Coming to recognize and appreciate these differences is one of the initial aims of experiential therapy. The relative infrequency of similarities in perceptions contributes to the acclaim we give to likeness. Such is the nature of social organization in essentially all its aspects. I've never heard of a group organized for the express purpose of bringing together those of unlike mind. Aristotle's observation concerning birds of a feather describes a natural law which applies to man's thoughts and behavior as well as his species.

The experience, the second aspect of psychological reality, is the sensory-motor sequence of the organism in time. The simplest experience consists of a stimulus and a response of equal and opposing force. This can be far more easily isolated neurologically than psychologically. Psychologically, the collected apperceptive mass, the current context and the anticipated future implications, all impinge to some degree in even the simplest, most spontaneous psychological experiences. This need not deter us, however, from attempting to define encounters—from the most elemental concordant nonverbal exchanges through the most complex intrafamilial discord.

First, it is necessary to acknowledge that every experience must contain both sensory and motor components. These are two sides of a coin which cannot exist singly. Thus, in every encounter, for every stimulus there must be a response, for every act there must be a reaction. We must know that acts and responses may be expressed cortically as nonverbalized ideas or attitudes, motorically from fighting to flight and/or viscerally, as alternatives to a direct, verbal exchange.

Next, we must consider the immediate context of the experience, for it is this context, composed of internal and external awareness, that determines the behavioral course. For example, when seriously challenged I may strike back verbally (a) if the challenger is smaller than I, (b) if I have supporting allies or available avenues of escape, or (c) if my internal structure permits me to confront this particular opponent. I'm more likely to be able to respond this way if the opponent is my child than if he or she were my parent, at home than in public, etc.

A person's awareness or perception about his own behavior often does not coincide with the experience as perceived by us, the therapist or others. As therapists, it is imperative that we come to know that everything said about psychological reality applies equally to us as therapists and that we have the additional task of attending to our awareness and the current experience we may be having with clients. We have no exclusive capacity for so-called objectivity but are merely somewhat more knowledgeable and aware, sometimes.

The person who has learned to be aware of his unfinished plate of food rather than his state of gastric satiety must now incorporate rationally this astigmatic awareness in current experiences. Suppose his stomach is full and there is still food on his plate. He may now become "aware" of other than stomach signals, such as something in the plate of food that makes it inedible, or his awareness may flee to another time and place to arrange the rescue. "I remembered I have a two o'clock appointment. What a pity I can't finish this delicious food, but surely you (actually speaking to his own self-concept) understand." This experience is couched in the framework of the astigmatic awareness. This person perceives himself differently than I perceive him in this scene. Thus, our psychological realities are quite different.

We can generally agree more readily that there is or has been an experience than on our perceptions (awareness) of what constituted the experience.

Why impinge my psychological reality on my patient? In all likelihood, he now sits in my office because he has complained of chronic indigestion for many years and no obvious medical basis for it has been found. It is my awareness that his chronic indigestion is part and parcel of a chronic psychological indigestion derived from earlier secondary adaptation. My own psychological reality is composed of experiences and awareness that compel me to conclude that returning his gastric eyes to his stomach will abate his symptoms. How this is achieved belongs to another chapter.

The third aspect of psychological reality is the evanescent omnipresent current moment that is ever constant and ever in motion and in which all awareness and experience occur. Awareness can shift, experience can change, but the existing moment transpires with unique stability. The depth with which we experience each moment is a composite of all the wealth and poverty of our past experiences that our awareness permits us to admit. The current moment is immutable. It is in this current mercurial moment that awareness and experiences exist. Though awareness may shift to other times and places or may narrow to focus upon a minute detail, and though experiences may be distorted or attenuated, the current moment flows unalterably. This moment contains all of the tragic wealth of our past experiences, conscious or not. It is in this inevitable moment that we exist.

During sleep, awareness is dimmed, experience paled, yet all three aspects of psychological reality continue to function. During sleep, movement occurs to accommodate circulatory needs; dreams occur to meet psychological needs; bedwetting and falling off that slim platform usually do not occur; and early awakening for vacations often occurs unheralded by alarm clocks. Evidence is rampant that psychological reality is operant during sleep.

Fantasy is *not* the opposite of psychological reality. Fantasy is a type of psychological reality whose prime characteristic difference is the attenuation of the experience. It differs from sleep in that awareness is not dimmed, but is similar to sleep in that awareness is directed essentially inwards. I say attenuation rather than elimination of experience, because it is not possible to eliminate completely our sensory-motor apparatus. Thus we can sit in a room with other persons and "talk about" or sit quietly alone in our reverie. When we do this, our awareness has taken off on a flight and does not attend the current experience. "Hereness" and "nowness" are temporarily ignored. When this occurs, the current experience, that is the stimulus-response interaction between organisms, is reduced in intensity. Those involved agree that attention to what each is doing to or with the other one is not of immediate concern, thus the experience takes on a specific quality of diminished intensity. This attenuated state is a special type of psychological reality called "fantasy."

The difference between fantasy and other states of psychological reality is the difference between relating a memory as a distant piece of data and experiencing the memory with all the flavor, sensations and affect of the actual incident. It is the difference between shouting joyously, "I have a perfect bead on the target," and pulling the trigger. It is the difference between saying, "I love you," and loving. It is the difference between living in the referential world of the observer-reporter and living in the world of being, feeling, experiencing and doing. Thus, all past as well as future constructs are in the service of fantasy: relating memories, future plans, five minutes ago, five minutes hence, hopes, dreams, expectations, the world of ideas, planning, thinking. Sitting around with colleagues discussing theoretical aspects of therapy is fantasy. "Talking about" things with patients is fantasy.

Is there value in differentiating fantasied from nonfantasied reality? If exclusively used, fantasied reality becomes a wasteland and had best be interrupted. In the referential, removed "aboutness" of the uninvolved world there is little opportunity for change. When the "aboutness" is changed to "beingness," the referential to experiential, then and only then can changes in behavior occur. As a respite from nonfantasied reality, such as in meditation, fantasy is a valuable integrative experience that enhances future nonfantasied experiences.

All therapists have experienced a patient reporting without affect an important childhood memory that, at this time, represents a meaningless discourse which alters nothing. The person exists merely as a reporter. The memory is presented in the referential world. The patient is referring to something that has occurred to him, something to which he holds on, yet something he will not touch. In other therapy models, the patient may return to this memory much later in therapy. On this latter occasion, however, the patient reexperiences the memory with all the flavor and affect of its original; only then do we begin the closure or finishing of a "real" situation for this patient. The person has shifted from reporter to vital participant. For any therapeutic endeavor to be successful, it is necessary for the patient to experience rather than to "talk-about" something; to live it, not report it. This is an essential principle of the experiential approach to family therapy. It is reflected in the techniques which are directed towards eliciting an experience in preference to talking about experiences. How this is done is discussed in a subsequent chapter.

4

The Therapist

At the inception of modern psychiatry, in the Freudian tradition, there was a beginning awareness of the therapist as a personal factor in the therapeutic encounter. This awareness was largely manifested in an effort to keep the therapist as a person out of the encounter. Awareness of countertransference—the therapist's beingness—was for the expressed purpose of excluding this vitality of the therapist from the encounter. It was considered a contaminant, hopefully nearly eliminated by prolonged preparatory analysis.

The explanation that this exclusion was to protect the patient seems erroneous when viewed from an existential frame of reference. More likely, excluding the therapist as a person was to protect the therapist, in this instance, Sigmund Freud. Another purported purpose of understanding countertransference was to clear the vision of the therapist to enable him to see his patients more objectively. This notion of creating an "immaculate perception" was consonant with Freud's era, an era in which objectivity—isolation of subject and object—was considered not only reasonable but downright scientific. The therapist purposely created

64

a no-encounter framework. This attitude of recognizing only one living person's presence, the patient, in some instances diminished and in others precluded the opportunity for growth and development.

A consequence, of course, was that therapy required a long period of time. That progress occurred at all might be considered surprising were it not that the therapist, being alive, could not totally and consistently exclude himself from participation in the encounter. Furthermore, patients, as all of us, have a tendency for psychological economy and, therefore, would tend to grasp what they needed in fantasy, if it were not available in fact.

People who could not fit into the no-encounter framework were listed as untreatable. The psychodiagnostic categories familiarly known as the character disorders, psychotics and schizophrenics—all those unable to function fruitfully in a no-encounter framework—were labeled as untreatable by psychotherapy. Patients able to derive benefits, despite the therapist's commitment to noninvolvement with them, were acceptable and given the label "treatable neurotics."

Today, our reasonable or scientific posture is predicated on a more unified theoretical construct in which subject and object, victim and victimizer, winner and loser, good and bad, are merely descriptive titles for polarities of unified or, at least, interrelated aspects of a single composite. In keeping, then, with our current philosophy, psychotherapy is evolving a model wherein the therapist and patient are similarly though not identically encouraged to impinge on each other, and the vitality of the therapist-person is welcomed. This new posture of the therapist has the distinct advantage of not giving the patient the conflicting message: "Learn from my words, not from my behavior."

This evolution to an existential, if you will, viewpoint in which the therapist truly becomes a person who brings to the therapeutic encounter merely a different set of experiences now provides a scene for growth and development for more people—character disorders, schizophrenics and even therapists.

What Does the Therapist Do?

Therapists have forces within them that operate to impede the course of therapy as well as to propel it on its way. Every patient similarly brings forces which propel therapy on its way in addition to those which impede it; in the past the latter commanded almost exclusive attention. This is not to say there are no differences between the patient and the therapist in terms of impeding and propelling forces, but rather to recognize a fluctuating balance in which the therapist and patient exchange labels perhaps more often than either would like to acknowledge.

Moments occur in therapy where neither identified therapist nor identified patient knows what to do. Such moments can be called an impasse. Acknowledging that an impasse exists and exploring the experience can be a fruitful off-ramp.

When there is persistently no change, therapy comes to a standstill, and a likely conclusion to the encounter would be the termination of the therapist-patient relationship. Whether this moment is due to the improved state of the patient or the inability of the therapist to inspire further developments, therapists and patients acknowledge it by termination of the financial flow—which has been, until this point, an integral part of the encounter, an added weight which establishes and maintains a balance in the encounter.

If the vitality of the therapist as a person is considered one significant aspect of the therapeutic force in experiential psychotherapy, the vitality of the encounter is another. Vitality of the encounter is sustained by insistent, preferential attention to the current moment, to what each person is doing in it, and to how each person uses the time.

During the course of therapy, the therapist initially functions merely as a catalyst, encouraging family members to confront one another more openly and directly. For example, behavioral nuances such as shrugging or grimacing are called to the attention of the person exhibiting them and the appropriate words for the gestures are sought. This catalytic effect of the therapist is largely one of enhancing awareness and encouraging more direct encountering. It includes suggestions for altered behavior, experiments to be tried, personal observations of how the therapist experiences what is occurring and sometimes simple directions or advice. Often such interventions are readily accepted, resulting in new, successful experiences without repercussions from within (represented by the unconscious) or from without (by family members).

From time to time, however, such dispassionate offerings are ignored, and the therapist may become frustrated. When this occurs, rather than retreat to a questioning "Why did you do that?" which would tend to disrupt the encounter in favor of sending everyone off to an historical retreat and search operation, the therapist hopefully will consider himself sufficiently worthy to demand that he not be ignored. Patients, of course, have the same right. All have the right to disagree and even to tell each other to go to hell, if they wish, but never to ignore. By setting such an example, a worthwhile aspect of successful encountering is demonstrated at the same time this encounter is being kept vital by remaining in the here and now.

This is not the only time the therapist's behavior may change from catalyst to passionate participant. Perhaps, while a parent and child are encountering, the therapist may become emotionally involved and choose to introduce his words and feelings for all to experience. This stimulus, when truly representative of the therapist at that moment, generally will have a salutary effect, even if later it is concluded that his expressed feeling was meant for someone else or that his charged words were inaccurate. The right to be, and the right to be wrong, as sometimes we all are, also serves well to keep the encounter alive and exemplary. Of course, to acknowledge such errors fully, with sadness or shame, if such feelings are present, protects the integrity of the encounter and, in my experience, has always been appreciated.

Experiential psychotherapy within families is not a method for teaching people merely how to improve their verbal communications. It is rather an approach which uses, among other things, the clarification of messages between and among people to enrich their life experiences. The assumptions inherent in this approach are: that the minds of people function only in the context of the minds of other people; that the significant "other" people, who are the environment in which we live, are most often found within the group called "the family"; that doing psychotherapy within the framework of the current family, therefore, comes closest to the treatment of the total individual; that the basic unit for therapy is the "organism-in-environment." It is further assumed that attending to what we do with each other, how we do it, and how we respond to one another in our current experience increases awareness of one's person in the meaningful context of the world of others; that this increased awareness, not in isolation but as experienced with others, leads to more meaningful exchanges; and that the more meaningful our exchange, the more profound are the satisfactions with which we experience our existence. It is in this framework and to this end that all of the technical aspects of experiential psychotherapy are dedicated.

In the comments that follow I am, of course, discussing largely my own experiences as a therapist. In discussing what a therapist does in this

approach, I am discussing what I do. I would feel I was creating an unnecessary distance between myself and the reader by relating my own
experiences in the third person. In one sense there is no such separation
of "the therapist" and "this approach," for during my hours as a therapist, I am my approach. "What" I do as a therapist is public domain,
so to speak; "how" I do it is uniquely me. "What" I describe can be
generalized and applied by others. "How" the "what" is manifest becomes the uniqueness of each therapist-person.

In this volume, personal reactions of the therapist are frequently discussed. They are exclusively for the purpose of exemplifying the general
premises of experiential psychotherapy. They are not recommended as
precise interventions. My behavior may or may not coincide with yours
in a given situation. The general premise which recommends active commitment of the therapist in the here and now always prevails. For example, aging increases the authority of the therapist. A casual comment by
an older therapist may carry weight equal to a more vigorous, repetitive
intervention of a younger therapist. Partially, experiential skill is responsible. The association by most people of age with wisdom has a
strong influence. A prophetic remark of a young man is less likely to be
heard than the grunt of a graybeard. Sensitive suggestions of a sage are
more audible than equally appropriate urgings of a novice. This influences the therapist's modus, the "how" of his therapeutic application.
The existential premises of experiential psychotherapy, however, remain
unaltered.

It is my impression that most obstacles that emerge during the
course of therapy belong to the therapist and not to patient "resistance."
It is my belief that the label "resistance" creates a poor attitude, born
of the therapist's frustrations; a simple statement by the therapist, such
as "I want to be more effective than I am at this moment and I don't like
it (you) when I'm not," is more honest and effective.

The existential influence in psychotherapy today has led to the frequent use of "I-thou" phrasing, acknowledging the therapist as a real
person in the therapeutic encounter. Yet, when the literature is scrutinized, encounters are still described in terms of individual behavior. It is
rare indeed for scenes to be reported in the literature in which patients
and therapist change, much less scenes in which the therapist alone
changes. Patients are still seen as individual pathological units, wearing
titles such as "depressed" or "paranoid." Rarely is paranoid behavior, for
instance, described exclusively in relation to the paranoid-evoking be-

havior of the therapist. It is still presumed that such behavior is largely an internal affair. To say that paranoid-evoking behavior of others, particularly of therapists, has not been elaborately explored in the psychotherapy literature is an understatement.

People labeled paranoid frighten me. This was more true in years gone by than today. I originally cajoled them casually and avoided closeness, clearly understanding that it was they who had the difficulty with closeness. I was unable to help them much, but always saw to it that I felt safe. When paranoid behavior was exhibited by attractive females of small stature, I fearlessly confronted them, often converting their paranoid behavior into depression and finally, with continued work, helping them. More recently, I have found myself confronting such people, male and female alike, with my own suspiciousness, offering them my feelings of being treated unfairly by them, and engaging their assistance to cope with my concern.

This behavior of mine has evolved since I have become less afraid of being momentarily the patient. An interesting consequence is that my perception of these people has altered; somehow I am not as aware of the paranoid traits in the fearful way that I once was. My experience has been that these people, perhaps initially suspicious, soon become interested in helping me. I like it and they like it. There is closeness. I am less sure now than I ever have been about the trait called paranoid.

An estranged couple was referred to me by a colleague who had diagnosed the husband as a dangerously paranoid individual. The couple had been divorced for two years but this man had been unable to detach himself from his wife and children, came around constantly, and harassed her boyfriends.

In the recent past one of her boyfriends had been shot after the husband threatened to shoot him if he continued to come around. Though nothing was proven, everyone suspected the husband. The wife was motivated to agree to a conjoint interview by a desire to disentangle herself from her former husband. He was obviously motivated to agree to conjoint therapy by his secret hope for reconciliation. As the initial session unfolded, the above information was revealed and the husband appeared extremely cooperative, constantly smiling, very friendly, almost to the point of being obsequious. He, of course, denied all of the charges made by the wife and, when he was unable to deny them flatly, he laughingly belittled them. He frightened me. I told him so. I explored with him my fear of him and my suspicions about him.

As I spoke, he seemed to gradually relax and relinquish his ever-present smile, which I had pointed up as one of my most serious concerns. As he responded to me, I began to feel sad and shared this with him. Soon we were both in tears as he revealed the terrible loss he experienced in this divorce. He began to share with me the sense of isolation that he had felt most of his life and his embarrassment about his tears. In the next session his wife reported that he had made out her alimony and child support check in her own name for the first time, rather than to "Mrs. George ......" Her comment both pleased and saddened me and I turned to him expressing my sadness. He again cried.

Sometimes during the course of therapy I yell and shout. I learned it from my father. I hope my rage is less impotent than his but I seriously doubt it. I am too close yet to know. My teenage son responds favorably to my rage, which makes me feel that it is effective. Effective means I get what I want. When he piles up a series of behaviors beyond my tolerance—staying out past my curfew limits, sloppy room, late for dinner, etc.—and my friendly appeals fail, I finally blow up with a righteous lecture in an angry voice and sincerely outraged gesticulations. He responds. For days, sometimes weeks or months, his behavior is altered. He is more cheerful and cooperative. He has, in fact, revealed to me that this is preferable to other ineffectual poses I have, such as imploring. After years of this kind of interacting with my children, I finally realized this stimulus and response is a cliché: Soft parental behavior equals unchanged child behavior; sincere rage equals cooperation. I taught him this pattern.

During therapy my enraged confrontations don't always produce this cooperative behavior, though when I try it I often expect it to work. One patient responds to simple offerings, another to an open request, a third to assisted self-exploration, still another only to vigorous, affectful confrontations. I must know not only my own behavior but that of my patient as well. I cannot know this in advance, nor is it necessary. It is only necessary that we interact; in the course of such interaction we will become aware of our differences and will inevitably affect each other.

I am not always the same. At times I sense quite correctly what elicits others' cooperative behaviors and at other times I do not. At times I am more interested in others and more willing to engage with them. When my confidence is dented or I feel slightly depressed, I am more likely to become angry and expect more. For me, this is recidivism; this is onto-logical repetition of earlier environmental influences. It is not necessary that I divest myself of these foibles in order to be a successful therapist. In fact, as certain behavior patterns of mine have been inevitably changed through the years, I have found an increasing effectiveness with people in more encounters, but also a diminishing interest and, consequently, a diminishing impact in other encounters.

PREPARATION OF THERAPISTS

At this point it might be well to ask: What preparation would be most suitable for a therapist who wishes to become experientially involved in therapy? The requirements for being an experiential psychotherapist are simple. Certification by any accredited professional, helping discipline is sufficient—sufficient to indicate that one is civilized enough to be in-terested in working for a living and capable of some studied behavior. Selecting one of the helping professions completes the requirements by revealing an interest in negotiating human behavior. A lengthy pre-analysis is unnecessary as the experiential approach not only allows but encourages the therapist's growth and development as a valuable and exemplary part of the therapeutic atmosphere.

The requirements are simple but the personal qualifications are per-haps not. A compelling need to meddle in the lives of others and an arrogant desire to be heard are distinct assets, if not absolute necessities, particularly when one works with families. Enough instability to encour-age experimentation and to take risks, coupled with enough rigidity to unyieldingly demand responsive behavior, are necessities. A curiosity about human behavior, leading to constant nit-picking at all nuances of behavior, a broad tolerance for differences, and a capacity to understand what it is like to be the other person are all valuable. To have lived vigorously enough to be scarred from bruises, rather than scared from the thought of getting bruises, is essential. A selective yet persistent con-trariness is most rewarding. To be suspicious and fearful enough not to trust manifest behavior and experienced enough to know intentions and motives cannot be labeled bad (or good) is wise. And finally, it is par-ticularly gratifying to be sufficiently self-critical to be suspect of one's own behavior, courageous enough to make mistakes, and loving enough to acknowledge them.

All therapists, appropriately, have some need for personal satisfaction from their work. "The money isn't enough," I have said to many a patient whose premise seemed to be, "I'm paying, now perform." I am available for a full, rich encounter. I choose not to be an entertainer. I want and need, among other things, altered behavior from my patients, not mere verbal and financial appreciation.

RELUCTANCE OF THERAPISTS

The reluctance of therapists to be intimately involved with their patients is expressed in many ways. Once, many years ago, I was to demonstrate a family therapy interview; the therapists, representing all disciplines, expressed concern when I suggested interviewing the family in our conference room in preference to using the one-way mirror. They worried about the fears and discomforts they were sure family members would experience. Their concern ranged from such simple comments as, "They would be uncomfortable, especially the children," to the most elaborate psychodynamic formulations which suggested that participation by the family would be limited by their presence. At no time did any therapist in the room acknowledge any personal reluctance.

The chairman of this meeting, himself an astute clinician, said, "Besides all of this concern about the family to be interviewed, I sense that among all of us there is a personal objection to such closeness, and I would like a show of hands to see if there are others here who agree with what I am saying." Every hand in the room went up. This question was followed with another, "I would like a show of hands for those of you who feel this resistance lies within you, yourself." Not one hand went up. Everyone looked around and, after a surprised moment, began laughing sheepishly.

Experiential therapy is a personal matter for each therapist. Terms such as "therapeutic techniques," "therapeutic skills," "tools of therapy" are useful only for distancing the therapist from the patients. There are no tools or skills; there are only people.

A prevailing notion is that there are two types of therapist behavior which should be excluded from therapy. First is the therapist's personal response to what is going on in the session. This may be expressed in such pertinent statements as, "I'm afraid of you" or "I don't know what to do at this moment and I feel embarrassed" or "You are so attractive I find it difficult to listen to you" or, perhaps, "I am repelled by your appearance and feel some shame in sharing this with you." Objections to making such statements are often expressed by therapists with remarks such as, "You shouldn't have such feelings" or "You are being unnecessarily cruel and, after all, it is just your opinion."

It is not important to me whether or not I *should* have such feelings but only whether or not I *do* have them. It is not important whether I am seen as cruel in revealing what I am experiencing in a session but whether or not *it is necessary for me* to reveal it. Am I saying it in order to avoid harboring the thought ‧and thus becoming preoccupied with trying to exclude it? Yes. This would diminish my participation, whereas simply expressing what I experience permits me to remain fully involved. Immediately after expressing myself, I feel differently. Expressing fear, for example, diminishes my fear, much like joy and relief often follow in the wake of sadness expressed.

The other kind of personal behavior that therapists have attempted to exclude but that, in experiential psychotherapy, is best included is the expression of feelings that are unmistakably unrelated such as, "I am tired today" or "I can't seem to tune in today as I am preoccupied."

During the course of‧a group session, I was having difficulty in attending what was occurring. I felt shallow and had no awareness of what was causing my difficulty. Finally, at one point I introduced this concern and began a personal search. I felt somewhat as though I were interrupting and expressed this. I felt that whatever was troubling me had absolutely nothing to do with them and expressed this also. After several minutes of ruminative searching I mentioned that I felt sad and could not think of anything that I might be feeling sad about. I mentioned that it seemed to have been coming on for several days but that today it seemed so pervasive within me that I could no longer avoid it.

Then it dawned on me that today was the fifth anniversary of my father's death. As I told them this, I began to cry. I continued to talk with them about my father and continued crying. The remainder of the time was spent with my tears, on this subject. Nearing the end of our meeting, others joined in with their reactions both to me today and to their own fathers. At the conclusion of our session everyone expressed appreciation to me for my willingness to share myself. In later sessions they repeatedly referred back to this meeting as having a profound effect in helping them to be (themselves).

It no longer occurs to me to think that what I am or what I experienced may not be pertinent to this encounter. What I am *is* pertinent to the encounter. It has no meaning to say that what I am may not have to do with "them." What I am has to do with the people I am with at that moment. That they may not be etiological factors is quite peripheral. Too much attention and importance has been given to genetic pertinence. I did not create their feelings of the moment either, but this does not mean that they do not have an effect on me, nor does it imply that I, in return, cannot become involved with them. In any encounter what I am must be considered pertinent to the others. If it is pertinent, to know it and include it will usually enhance rather than diminish the encounter.

Someone once said of me critically, "You sometimes get more out of the treatment than your patients." By "more" I presume they mean greater self-awareness and fulfillment, for this is the "more" for which we all strive. I feel flattered, not criticized. I would hope this critique were true. Somehow I see this as consonant with greater self-awareness and fulfillment for my patients as well. Such criticism seems rooted in a seesaw philosophy which conceives that the enrichment of one is necessarily at the expense of another. This is often witnessed in families where a parent or spouse feels dwarfed or diminished in the wake of someone else's achievement. Or perhaps it is expressed as feeling less loved when another member of the family is, for the moment, being appreciated.

A child graduates from school and a parent cries for many reasons— appreciation, gratitude, pride—but the tears also represent loss. The self-image as parent is diminished as graduation brings the child a step closer to separation from the parent, as a child. We all know that this is just a transient gap that is bridged; we lose the child and regain him later as a person or a friend. Yet at these times we are often aware only of the loss. The image, role, posture of parent is in fact diminished. The totality of that person of whom only a part is labeled parent is in fact enriched by both the graduation and the sadness. And so it is also in therapy that the therapist may at times become upset with the loss of his self-image as therapist, but it is in experiencing and sharing this loss in its fullest measure that all requirements are met for a therapeutic encounter which is available to everyone.

The richest distillation of the therapist's person at any given moment carries the greatest therapeutic impact. It is the clearest possible statement of who I am. It is the statement of who I am, carried in such a manner that there need be no mistake about it. I may come out in a simple, calm statement beginning with the words "I am . . ."; I may come out angrily critical and accusing; I may be expressed distantly with an indifferent pronoun such as "It seems . . ."; or I may be expressed as a fantasy that I am having at that moment, which I identify as a fantasy first and then pursue. At times, knowing only that I am dissatisfied with what's going on, I interject this comment as an opening for further exploration and clarification of who I am.

Dissatisfaction is a painful feeling for me, one for which, like a child, I have no patience. I am dissatisfied when I feel unaccepted, when I am not appreciated, when I do not feel effective. For me, dissatisfaction elicits action. During therapy this means verbal action, vocal range finding, "speaking my mind" aloud to a shared exploration of our dilemma. Yes, *our* dilemma, for the dilemma cannot be mine alone any more than my clients' distress is solely theirs when we are together.

If I am uncertain about what troubles me, I will share my uncertainty. If I am dissatisfied with the ongoing scene, I will spell it out to each participant with whom I feel dissatisfaction. If I am concerned with our effectiveness together, I am likely to express this, not as an idle observation, but as either an aloud self-exploration or an attack upon specific members whom I hold responsible at the moment. Should such a member fail to answer the charge, I will invite his response. During a family interview, a dilemma is always *ours*, never solely *mine* or *theirs*.

I recall a first interview with a couple in which the wife rambled incoherently and the husband kept responding to her aimless remarks with answers, attempting to establish a reasonable discussion. Ignoring her nonpertinent responses, he would continue to pick up her comments and attempt to negotiate a conversation. At first I was slightly anxious, as I often am in the presence of an unfamiliar interaction. For a brief time, this kept me rather quietly searching. As their exchange continued I became amused, sad and then distraught, not knowing what to do or say. Finally I said just that and then continued, "Since I don't know where to begin I'll just tell you how I see us here."

To her I said, "You're crazy. You make no sense at all with all your trying." And turning to him I said, "You're not crazy, you're a fool for trying to reason with a crazy one like her. And me, I want to do something in this very sad scene, but I don't know what else to do with my interest and sadness at this moment." He said nothing and she began to look very sad. "Your sadness is a welcome relief for me," I said, "that I can understand." She looked up and said, "He tells me I shouldn't cry." I replied, "That's crazier than anything you've said today." I spoke with distinct resentment. She bawled. When she finished, she began to speak without her craziness. We continued to work from there.

Therapists are often reluctant to state clearly what they do not like about a person. Again, these objections are expressed in many ways, ranging from "Isn't it bad to criticize a parent in front of their children?" to "Isn't it necessary to like patients in order to be able to help them?" My answer to the second question is, "I must be able to openly dislike people in order to like them enough to remain with them. I must be with them before I can help them." Saying what one does not like in front of children is one of the nicest things we can do for children. How else can children learn to argue and negotiate without losing their integrity? I argue and criticize in front of the children and urge families to go home and do likewise. When I say *argue* I don't mean *bicker*. Endless bickering is stupid and fruitless. Arguing means expressing how one feels and what one believes from moment to moment. When this is done, feelings change and the content is altered. Bickering has nothing to do with this. Bickering is merely taking a position and deciding stubbornly to defend it.

I have often heard parents say, "I love all my children equally." That is an unnecessary lie. We are not sticks of wood. We cannot feel the same to all environmental stimuli. Each child impinges differently and our responses must be different. I do not like my patients equally, either. I do not have to, and I suspect there would be something wrong with me if I did. To me, people are not all gray, but each person carries multitudes of colors and shadings, some of which appeal to me not at all. Can I be effective with them? Only on one condition. That condition is that I am able to express fully at all times what I do not like about them. The freer I am to say what I do not like about a person, the more comfortable I am with them and the less desire I have to leave them.

"Who am I to judge?" you might ask. I defend myself by saying, "I am not judgment, I am merely opinion." But I think that both the terms judgment and opinion beg the question. I am what I experience and I must have my right to that. This is me and my expression of me and need not have anything to do with my patient. This is not for me to decide but for them to decide. It is an unfair, encounter-diminishing tactic to attempt to turn off someone's expression of himself merely because you cannot see him as just another person in the world. I will defend my right to my expression and offer my patients that same privilege. In such atmosphere, good experiences occur.

I am not heedless. I am certain that no therapist is heedless. I am not advocating heedless or thoughtless expression. I never lose sight of my desire to be in better touch with people. However, I have confidence that this factor operates in all of us more automatically than we realize, and that it is the lack of confidence that we, as therapists, have in our good intentions that causes us to err on the side of excessive caution.

One wife presented herself as an intelligent person living constructively in social ways, but her appearance and obesity were disgusting to me. My disgust was expressed as frequently and as profoundly as I experienced it, and it took a great part of our therapy time. At first she objected in many ways, including, "That's your problem and that's not what I came here about." I could not yield to her objections, and in the course of our work together she came to the conclusion that my position was, in fact, more loving than her husband's attitude of indifference to her obnoxious appearance. There is no doubt that I tempered my remarks or couched them in such a way that she would not withdraw from treatment. I'm sure that many observers would have expected her departure. However, from experience, I find that it is rare for someone to run away from honest expression, sincerely offered, regardless of whether it is positive or negative, or calmly or vehemently expressed.

Working with families itself is a compelling force toward the therapist's full participation. It seems to me that family therapy and an experiential approach cannot help but be combined.

A colleague who had decided to try family therapy reported to me after his first experience: "It was astonishing. Things were happening in the first session that I would not come close to for six months or more in individual therapy. It was even a bit frightening. Some of it reminded me of my own family life and I was not sure of how I should be."

The reluctance of therapists to try family therapy has two bases: The first has to do with what has just been discussed, the fear that action in therapy might carry with it that terrorizing label "acting out." This will be discussed further subsequently, when we explore the possible hazards of the experiential approach. The other reluctance, born simply of inexperience, derives from fears of what might happen in such exuberant interactions and from fears that the therapist might not know what to do.

Hopefully this text will provide some answers about what to do. The therapist's fantasied concerns, however, are a different matter. The difficulty in coping with these fantasies is that, in the therapeutic experience itself, these fantasies and their horrendous complications simply do not occur.

Let us consider for a moment a popular "what if" question that I encounter in discussing with colleagues experiential psychotherapy within families: "What if you are working with a mother, a father, and a daughter in her teens and incestuous material surfaces?"

First of all, this has never happened. But, should there be a serious concern about overt or covert incestuous behavior, it is more likely to manifest itself as a conflict between the parents and not be identified as a problem of the child's. Therefore, it would be the parent who would be seeking help and the children or involved child would not likely be present at such an opening session. If it does not come up openly, then it is in the therapist's mind that it exists and may more accurately reflect his training rather than what he is experiencing in the session.

A mother, father, and an attractive 16-year-old daughter presented themselves to me with the chief complaint that mother was always depressed, while father and daughter were allied in an endeavor to help her with her depression. The mother identified her depression as related to the strong alliance existing between father and daughter, an alliance in which the father reportedly advised the daughter not to listen to her mother and preferentially invited the daughter to assume mothering and wifely tasks around the home. The father vehemently defended himself, accusing the mother of not being responsible in the home. When she tried to be responsible she was still considered a bad parent by this husband. Thus, he saw his own behavior as being a dutiful father in defense of his very fine daughter. The daughter sat sweetly, smiling at the father, scowling at the mother, and nodding approval of whatever father said.

I confronted the visible postures that each presented during our interviews. As her ally, I encouraged mother to "take on" the holy alliance of father and daughter; as her forthright critic, I castigated her woeful posture. Father was not only critical of his wife but also genuinely concerned for her welfare. With this evidence, I encouraged a more direct expression of his obvious accumulated resentments towards his wife and then supported his now almost obliterated desire for the effective helpmate he admittedly once enjoyed.

Heartened by these experiences, in a matter of weeks (according to her husband she had been hospitalized a year before as a chronic depressive) this woman began to repair her self-esteem and resume her rightful place in her home. As father more capably confronted his wife with both his anger and his needs, he spontaneously became aware of how he used his daughter as a treat and retreat from his wife. Daughter responded with obvious relief and gratitude now that she was once again free to become friends with her mother.

A satisfactory equilibrium was established in the family in a matter of months, and at no time was incest raised as a topic for conversation. I am convinced that to have raised such a topic would have been a diversion from the necessary work required to bring these people together.

"What if an individual calls for individual therapy, identifying the difficulty as intrapsychic, but the therapist believes that family therapy would be a better approach? How can the spouse be involved?" This is akin to another question offered by a colleague, "With people geared to the idea of individual therapy, how can you get the rest of the family in?" My response is, "How can you manage to keep them out?" In other words, it is the therapist's orientation that determines how he will work. If he believes in what he is doing, he will find that his patients will probably subscribe also.

Remember, we are speaking of how an individual perceives his problem, not how his problem actually exists. How the problem exists has to do with the theoretical framework in which the therapist works. Therefore, for me, any identified intrapsychic problem immediately can become an interpersonal problem by asking a spouse how he feels about his mate's problem. Regardless of his answer, we have now exposed his posture toward the so-called identified problem and this posture must have an effect on the mate's identified, intrapsychic conflict. Even an attitude of indifference is an influential position.

A therapist reported a conjoint interview between a mother and a 20-year-old daughter in which the mother began with a long list of complaints about her daughter's behavior. The therapist appropriately redirected the mother's criticism to the daughter where it continued for the next 15 minutes, unceasingly. The therapist invited the daughter's response to the mother's harangue. The daughter merely shrugged, and the interview seemed to break down.

At this moment in therapy, the therapist was aware of his mounting exasperation towards this mother and, at the same time, realized that he was not holding the daughter equally responsible for the failure of the encounter. He was concerned that expressing his anger towards the mother would be unfair, yet that was how he felt. The failure to express his "unfair" feelings was the unfairness responsible for the arrest of this therapeutic encounter at this time. In whatever form he could have expressed it, his resentment towards the mother would have been a living example of a response that was probably felt for years by this daughter. By now she had probably learned to tune out the mother far better than the therapist and probably felt, at least for the time being, less disturbed by her mother's behavior than the therapist.

This is not to say it was *necessary* for the therapist to become angry with the mother and set an example for the daughter. But this is who he was at the moment. His expression of his feelings could have been a valuable experience for the daughter. Had he become aware of his discomfort earlier, he might have used it to encourage the daughter more vigorously to utter her own dissent. Instead, the longer he waited, the shorter his temper became. The shorter his temper, the more unreasonable and unfair he felt and, therefore, less willing to become involved.

Another therapist, developing interest in family therapy, reported an experience he labeled a failure, explaining, "I reached a point with the father where I was so angry with him I felt it would be useless to say anything to him. I didn't know what to do. The rest of the family just sat there saying nothing. I wished I had never started this session. I felt all alone with no one to turn to. I felt everyone was waiting for me to do something."

This beautiful statement was made to me at the very point in the description when it would have been most appropriately made in the original session. Sharing these thoughts could have been the beginning of a fruitful search for a way out of this dilemma. It would have allowed the family members to help themselves at the same time they were helping the therapist.

So often we are needlessly fearful of exposing our helplessness. In this we are identical with our patients who also often connect transient help-lessness with diminished self-esteem. The primary value, for me, in such exposure lies in the fact that it frees my energies and permits further attention to our experience together. If I did not air my feelings of help-lessness, much of my valuable attentive energy would become tied to an attempt to exclude awareness of my frustration and helplessness. Also, when speaking up honestly, I become different as a consequence of the overt expression.

I had been seeing a husband and wife for some weeks when the wife said to me, "Don't just sit there, help me." To which I replied, "I don't have anything to offer you at this moment other than my attention." She became angry and told me that was not what she paid me for, accus-ing me of being a charlatan. I laughed. This infuriated her further and she attacked me for being so comfortable with my impotence. I began to get annoyed with her and told her so, saying, "I'm not as comfortable with my helplessness as I would like to be, for I am getting resentful about your unjustified tirade." We argued till I found myself shouting at her, "I don't know why in the hell you can't leave me alone. It is my helplessness, not yours." Like a boomerang my own words struck me. I softly invited her to explore her terror of her own helplessness. She broke down, and sobbingly told me of how she had always been depre-ciated and scorned for feeling helpless.

A question I am often asked is: In this experiential approach, aren't there some hazards to this impulsive interacting with patients? The an-swer, of course, is that what is called for is spontaneous behavior, not impulsive behavior. Impulsive behavior is compelling and heedless, ex-pressing a limited aspect of the individual, with essentially no opportun-ity for choice. The prime characteristic of spontaneity is that it represents an enriched distillation, an essence of the person at that moment. It has to do with the *fullness* of expression, not with the speed alone.

The following exchange will show what I mean:

Wife: (*Starting a session*) I feel confused. I'm not sure of myself.
Husband: (*With sincerity and warmth*) Any lead as to what brought it up now?
W: (*Quickly*) I suppose it has to do with us since we are here.

Therapist: *(To wife)* That was such a quick guess, you didn't seem to take time to search for an answer.

W: I was spontaneous.

Th: You were quick. His message went up to your head and your computer-like brain relayed a clever, seemingly appropriate response. It didn't go down to your guts to search.

As we explored, we became aware of how necessary it was for the wife to push away her husband's affection and her own sensibilities in favor of a posture of an intelligent, quick-witted woman who needs nothing from anyone.

W: What's to search? I knew the answer.

Th: Do you recall Chekhov's "The War?"

W: No.

Th: It is a story about a conversation among a trainload of peasants during the war. Several mothers were distressed that their sons were going to war. A man readily joined in, light-heartedly extolling the virtues of dying for one's country in preference to dying insignificantly, adding with pride that his own son, who was recently killed in action, agreed with him. At the conclusion of his loud and proud speech, one of the women quietly looked at him and said, "You mean your son is dead?" The man looked silently at her for a brief moment and burst into tears. This is spontaneity.

My patients were quiet. This is also spontaneity. They were both now responding from within. Webster defines spontaneity as "proceeding from natural law without external force."

It is remarkable how little spontaneity exists in the average social intercourse. Often we are merely *re*sponding rather than "sponding" or "spontaining."

A: How are you?

B: Fine.

A: What is new?

B: Nothing.

A: Wasn't that one helluva ball game?

B: Sure was.

Now let us consider an alternative exchange.

A: Hello, how are you?

B: I'd tell you but I don't feel you are really interested.

A: (*Smiling*) Oh, it's just a figure of speech.

B: What are you smiling about? Are you happy?

A: I'm rather amused by your response.

B: I wasn't amused by your insincere inquiry.

A: I *said*, "It is just a manner of speaking."

B: You seem annoyed now.

A: Naw! Why should I be annoyed? (*turning slightly away*)

B: You're a liar. You are turning away and your attitude tells me you are annoyed. I don't like your pretense of affability.

A: (*Emphatically*) I tell you, you are wrong. I'm not annoyed. (*with vehemence*) It just seems like a strange conversation. All I said was "How are you?" That seems friendly enough.

B: I needed someone to be interested in me and your inquiries felt so empty.

A: Are you on drugs?

Reluctance by therapists to fuller participation is very often expressed in terms of the omnipresent dangers inherent in being involved with others, sexually or hostilely. "Not that either one is bad per se," they hasten to add, "but in therapy you must admit it's inappropriate acting out at best." The implication here is that, as soon as terms such as "involved," "genuineness," "intimacy," "commitment" or "spontaneity" are introduced, terms such as "professional competence" and "responsibility" automatically are eliminated. More "see-saw" thinking.

There was a time when I was concerned about my sexual and aggressive potentials and their deleterious impact on my patients. (But then, that really included family, friends and strangers as well.) Then somehow I learned something. It was not rape and murder that concerned me, for in this time and place of my existence, my capacity for murder and rape had long since left the warehouse of my potential behavior. It was the idea that troubled me. In fact, it wasn't even the idea, it was my self-criticism for even transiently harboring the idea that pressured me. Such is the madness of sanity, of thinking, in preference to experience. I was thinking of my intolerance of my own ideas. I was experiencing nothing.

Then I began to search, to experiment, to dare to know what I experienced with patients. I found fears and embarrassments more often than lust and larceny, though I found those also. I found it was far more difficult for me to expose such tender parts as my sense of inadequacy at a given moment, my empathic tears, my wish to embrace a man in his moment of sadness, my petty envy, my embarrassing flatulence or my own unacceptable disinterest in my patients at a given moment.

I feared expressing my irrational, seemingly "inappropriate" thoughts and was often too embarrassed to share my petty irritations and absurd fantasies. In short, I dared not reveal who I was. I told myself that my patients could not stand me if they knew and that it was unfair to burden them with who I really was. They were too weak and helpless to be confronted by what I experienced, no matter how transient the little madnesses might be.

Then I discovered my projections. No, it was not my patients who could not stand these awarenesses of me. Patients cope with such matters readily. Even today it is still more difficult to admit to a patient my ephemeral feelings of incompetence at the time I feel them (it is always easier to talk about them *later*) than to express anger or sexual excitement. Intimacy does not mean merely the privilege of raging or fornicating. Genital sexuality and anger are more often devices to avoid involvement with others. Intimacy, genuineness, involvement, whatever word you chose to use, has to do with a willingness to expose ourselves, particularly our unacceptable and vulnerable qualities, rather than our genitals.

The reward for such behavior, as has been suggested above, is the recurrent expression of gratitude for what patients refer to as "refreshing realness, openness, and honesty." My reward is double. Not only do I get the increased satisfaction from being more fully with people at work and elsewhere, but I also get accolades such as the one expressed by a patient who simply said, "I can't explain it, yet I know I get more from being with you than what is in your words. I try to understand, but something more important seems to happen."

5

Individual Encounter-Diminishing Behavior

Once the orientation for successful encountering is established—the clearest possible identity for each encountering person striving actively in the here and now—all behavior can be viewed in relation to these premises as either encounter-enhancing or encounter-diminishing. Earlier, encounter-enhancing activities were touched upon as the criteria for satisfactory encounters. In the chapter on Interviewing, where therapeutic interventions are discussed, the story of successful, encounter-enhancing behavior will be completed.

Encounter-diminishing activities will be considered from two vantage points: individual encounter-diminishing tactics and familial combinations that, wittingly or not, serve to diminish encounters, preventing satisfactory completion. This chapter will consider some of the more popular individual tactics used to diminish encounters.

Interactions may be thought of as simple sentences containing a subject, predicate and object for each participant. Any person may diminish his or her part in an encounter by obscuring any one of these three components. To obscure the subject or object in the encounter, the individual merely needs to substitute some word other than "I" or "you." Words popularly used to obscure the identity of the subject or object are: it, they, circumstances, the facts, the situation. All such terms have the effect of obscuring the subject or object of the encounter, namely, you and me. The predicate—what the person is doing to the other person—can often be obscured by drawing attention to other times and places. Thus, telling stories about what one did yesterday can serve as an excellent cover for what one is doing right now. Other tactics for diminishing encounters are the use of social amenities to avoid honest confrontation and the use of emotional and physical behavioral substitutions. Actually, these can be considered variations of the "masked I." The sampling herein is admittedly sketchy and is intended merely to encourage readers to become familiar with, and perhaps interested in, their own further exploration of such activity. Encounter-diminishing behavior is rampant and readily discernible to the attentive therapist, often with amusement, sometimes with amazement, and frequently with chagrin.

The clearest identified subject in an encounter is one who essentially starts each statement with "I": I am, I will, I won't, I want, I don't, or some other variation on a direct expression of one's own person. It is truly astonishing to discover how few people, both in and out of therapy, can clearly state who they are and what they want in each encounter. These two criteria, who I am and what I want, when coupled with the capacity to negotiate successfully to obtain what I want, are the criteria upon which the definition of mental health is constructed.

The most common verbal social device to disguise individual identity is *the question*. It has been said that to ask a question one must already have the answer. This seems a bit stringent, yet worthy of consideration, particularly when observing the use of the question in an average encounter. In the judiciary system the masking value inherent in the question-answer interaction is well-known and well used by lawyers. Despite a multitude of righteous protests to the contrary, questions are more often used to obscure the interrogator than to elicit information, both in and out of court.

A gregarious college friend, who never quite developed social aplomb, always carried chewing gum. "Would you like some gum?" he would inquire to engage people at bus stops, in the bookstore, between classes and at any lounging area. Others avoid isolation by asking: "Do you have the time?" "Nice weather, eh what?" "Did you see the ballgame last night?" Hitchhikers never ask you to take them. They inquire, "Are you going as far as. . .?" If you answer, "Yes," they hop in.

Through questions, an individual can covertly criticize: "Whatever made you do that?" (stupid!). "Do you believe it's good for Johnny to stay up so late?" By questioning, a person can readily hide other feelings and attitudes: feelings they believe would be unacceptable or feelings they are unwilling to face the consequence of.

"I must be going now. Will you forgive me?"

"Isn't it getting rather late?" she informed him.

"Did you enjoy the movie?" instead of, "I'm reluctant to give you my impressions until I know where you stand."

"Why did you hurt me?" instead of, "Ouch, you clumsy oaf!"

"What do you mean?" Rarely is this a legitimate question when used more than once in an encounter. Its repeated use should signal the therapist that the individual is not fully participating in the encounter. If he is sincere, he will readily respond to the suggestion that the question be turned into a statement. When this is overlooked by the therapist, the person is likely to continue using this question until his opponent, whether family member or therapist, says something that he can safely contest or disparage.

A humorous example of the use of questioning to avoid identity comes to mind. Three ministers at a convention are secretly playing cards in a hotel room. A knock at the door makes them hide the cards quickly. In comes their clerical superior who asks suspiciously, "Did I hear card playing going on in here?" The first minister replies, "Would I do a thing like that?" The second says, "Look, Father, do you see anything suspicious?" The clergyman turns inquiringly to the third minister, who simply shrugs his shoulders and asks, "With whom would I play?"

Another exchange which illustrates the same point:

A: What do you mean by that?
B: What do you mean "What do I mean by that?"
A: Are you trying to tell me something?
B: Like what?
A: Don't you know?
B: If I knew, wouldn't I say?
A: I don't know, would you?
B: Why wouldn't I?
A: Then tell me, what do you mean?

B: Are you kidding?
A: Would I kid you?
B: Do you really think I meant something by that?
A: Why else would you look that way?
B: What way?

In therapy, questioning is a device used by patients and therapists alike. The therapist's claim to the device comes quite naturally from the myth that questioning is a part of the scientific model. True scientists are curious observers and experimenters, not questioners. They don't ask questions, at least not of other men. Yet questioning patients for historical data is considered so consonant with good medical practice that questioning is never questioned. Questioning patients in psychotherapy is the long hand of learning. By matching the answers with previously learned data, connections are made that, by the familiarity they breed, relieve the anxiety of the therapist. The therapist is then free to apply other tricks of the trade, to his now categorized patient.

"But there isn't enough time or opportunity to learn everything first hand," some might argue. Observation and experimentation are a function of interest, not of time. They are chosen by therapists who wish to make their own astigmatic observations rather than learn from the erroneous observations of others.

If we assume that patients come to treatment in search of greater knowledge of themselves, then there is little need for questions from their side also. Questioning the therapist can only serve to give them greater knowledge of the therapist and greater skill at questioning. Admittedly, sometimes people learn about themselves by questioning others and comparing, but this is a far less incisive method and fraught with hazard. Better they should observe and experiment with their therapist.

By refusing to answer questions and insisting on "I" statements, three chronic questioners in a group were unmasked, and three quite different uses of questioning were discovered. The first person, intelligent, friendly and seemingly curious, asked another group member, "Since you seem so well-informed and confident, why are you in the group?" When urged to convert the "I" statement, she was initially still friendly: "I would like to know about you so that I might use the knowledge probably for myself and at the same time be helpful to you." Being unsatisfied with this cold, intellectual and reasonable statement, I urged a further reappraisal, hoping for a more personal and intimate comment. It arrived with envy and resentment: "You think you're so smart offering others help when you can't even help yourself. I wish I could have your confidence, but I don't envy your arrogance which accompanies it." At this, the other person, who had indeed been arrogantly handing down well-thought-out interpretations, stopped smiling and began a profitable and thoughtful search, which ended in her expressing, with great concern, a desire to be appreciated. These two people continued an enriched encounter and deepening friendship.

The second interrogator presented her questions as a sincere search for useful knowledge. She collected sayings and reasonable attitudes as a philatelist collects stamps; never did she say anything about herself; never would she offer an opinion about anything. She lived by incessant questions. Her conversion to "I" statements was extremely difficult to obtain, but she finally said, "I am so lonely. I want people to talk with me and I know they really couldn't be interested in me. When people are talking I don't feel so lonely, and besides, I learn 'things' that way." When encouraged to talk with us about her gigantic and unfillable pit of loneliness, which she continuously tried to stuff with words of wisdom, she cried and abandoned her most offensive air. By always questioning she was herself being a "thing"—a collector. When speaking for and as her loneliness, she became a person. In so doing, she discovered how her well-intentioned questioning actually aggravated her loneliness. By denying her "I"ness she was, in fact, abandoning her own beingness and at the same time driving others away with her dumb questions. No one wants to be someone's encyclopedia, at least not for long.

The third person, a bright young girl, was generally quiet. When she spoke, she asked questions with grimaces and gesticulations suggestive of an apology. She was invited to pay attention to her motor activities and urged to convert her questions to statements which might include the words tied up in her gestures. As she began haltingly to make statements, she constantly, critically interrupted herself with remarks such as, "That's not right. . . . What I mean is . . . I'm saying it badly . . . I'd better just shut up." She then fell silent as tears came to her eyes. She couldn't even cry without a critical inhibition. Questioning was her only device for being with people without criticism from her self-image. She could listen or veil an intelligent, sensitive comment in a question so that her capability would not be seen. It was not until her questioning was obstructed, her statements patiently and gently encouraged, and her despotic self-image challenged, that she began to regain her right to speak.

In this group one person was hiding her envy and resentment, a second, her loneliness, and the third, her sensitive expressiveness—each by using the same device, the question.

A most common opening gambit during initial family interviews is someone, usually the mother, turning to another member of the family and asking, "Would you like to start?" Often a parent will turn to a child and ask, "Don't you want to tell the doctor why we brought you here?" On other occasions, a family member may turn to the therapist and say, "Well, here we are. What do you want to know?"

By such interrogation, the questioner avoids any comment about who he is or what he wants from this meeting and is asking others to do what he himself won't do. This popular tactic pretends to be responsible but in fact keeps the questioner outside of any encounter. An appropriate response by the child might be, "If I had wanted to tell the doctor, I would have spoken." This is not likely to occur, for where would they have learned to speak this forthrightly? More likely, having learned from the parent, the child might respond with another question, "Why don't *you* tell him?"

In asking the therapist, "What do you want to know?" the same avoidance is seen, for it is obviously what the patient wants that is of concern to him. While admitting that there are some exceptions, as a general rule, during therapy, whatever the particular words a therapist actually employs, questions are best met with a remark that conveys the idea: "Please convert that into a statement starting with the word 'I.'" To this patient, I might reply: "I would like to know what *you* want."

During a family interview, a mother repeatedly asked her daughter, "What do you think of me?" The daughter tried several answers, intended generally to reassure the mother, but they were all to no avail. It was only when the mother was encouraged to make "I" statements to her daughter instead of repeating her questions, that we were able to pursue this encounter to a fruitful conclusion. The mother's conversion went something like this: "I want you to think well of me, to assure me that I am a good mother. I live in constant fear that I am not. I see your behavior and it is acceptable to me, and yet somehow it does not reassure me. I have such terrible doubts as to what a good mother is. You see, I never had one. I guess that's what I am really saying."

At this point the mother was encouraged to direct her further remarks, in fantasy, to her own mother for whom they were so clearly meant. She began to cry and, in this fantasied encounter, began to complete the unfinished business that never could have been concluded by asking her daughter, "What do you think of me?"

Gossiping, like questioning, is a popular method of escaping from pertinent encountering. Gossiping describes any remark made *about* rather than *to* the other person. It differs from questioning in that it operates by obscuring the "you" as well as the "I." There can be no vital encounter with "you" since the gossip is still involved with a prior encounter—existing, as it were, in another time and place. Thus, there is a diminished "I" and, as the recipient of gossip, "you" are a mere receptacle into which leftovers from a prior encounter are being dumped.

Consonant with this approach, if a remark is directed to the therapist about another member of the family present, the therapist should urge that it be redirected to the involved subject. Should the gossiper refuse, the therapist can suggest that the refusal itself be directed to the other member.

It seems easier for many of us to tell strangers that we like them than to tell intimates that we do *not* like them. Sometimes the gossip emerges subtly as a positive comment to and about the therapist: "You sure are understanding." It behooves the therapist to beware of such activity and refuse to accept a positive statement to him as a substitute for a negative one to a primary person in the individual's life. Such remarks should be parried with something like: "I would like you to say something to your spouse (or son, or daughter . . .) about understanding."

Sometimes the would-be gossip complies, turning to another family member and saying, "I don't really expect you to understand me. You never do. You always twist things around." To this the other may respond, "I don't know what the hell you're talking about. You're the one who doesn't understand, not me." Now we have the beginning of an encounter.

Less subtle and more common are comments made to the therapist about the other member: "Marcy won't mind." "He never will cooperate." "She refuses to. . . ." All such comments are best confronted: "Tell him (or her)." "What can you say to them about (whatever the topic happens to be)?"

During therapy, when the person being talked about is not present, the alternatives are to diminish the intensity of the encounter by a brief discussion (gossip) or to use a projective technique, reminiscent of psychodrama, in which the individual engages the absent other in a contrived encounter, the individual himself playing both roles. Sometimes the therapist may try having another family member play the part of the absent person, or the therapist may choose to do this. In my experience, these latter alternatives have been less productive.

The well-known and much abused *editorial we* is, of course, another means of remaining nameless. "We don't seem to be getting along." "We have trouble understanding one another." Or, what I always look for and never quite hear, "We don't like him (or her)." The rule is: Everyone speaks for himself. There are no "we's" in therapeutic encounters, only "I's."

And then there are those people who live in *quandaries*. These people have difficulty knowing where they are and manifest this problem with vagueness, indecisiveness, uncertainty, innocence, naivete, and in its simplest form, the repeated use of the phrase, "I don't know." As long as the person remains in this quandary, it is impossible to find him for an encounter. "I don't know" is indeed a decisive and informed posture. It requires much knowledge to achieve such a position of "ignorance." It takes sufficient knowledge of the subject at hand and considerable knowledge about oneself in relation to the subject at hand to make the observation, "I don't know."

It is conceivable, and should be kept in mind, that this position may be a sincere expression of some concise, limited area of ignorance, but more likely and more often it is used as a social manipulation which permits the speaker to remain obscure and nonresponsible. Were it simply a matter of not knowing, the person would probably be interested enough in the subject to stimulate either an inquiry or a self-search for greater comprehension. "I don't know" is used as a refuge. "I *won't* know" is usually what is meant, and the therapist can offer this to the patient to try on.

By the same token, *indecisiveness* requires a decision to be indecisive. Furthermore, it requires repeated and frequent decisions to remain that way. Indecisiveness is an active, time and energy consuming posture. Denial that such behavior is decisively arrived at is in itself a position that the person has decided to take.

This quality of denial ranges from simple social operations, as suggested above, to and including what we often call schizophrenia. The difference is largely one of degree, the variations having been learned experientially in each parent family. Regardless of the degree to which this operation is used by a patient, the gross therapeutic approach remains the same: be decisive. The greater the indecisiveness and uncertainty of patients, whether diagnosed as neurotic or psychotic, the greater is the therapeutic impact of a decisive approach to them. An "I don't know" which is not held tightly by a patient may be treated with a simple offering of awareness and suggestions for alternatives. With patients labeled schizophrenic or psychotic, a most decisive and imposing attitude on the therapist's part is necessary.

A mother, father and their tranquilized 19-year-old daughter, who was recently released from a state mental hospital, were seen for the first time. Mother spoke for the family; father was constantly agreeable; and daughter, appearing more stoned than tranquil, responded "I don't know" —that is, when she responded at all. Mother revealed several situations in which she overextended herself for daughter, then carped resentfully for daughter's failure to be appreciative, submissive and cooperative. For example, she provided cartons of cigarettes and complained that daughter smoked too much; she insisted that daughter have a car and complained that daughter drove around too much; she did anything daughter asked and then complained that daughter was too demanding. Mother asked daughter to verify the charges by concluding each one, "Isn't it true, Alice?" To this, Alice sometimes shrugged, sometimes said, "I don't know," and more often failed to respond visibly at all. When urged by the therapist to respond, Alice grunted without looking up from the floor and said, "I don't know what to say."

I asked Alice if she could look at me as we conversed. She nodded affirmatively but had difficulty. Since she had said, "Yes," I held her to it. Then I told her what to say: "Tell her to get the hell off your back. Tell her to quit buying cigarettes and accusing you of smoking too much just because she's too damn weak to refuse to supply them. Tell her to mind her own damn business instead of trying to be so good. You damn well know what you want to tell her. You just want me to do it for you. Now tell me you 'don't know' what the hell I'm talking about since 'I don't know' is such a favorite expression of yours." By now, Alice was smiling. "Now what do you say?" I asked her. She responded, "You're right." With this a most profitable session began. "You will damn well learn to say what's on your mind if you keep coming around here," I said in appreciation.

Circumstantiality is a variation on the theme of remaining obscure through indistinctness. Here, however, the haziness is not of the person but of the subject matter. There are three traditional gambits in this strategem: subject hopping, conditional uncertainty and preambling.

Subject hopping, to be successful, requires a cooperative partner:

Mother: You didn't put your socks in the hamper again yesterday. I'm tired of picking up after you. We've got to do something about it.

Son: I thought I did. Anyway, don't you wash on Thursday? It's only Tuesday.

M: This week I had a doctor appointment on Thursday and I did the wash a day earlier.

S: I didn't know. What did the Doc say?

M: I'll be okay. Just need to rest up for a few days.

S: You and Dad ought to get away for a few days.

. . . Like the subject did. This way mother need not be identified as the taskmaster and son need not be identified as the slob. Such subject hopping is best approached by an initial confrontation of differences between the therapist and the others as to what each considers pertinent, or what each believes should command attention in the conversation. By attending to how this particular encounter progresses, the therapist will learn whether this is a social device for avoidance or a pervasive, existential ignorance for that person that would require an explanation rather than a confrontation.

Conditional uncertainty is expressed in remarks which begin with the word "if." "If only you were a foot shorter and your name were different. I could really like you" in place of "I don't like you." "If there were only (miracles?), I could be (successful?)" in preference to "The task is too difficult for me."

Many *preambles* also serve to avoid full encountering: "Maybe . . ." "It seems to me . . ." "Somehow . . ." "Perhaps . . ." "Possibly. . . ." Such preambling makes clear discussion of a subject difficult, if not impossible. "I'm not sure, but it seems to me that it would probably be better if everybody (whoever he is) could maybe be more or less kind of direct, at least one could perhaps try, if you know what I mean, huh?"

The use of the indefinite pronoun "it" (or "they") has been mentioned elsewhere as a familiar method of avoiding responsibility for what the speaker is expressing. Other *indefinite subjects* can be used instead of "it." "Time" (as in the phrase, "If I only had the time") "the situation," "circumstances," "factors," "pressures," "things on my mind," and endless other "things" can be called forth and identified as the responsible subject, should the speaker choose to remain cloaked. "Gee, I had so much on my mind I just forgot to call." Or, for the more sophisticated executive, "Were it not for innumerable unforeseen pressures (those are the best kind of pressures there are!) I would have called sooner."

In such instances the speaker pretends to represent or merely submit the information much as a reporter. "Reporting," "announcing" and "broadcasting" are terms for this behavior. Of course, should the announcement be well received, the announcer is likely to accept a more personal responsibility.

Substituting one emotional posture for another is a device often used to obscure one's person. Most of us are taught that anger is a bad thing; some of us believe it. If so, some alternative behavior must be found to express negative feelings. One of these may be the use of another emotion, such as fear, as a substitute for anger. In one family the mother expressed her displeasure exclusively through her fear. Every "I don't like . . ." became an "I am afraid of. . . ."

Brusqueness, irritability, outbursts of temper can all be substitutes for tender feelings, much as the provocative "bad boy" who seeks attention and interest by being irritating. This is seen particularly among men who cannot permit themselves awareness of their own sadness or needs for closeness. Cheerfulness as a substitute for sadness is well known. I have witnessed it so often now that, when a family arrives and everyone is laughing and joking with one another, I know they all will be in tears shortly after we begin.

Interrupting is an excellent method for altering the direction of an encounter that is becoming too intense. It very often becomes a familial activity and is helped along by others who do not challenge the interruption. For instance, in a family where interrupting is used to prevent closeness or to disrupt completion in encounters, the others always collaborate to permit the interruption. This is generally done on a verbal level but patterns for interrupting can be behavioral as well. Verbally, interrupting is, of course, done by starting to talk while someone else is talking, either on the same subject or on what appears to be a peripheral aspect of the same subject but really is moving towards something else. Nonverbally, interrupting is done by picking up a book and starting to read, by picking up the telephone, or simply by diverting one's visual attention and interest.

Where the therapist impinges in such a situation depends exclusively on where the greatest effort can be made to disrupt this pattern. "You interrupted," and to the others, "You permitted the interruption," is the simplest and might appear to be the fairest intervention. However, in the context of the experience, the therapist's strategy will vary. Attention may be focused persistently on those who permit the interruption, or the therapist may take the more familiar position of holding the interrupter solely responsible.

Silence is used almost as frequently as talking for obscuring the individual and preventing an encounter from being completed. Obscuring silence can be applied by simply ignoring a comment as though it had not been heard. Although this is too crass for most, if frequently used it can result in an actual deafness. In one family, the wife, a compulsive talker with a particularly grating voice, came in with her husband, whose deafness began two years after their marriage. I was not surprised to learn from this man that his physician was mystified about this organic deafness for which no cause could be found. A hazard of specialization is the doctor's desire to explain etiology without leaving his field of expertise. The otologist had never met this man's wife.

Screen silences occur when a person has something to reply to a statement but, for whatever reason, elects to withhold it. The withholding may be detectable in a grimace or shrug, but often it is so well masked it is missed by the most sensitive observer. This type of silence is generally associated with gossiping, for at some later date the silent individual is likely to seek a third party to whom he can say what he dared not say earlier. A shunting of responsibility often accompanies this, for example, "What could I say, they wouldn't listen to me," or perhaps, "I wouldn't give him the satisfaction of . . ."

Garrulousness and *loquacity* often obscure the person's intended statement. This was most eloquently expressed by a woman who turned on a voluble member of her family and screamed, "Shut up and talk to me."

Harold Pinter, the English playwright, whose plays are beautiful examples of incompleted encounters, has commented on silence and the tyranny of words in another way.

> There are two silences. One when no word is spoken. The other when perhaps a torrent of language is being employed. This speech is speaking of a language locked beneath it. That is its continual reference. The speech we hear is an indication of what we don't hear. It is a necessary avoidance, a violent, sly, anguished or mocking smoke-screen which keeps the other in its place. When true silence falls we are still left with echo but are near nakedness. One way of looking at speech is to say it is a constant stratagem to cover nakedness.

Obscuring silences need to be separated clearly from working silences. The simplest and clearest detectable difference lies in what the person is doing during the silent period. In working silences, the therapist and all others are ignored. The person sits quietly, staring fixedly at nothing, and is largely expressionless. There may be transient frowns, a lifted eyebrow and then once again no motion. The time is not yet ripe. At the moment the person looks at someone or begins gross motor activities, whether it be a marked and persistent change in facial expression or a change in posture, I assume that the work is shifting. I am interested in what has happened, so I will usually make an inquiry such as, "Where have you been?" or "Where are you now?"

By contrast, those silences in which one's identity is being masked are generally characterized by deliberate motor activities and either casual or studied attention to others. This "masking" type of behavior demands that the therapist confront the person bluntly with the silent behavior. Any softer, persuasive questioning will not produce an effective response.

We could explore types of encounter-diminishing behavior indefinitely, but the examples given here will hopefully serve their primary purpose to stimulate awareness and perhaps interest in seeing behavior in terms of encounter-diminishing potentials.

By *avoiding attention to what is going on in the current moment*—the here and now—encounters can be diminished. "I was sure mad at you last week" is an example of a remark that may serve to initiate a new and more rewarding encounter. However, it can also be a device to avoid a more current feeling of either the same or a different dimension. One possibility is that the person's anger has been recalled at this moment because of something that occurred at this moment that also angers. Instead of a here-and-now confrontation the person chooses a less hazardous course (in his or her estimation) by choosing a similar scene from the past to "talk about" instead.

Another possibility is that the anger is recalled now because it feels safe to do so; there is sufficient distance from the original set to make heated conflict unlikely. When such a remark is offered to me, it arouses very little affect, consistent, I am sure, with the announcer's intention. I might be curious, at best, but certainly removed enough from that earlier period that, even with further explanation, it is not likely to elicit any great surge of current emotional involvement—for either of us.

Deserting the here and now in favor of seeking an historical reference is quite popular with both therapists and patients. It includes the gamut from childhood memories through the experiences of last year, last week and even earlier moments during the same session in order to avoid a more highly charged current moment.

An emotionally constricted, professional man approaching his forties, on the verge of crying for the first time in his adult life, interrupted his experience with a gesture of appreciation: "You know, when you said a few minutes ago that I appeared to be holding up a pretense of cheerfulness, you sure hit it on the head. I didn't realize that was what I was doing." Then he added, "I must do that quite a bit . . ." I responded to his anguished expression, "And *now* what are the words that go with the expression on your face?"

For another person less familiar with this tactic of tuning in to one's bodily expression, I might prefer a less sophisticated intervention, such as, "And what are you aware of about your pretenses at this moment?" When I am concerned that such a question might be intellectually abused, I might suggest a "try on" statement like, "I would like you to try saying to me 'I won't show you my sadness.' " If the person experiences difficulty with this "try on," I know that I am on target. Should this not fully mobilize the person's expression of sadness, I may ask that he repeat this statement over and over, louder and louder. When he is able to identify with the objection, the underlying affect often breaks through.

Regardless of the reason the individual is unwilling to proffer an unacceptable affect at the time it is experienced (such as fear of jeopardizing our relationship), it is inadvisable to collaborate in this encounter-diminishing activity. When confronted, more than one patient has responded, "But I'm not even aware at the time that I am angry." My answer, "That's too damn bad. Now, how do you like that? Or will I get this report next Tuesday?" The innocent protest makes me angry and I respond now. My response satisfies me. I'll not be coming to them next Tuesday saying, "You know, last week you made me angry." Further-more, by expressing my resentment in a grossly challenging manner, I offer the patient an opportunity and an example, which are often accepted, to try on a new form of behavior. Patients have often subsequently responded with appreciative comments such as, "Your behavior creates a good atmosphere where I feel freer to try on more honest behavior." On both counts I appreciate the appreciation.

Time can be used in a multitude of ways to avoid the current moment. Talking about it, as in, "I hate deadlines," can use time as an object to blame. Deadlines become a tangible patsy, while the current moment whisks by. Stuffing a current moment with tomorrow's fear, as in, "I'm afraid of what tomorrow will bring," conveniently takes today's fear of the moment and attenuates it by placing it in tomorrow's context so that nothing can be done with it *now*. "Let's do something exciting tomor-row," she said to him, assuaging her ennui.

In the fifteenth or the fiftieth session, the working premises remain unchanged. Though the total gestalt of each of us has changed and the content has ranged widely, the therapeutic effectiveness continues un-remittingly as long as the therapist attends the current encounter and uses his current awareness as a fully committed person. There is no such thing as working with a "deeper" level. The deepest level at all times is attained when one is attending to the obvious.

In a first session, I confront a hapless, demoralized, degraded, di-sheveled mother with her self-destructiveness, with all of the rage and disgust she elicits from me. She responds with tears, apologizes agreeably, saying, "Yes, I know." She sobs on abjectly as I continue storming. About the fifteenth session, she reports, "Yesterday I spoke up to the milkman and the day before I bought a new dress."

I respond softly, telling her that I am both aware of and delighted with her improvement and add, "I feel some discomfort with your presenta-tion. The fantasy I have is of a pagan sacrificial offering being made to appease an angry god." She now responds in anger, attacking me for being so suspicious. I laugh with delight. I am doubly delighted. Her anger tells me that I was correct and her angry response reveals indeed that she is better.

Each session, almost each existential moment, is complete unto itself.

What has transpired in prior sessions, as in our life history, is a fundamental aspect of our current existence. This approach requires no new orientation for subsequent sessions or for the achievement of "deeper levels" of therapy. Each moment plumbs the depths of our capacity for interaction, and that is all there is. Were I to sense in a later session some shallowness or sameness to our encounter, I would be likely to introduce this current feeling and explore it as an essential feature of our current encountering.

Deserting the here and now can occur in two directions. There are the various retreats to the past, to anecdotes, memories, etc., and there is the escape to the future, through planning, anticipating, discussing expectations, etc. Admittedly, sometimes "talking about" is a necessary step; in some instances it may represent the total distance that can be crossed in this particular encounter, but it is well to keep in mind the encounter-diminishing potentials of such behavior.

"Tomorrow things will be better," signals psychological desertion of a painful today. "I'll never lend you anything of mine again," a mother coldly announced to her daughter, who returned a borrowed blouse, now torn. Mother has moved to finish today's anger in the future. A better choice might be a negotiated restitution here and now, beginning with, "This is unacceptable. I want the blouse returned as originally loaned, or replaced." And, if necessary, "Damn your careless hide" may be constructively appended as richly as needed to discharge the disappointment. Mother can then decide about future borrowings at the time future requests are made.

Too often we have learned remarks for flight rather than phrases that might encourage completion of today's encounter.

In a semisocial encounter with a university department head and one of his staff members, the chief complained that this staff member had not played it fair at the time of his application for his current job. The department head thought the other man should have confessed at the time of his application the personal difficulties he had met with in his relationships in previous positions. The staff member rightly and righteously proclaimed, "When I am looking for a job I am going to put my best foot forward. I am not going to wash all my dirty linen publicly. That would be kind of stupid of me and it is stupid of you to expect it." The department head agreed with this reasonable, if provocative, response.

As the three of us pursued this subject, it became apparent to me that the department head had created his own difficulty by not living in his current experiential moment. Even now, in this current encounter, I could see he was not coping with his mounting resentment at this young man's arrogant confrontation. Rather, he was acting the role of the intellectual department head who could only respond "reasonably." During the earlier job application interview, he had chosen to retreat to history, studying the man's credentials, which merely represented some of the scars of his past history, instead of paying attention to his experience with this person during the interview. By poking around as one person with another in a current encounter, he would probably have elicited behavior from his would-be associate that would have provided him with far more valuable information than he obtained from scrutinizing his credentials.

When I confronted the department head with my thoughts on the matter, he responded with the explanation that he felt obliged to use proper social amenities and courtesies because of his position, rather than to "poke around."

A plea for intimacy can be an encounter-diminishing tactic; ask any woman. Actually, such behavior pervades the entire range of social intercourse and need not be applied only to the use of sexuality to obtain emotional distance from other people. The advisability of using first names in therapy has been toyed with at least once by every therapist. I usually call people by their first names and do not insist that they do the same with me.

While working with one couple, the husband, who had been depressed for several years, had been getting a rather severe drubbing from me in an attempt to mobilize his aggressiveness. His depression felt more like an iceberg to me than weight. He had, on rare occasions, over these first few weeks of our working together, feebly protested that my "approach" was "unsympathetic."

On this day, I pushed once again, calling him by his last name, without benefit of title, saying, "Smith, you're dead, stone cold dead. I feel absolutely nothing for you." He pushed back, "Could you please call me 'Smitty.' That's what everyone calls me. I don't like being called just 'Smith.'" Candidly, I told him that he felt just like a plain Smith to me— a thing—not Mr. Smith or Smitty. "I couldn't call you Smitty at this time. I don't want to." He submitted incompletely, "Okay, I understand." The encounter was unfinished for me also, but I decided to drop it at this time.

Several minutes passed during which his wife and I had a brief, rather shallow encounter. Then he turned to me and said, "Dr. Kempler, I . . ." I interrupted, "You can call me Walt." He stared at me in dead silence for a moment, and I caught the first glimpse of a smile as he said, "I don't want to." Now for the first time I felt something towards him and almost wanted to call him Smitty. I mentioned this to him, although I didn't call him Smitty; I wasn't quite ready for that yet. I suspect I wanted to goad him further with "Smith" and wasn't prepared to relinquish so valuable a weapon at this time.

In this kind of therapy, the therapist must be ready to parry subtle, socially acceptable gestures that are designed to diminish encounters. My unscientific observation, supported only by a lifetime of consistent experiences on the matter, suggests that the social amenities have been created expressly for the purpose of avoiding involved, emotionally laden encounters. Smile, whether you are happy or not; say thank you whether you are appreciative or not; say you are sorry even though you are glad; never be rude and always be kind. Remember, courtesy conquers. The integrity of an encounter depends on the integrity of the individuals who are expressing themselves in the encounter. Any behavior, socially approved or not, that distorts or diminishes the accuracy of what the individual is, in favor of presenting some social face, is to me a most rude and unkind behavior.

"Well, you wouldn't go visit a friend in a hospital and say to him, 'You look like hell,' would you?" is a sample of the counter arguments. I probably would say it, as I enjoy sharing the sense of relief that we all get, my sick friend included, from the openness of our exchange. However, I am sure there are times when even I would avoid such a comment. This blunt comment, however, need not be exchanged for a dishonest, social amenity. There are many other alternatives that do not require the abridgement of one's integrity. A simple "I" statement that best summarizes who one is at a given moment is the best possible encounter-enhancing statement, whether in therapy or in any other social situation, including the aforementioned scene with a hospitalized friend.

In response to an undesired social invitation such as, "Perhaps you can come over this evening?" one might respond, "I would really love to but I just can't tonight. Perhaps another time." This response suggests a helpless pawn being denied a great pleasure by some unseen, cruel and whimsical overseer. The concomitant, covert message is more likely,

"Don't see me as the one who does not accept your offer."

A sister says to her sibling, "You are selfish. I am willing to let you use my clothes and share them with you, while you, on the other hand, will use my clothes and refuse to let me share yours." Superficially it would appear that this child begs merely for fair play. In reality, she "selfishly" attempts to impose her position on her sister, using the social amenity called "fair play" and a pretense of selflessness. In this family, she was supported by her parents in this attitude, which in reality was saying, "Damn it, you better share with me according to my rule since my rule is based soundly in the social grace called fairness."

A student in a conference attacks me with, "You have been unfair. You bludgeon us with your openly expressed opinions and attitudes and defend yourself by saying we do not have to accept them if we do not want to and that we can openly disagree with you if we choose. This is not the way it is supposed to be. You must recognize your position as an authority and teacher. This means that you should use your position more gently and judiciously. This is an accepted social custom, established to protect us from your abuse, which you refuse to follow. For this I am justly angry with you."

Although it was five sessions late in coming, this was a welcomed comment from this student with whom I had been candid in my dislike of some of his behavior. My reply: "I'm delighted with your ability to express yourself to me, finally. You have broken a social amenity of ancient origin which advises you to respect your elders, particularly your teachers. I am pleased with your violation and I like you better for having spoken."

On another occasion, in an interview with a husband and wife, I notice that the wife is wearing an eternal smile. I point out the discrepancy between the content, which is rather painful and serious, having to do with the survival of their marriage, and her smile. Until now, she has remained comfortable, animated, and the conversation seems to have gone no place. Now, in her attempt to comply and cooperate with me, she stops smiling and I notice that as she continues to talk with her husband she is no longer able to look at him. As we continue, she alternates between looking at him with her smile or turning away as she catches herself smiling, and continuing to speak without the smile. This becomes the next point of focus for my attention, since her husband still seems ready for more of an encounter. I point to her new behavior—her apparent inability to look at her husband without her mask of comedy. She looks at me intently and soberly for a moment and then returns to her conversation with her husband. Now the way in which she speaks changes markedly. Whereas before, she spoke with confidence, simply and eloquently, appearing to be most intently involved, now she speaks with great hesitation and preambles everything with comments like "I wonder."

Her husband is not particularly aware of these changes in her behavior, but seems perplexed as to what is going on. I choose to ignore this at this time in favor of bringing his wife to a more negotiable posture. I point to her uncertainty in her speech. She also becomes perplexed and seems to be at a standstill. She again tries to continue, but her speech is vague and her look uncertain. As she continues her fruitless searching and rumination I share with her something new that has emerged in me at that moment. I feel cheated. When she arrived on the scene I was impressed initially with her demeanor and felt that she was capable of considerable involvement and commitment. Now, when I disrupt a few social facades, she seems to be left with little. After I share these thoughts with her, she responds rather clearly, confirming that what I have said feels appropriate to her. She continues with quiet conviction, "I've never discussed this with anyone before, but very often I have felt like a cheat. However, I didn't think anyone ever noticed it."

Her husband didn't like what had been going on in their marriage and could not understand what it was all about. He just knew that he didn't like their marriage. She begins to weep, and he turns warmly to her and with obvious interest says, "I've never thought of you that way before, and I never knew that you had such feelings." When a form of counterfeit social behavior, her smile, was confronted, therapy was under way.

Not all social amenities are for the purpose of obscuring encounters or distancing individuals from each other. When we consider the origins of social amenities, there is plausible evidence that they began as protective devices to provide safety while permitting greater intimacy. It is only as they become overprotective or obsolete that, instead of allaying anxiety, they serve as distancing mechanisms and often generate anxiety.

The handshake is a good example. Originally, this behavior served to expose the weapon hand—usually the right—to each confrontee, thus allaying anxiety. By comparison, I can recall as a child learning this outmoded amenity and feeling, not relief, but anxiety and concern about whether I was doing it correctly. I was not concerned with what other people had in their right hands, for this in fact represented no great hazard. The hazard had now moved into the heads of my parents, my source of approval. Disapproval was the hazard to me. Later, handshaking provided a superficial pride, telling me that my social image was correct. This provided thin satisfaction. Finally, it became an almost comical bore. I have now replaced handshaking with a simple greeting sans motor-response, or, when the feeling is marked, an embrace.

Saying and waving "good-bye" is a more functional social operation which permits the individual to tie up appropriate and immediate feelings of impending loss in nonverbal and verbal behavior. This activity, when the feeling runs high enough, is often accompanied by crying. Crying is especially evident when there is love and a question of possible finality to the departure, such as when a child goes into service or when a parent leaves the very young child to go shopping, the child being too young to comprehend the transient nature of the separation. When one of my sons was approximately one year old, my wife reported that he cried when he saw me leave in the morning to go to work. However, when I said goodbye and waved to him, which he had just learned, he smiled. As I drove away, he often continued waving toward the door, intermittently, for five or ten minutes after I had gone. Now he did not need to cry. This behavior was, of course, transient and changed as he learned that I would leave and return with some predictability. There is nothing in his behavior to suggest that departure means rejection. This seems to be a more adult and intellectual type of conception. As his comprehension grew, waving and saying goodbye became a casual habit or game that we were free to play or abandon at will.

Usually, however, the social amenity is part of a system of recommended rules for (diminished) encountering. Such rules are often individually embellished or interpreted and may become part of the entire operation within a family. "Always be fair" is a popular parental amenity. As soon as you show any emotion, particularly anger, you lose. I will be polite and let you get away with it this time, provided you do the same for me next time. Honor thy mother and father, meaning never disagree openly. These and other samples of social amenities, familially adapted, will be discussed in greater detail as we look into specific familial patterns of encounter-diminishing behaviors in the next chapter.

For all practical purposes, every bit of human behavior, verbal, emotional, visceral and motoric, may be used to diminish encounters. Up to now, we have considered mostly the verbal mechanisms. Familiar emotional responses such as sadness, fear, anxiety and anger may also unintentionally diminish encounters. Pseudoemotional behaviors such as pouting, temper tantrums and whining usually, and intentionally, diminish encounters. Some evidence of "You hurt my feelings" is generally sufficient to prevent further confrontations when one is dissatisfied with the encounter.

Anyone may have his feelings, but no one may use them to manipulate another person. Anyone may try, but the other is under an obligation to prevent being manipulated. In the course of therapy, individuals are encouraged to express their feelings and the remaining family members are discouraged from responding. Often, pseudoemotional behavior is mistaken for the real thing by other members of the family; for example, whining and tears are often mistaken for sadness and crying. The therapist, by enlightening the family and rejecting such behavior, encourages its early abandonment in favor of something more effective.

I was consulted by a colleague who needed help with a couple. The wife had, for several weeks, been determined to get a divorce. The husband, alternating between murderous threats and fits of crying, had the wife and the therapist stymied. All three came to me looking quite serious. The husband readily started, reinforming me of the above information, concluding tearfully, "I don't know what to do." These words were coupled with dramatic facial grimacing. He never once looked directly at anyone. Tears rolled down his face as he wailed on, bemoaning his fate, expressing his remorse and sense of failure, coupled with a seemingly submissive plea for personal aid. He was eloquent. In fact, he seemed to be more eloquent than sad. His total behavior suggested an act to enlist my alliance rather than genuine sadness. I told him this.

As he stopped crying and put his handkerchief away, he said, "You're wrong Doc, I'm really very much involved with my sadness." His handkerchief told me the truth. My impression was confirmed, and now I felt annoyed that he was denying his attempt to manipulate me. "I'm not impressed with your sadness. If anything I'm angry. I don't feel sorry for you, and I suspect you're an actor trying to manipulate me into making your wife like you." I told him how I felt and what I thought. He acted grossly offended and, again, more involved with me than with himself. I knew I was on the right track. I chuckled at him and suggested sarcastically that he was wasting talent in my office and would be better on stage. I was intentionally provocative. He grimaced.

· "What does the grimace say?" He replied, "I don't know what to do." "That's a lie," I pushed, "What do you think of me?" I suspected his grimace carried off his resentment and I wanted the words. "I think you're a heartless bastard," he said angrily. I laughed. "That's the first honest thing you've said the entire hour." I told him of my empathy and my lack of sympathy. I suggested he get some help for himself rather than waste his time trying to manipulate his wife, who was quite firm in her decision to divorce. When they got up to leave, he said, "Thank you, you've been helpful and you're really not a bastard." I knew it. I replied sincerely, "You're back to lying again, I see." We parted. The next day he called. He asked if I would consider taking him as my patient. He had decided to stop pursuing and badgering his wife and wanted to "get myself straightened out. You seemed to know what you are doing and also what I am doing."

With another couple, the husband brought his wailing and complaining wife to therapy out of desperation. He did not believe in it, but he had tried everything else. She moped endlessly around the house, doing none of her housework. She expressed such fears at leaving the house that he had to do all the shopping. When he went to work, she would frequently call him to tell him how frightened she was. She was a bright woman who seemed to have a spark even through her miserable behavior. He was an aggressive, outspoken and capable fellow who worked as a lawman. He readily admitted that he had no confidence in me and, at the same time, expressed his promise to be grateful if I could do anything. After poking around a bit, I decided that he was sturdy and trustworthy and that her spark could be ignited.

I abruptly confronted her with her whining, hangdog expression and posture and told her flatly that all of this was a pose to avoid calling her husband a bastard. I told her she could continue to talk if she wished, but she would have to look up at the person she was addressing and end each sentence to me or to her husband with the words, "you bastard." She laughed sheepishly and protested mildly. He said, "It sounds crazy as hell to me, but if it works it's okay." I firmly held my ground, reminding her whenever she tried to forget the epilogue.

Soon, her whole posture changed, she sat up, began talking about many things, and her husband was more astonished than she was. They both quickly became aware of what her behavior had meant, and each of them, without a profound analysis or understanding, seemed readily to assimilate the implications of our experience. The husband realized he had been unwittingly helping in their defeat by his kindness and by curbing his resentment. She was surprised at how much better she felt immediately. Although she was somewhat reluctant to acknowledge that she was so angry, she was willing to experiment further with it. The progress this couple made in a couple of weeks was remarkable. It was even more remarkable when one considers that two months before she was heavily tranquilized and preparing for admission to a state hospital. Her husband was quite ready for her improvement, was most cooperative and appreciative and certainly demonstrated that spouses don't always "need" the sick behavior.

I have been asked if I could find less offensive terms than such crudities as "fool," "bastard," "louse," "slob," "S.O.B.," "hell" and 'damn" to express myself. I cannot. I will not. I choose the strongest words possible, short of ostracism, for each person in the context of my encounter with him/her. Of course, in front of children I tend to choose other words. This does not necessarily mean that my impact is diminished since the children's presence itself serves as an impelling force. It seems more difficult for people to be devious in front of their children, just as it seems more difficult for people to be devious in front of an audience or even in the presence of a tape recorder.

I have considered using words like "rogue," "scoundrel" and "bounder." Unfortunately, such terms, for me, would lend a distorting sense of comedy rather than convey my serious displeasure. The reader may then suggest the alternative of avoiding name calling entirely. I sometimes, though not often, wish I could. However, I have found such actions as name calling, sarcasm, ridicule, mockery and even exaggeration extremely effective in mobilizing some people to engage with me in an encounter and, therefore, I cannot abandon them.

I am discriminating, nonetheless, and will not speak this way to everyone. I am interested in effective impact, not alienation. Judicious application is what I intend. In encounters where I can see the other person, thus getting a more complete message than what may be conveyed by words alone, I can measure my behavior more discreetly. With readers, I cannot be so specific. Therefore, I wish to remind you, the reader, that such blunt comments, which may be offensive to you, might never actually occur in my encounter with you. I must also add that your offended behavior may be insufficient to deter me.

Emotions can be worn like magical shields to ward off disaster. For years I clutched anxiety like a security blanket in nearly every encounter until I discovered how I used it as a catchall instead of being who I was— angry, sad, needing, fearful and even anxious. In my family, mother preferred anxiety and could be manipulated by it more than with any other emotion.

Does it seem strange that anxiety can be used to ward off anxiety? It can. In the same way "being afraid" can be used to ward off the feeling of fear. "I'm afraid to let myself be afraid," one woman finally revealed with a great sense of relief as that awareness touched the bottom of her seemingly bottomless fearfulness. Originally she had complained of many fears—of going crazy, of being abandoned, of being locked up.

In another patient-family, a mother wore dread like a suit of armor. She "dreaded" everything, most of all, disease. She offered her dread to all members of her family couched in remarks such as, "Put on your sweater"; "Let me see your tongue"; "Rest this afternoon, you look tired." She never insisted, however. It was as though the dread itself was the magic. She functioned under the banner of "Dread Kills Germs." When she was confronted in therapy, her teenage children, tainted and burdened by her constant admonitions, drank this awareness with alacrity, converting their ill-fitting fears to excitement and glee. Although mother persevered, she was able to take her self-image amulet less seriously. In time, I knew it would wither now that she had lost her most important playmates for this endeavor.

The most common somatic manifestations of encounter-diminishing activities are grimaces, shrugging, body movements which turn the individual away from the encounter physically, and avoidance of eye contact. The latter seems to be one of the most significant mechanisms, and consistent confrontation of such behavior has produced most rewarding results. Unless someone has a serious eye condition, I will not allow him to wear dark glasses. In response to a comment such as, "But it's very uncomfortable for me to look at you," I will answer, "You may tell me all about your discomfort if you wish—while you are looking at me."

I will pursue this matter through several sessions if necessary, and such pursuit has always been extremely important and useful. Remember the precept of the mule trainer: "First, you must have their attention." The absence of eye contact preestablishes a diminished encounter. The importance of eye contact cannot be overemphasized. A woman in her late forties, with acquired blindness of seven years' duration, was no exception.

When, like a sonar system, her blind eyes were directed to me by the sound of my voice, we negotiated. When she looked away, she was hiding. I demanded she look at me when we worked. With another woman, congenitally blind, I discussed this matter and learned that she didn't know where her eyes pointed. I discovered that she looked to about 1 o'clock when she was negotiating directly and this became her "looking at me" which I demanded.

So-called psychosomatic manifestations are more subtle but no less important than other more visible and more evidently controllable behavior. Hypertension, asthma, ulcerative colitis, obesity and, at times I suspect, all illness represent attempts to finish encounters internally.

Encounter-diminishing behavior is not always actually encounter-diminishing. Each individual has the obligation to finish an encounter for himself and the exclusive privilege of deciding for himself whether the encounter is completed and whether any of his own behavior is or has been encounter-diminishing. Completion is an individual matter, and the interpretation of one's behavior is uniquely personal. It is possible for one person to complete all of his encounters one day and yet each other person who encountered him could feel "unfinished." If such unilaterally satisfying behavior were in fact true, the satisfaction to the person who believes that he has been completing his encounters will eventually prove to be ephemeral. There are those relationships in which each person has, in a sense, agreed upon incompletion, thus permitting the relationship to be sustained, albeit attenuated. However, if there is inequality, if one person continually completes his business with the other while the other fails to do so, eventually there will be discord. Remember, each person decides what is completion for himself; therefore, there need not be agreement on what is completion for both, there need only be the experiential completion for each.

Suppose I am negotiating with someone and come to the conclusion that I do not wish to negotiate any further. I conclude that it is a waste of time, that my need will not be fulfilled in this encounter and I am disappointed. I tell this to the other person. He, in turn, feeling incomplete, urges me to remain and negotiate further. Each of us has the right to fulfillment, but neither of us has the right to demand it from the other. Therefore, as long as I am unreservedly satisfied that fulfillment cannot be complete here, and as long as I have completed the expression of my regret, I am now free to move on in search of fulfillment. The other person has the same recourse and can express, as fully and vehemently and emotionally as he wishes, his disappointment at my decision, thus completing the encounter for him. Insofar as he is unable to do this or refuses to do it in favor, let us say, of a clinging, imploring action designed to manipulate my behavior, he is responsible to and for his own incompletion and will bear the consequences thereof.

At the point that two parties terminate an encounter, perhaps both shrug. For one, the shrug may represent a part of his total expression of completion, finishing the last bit of wistful feeling, motorically. For the other, it may be part of the statement "I don't know what to do now" and may be associated with other internal evidences of incompletion such as a headache. For one, then, the shrug signals completion, while for the other it signals an unsatisfactory disruption. It might be claimed that as long as a shrug exists at all it represents something less than completion. In the purest sense this must be true. However, personal integration, like any other ideal, is a goal to be striven for, not necessarily one that is always achieved.

In an earlier example, I insisted a patient add the words "you bastard" aloud every time she spoke. This began the process of completion for this woman. Every bit of resentment expressed in that statement helped her to finish a little bit of her frustration and thus also opened the door for a freer exchange and a furthering of her awareness. As we continued to work, the epithet "you bastard" became a recognition of her capacity for hatred and the permissibility of expressing such hatred without fearing the loss of relationship. She could then recognize, "You mean you can tolerate me even though I am not all sweetness and light." This was followed by the awareness that the intolerance was inborn.

On the other hand, the epithet "you bastard" accompanied by departure would signal incompletion of the encounter for all concerned. This is a familiar hit-and-run behavioral tactic. Expression is for the purpose of permitting the individual to remain in the encounter with his frustration and should be used to *increase* the opportunity for completion within the encounter. Thus the encounter-diminishing behavior need not accrue from the epithet itself, but instead occurs because the subject bolts after making an angry charge or because the recipient ripostes with some other encounter-diminishing response such as, "You hurt my feelings. How could you talk to me this way after all I've done for you?" Or it may stem from the recipient's decision to mobilize and retain a silent bitterness.

Unexpressed bitterness, a compromise between sadness and rage, will likely have more of an encounter-diminishing effect in a relationship than a ridiculous epithet which serves to express one's anger. Granted, an "I" statement representing the most accurate distillation of an individual at any given moment is the optimal encounter-enhancing expression. However, this avenue is not always available to us and need not be. Irrational labeling and accusations, when used in an encounter to convey distress, thus permitting the person to continue in the encounter, become encounter-enhancing as much as an "I" statement. A calm shrug accompanied with bitterness or visceral distress may ultimately represent a far greater encounter-diminishing action.

Thus, we can see that any and every bit of human behavior, socially acceptable or not, seemingly cruel or sincerely nice, can serve the interest of enhancing and completing encounters or, alternately, may help to diminish encounters. The decision rests solely with the subject and does not exist in perpetuity. At any time, the individual has the right to review and to reconsider his behavior. And, of course, there is always the recourse of renewed negotiation. Each other person then has the same privilege of considering whether renegotiation is of possible interest to him. Such is the matrix of our encountering existence.

6

Familial Encounter-Diminishing Behavior

For every piece of encounter-diminishing behavior there is a matching counterpart. It takes two to join in the shameful, though usually unwitting, plot to attenuate their experiences. For every interrupter, there is an interruptee; for every questioner, a reasonable answerer. Contrary to a popular myth, this does not mean that the collaborator "needs" the other for this painful interlocking. They do it, yes, but it does not follow that they always do it out of necessity.

Often, in families, merely calling attention to the pattern is sufficient for one or more members to stop their part in it, thereby eliminating the possibility of continuing that interlocking behavior. The task then is to assist the remaining member or members to cope with their resultant frustration until they also can relinquish the unsatisfactory behavior. Otherwise they are likely to seek others, or other ways with the same person, to reestablish a dwarfed relationship. Sometimes there is a tendency merely to exchange old tactics for new, perpetuating the same experiences with new devices. For instance, a depressed tearful wife/remote reasoning husband interlocking pattern may be exchanged for a now angry wife and

113

a less reasonable husband without altering the deadlocked relationship. If this change is a necessary step along the way in which each is in the process of becoming more negotiable, then fine; they should be encouraged. Should, however, this represent a change, possibly more for the purpose of pleasing the therapist than for altering their relationship, it must be vigorously confronted. The objective is completing encounters for greater personal satisfactions, not merely altering patterns for whatever reasons.

Frequently an entire family group is interlocked in some encounter-diminishing behaviors that ultimately produce sufficient anguish either to generate recognizable symptomatology in one of them, or to provoke a separation, by a spouse seeking divorce or a child running away from home. The subsequent examples, excerpts from interviews, are single and usually initial patterns of interlocking seen in families. Rarely is there only one such pattern in a family, although there can be one fundamental premise upon which many constricted encounters hinge. Implications and ramifications from a single encounter-diminishing premise or operation can reach, like tenacles, into many aspects of people's relationships.

A family, when first seen, usually identifies the "problem" as resting in the individual behavior of one member, with the rest of the family coming along merely to assist. The picture of what the problem is in a family is not always uniformly agreed upon, although initially the members usually present themselves as a unified group. Sometimes the painful interlocking is seen by the entire family as existing between two members, with the other members involved only by their proximity. For instance, one parent and one child may be locked in conflict; the other parent may be unintentionally contributing by not becoming involved in the conflict, while the other children, also unintentionally, enjoy being favored because they are not causing any trouble.

The operating premise in this family might be, "each parent must settle his or her own conflict with each child." At times, this is a correct premise, for example, when referring to the discipline of young children by the mother. It is generally deleterious for mother to admonish the child to, "Wait till Daddy comes home and I tell him what you did. He will punish you." This behavior diminishes mother and makes home a nightmare to the usually exhausted father who is coming to his sanctuary for rest. Yet, there are times when one parent and one of the children are continually in combat; then it is not only wise, but a necessary family function for the other parent to intercede and mediate. If this rescuing operation becomes a recurrent pattern, it must be examined.

Less frequently, the presenting complaint is a "mea culpa," with one parent, usually the mother, beginning, "I know I must be causing Johnny's terrible behavior, but I don't know how or why." Why is unimportant. What is important is whether her behavior in the interview verifies her attitude. Often this opening comment is a hollow statement as is proven by her subsequent condemning behavior, such as placing blame on Johnny at their first impasse in the interview. If this is the situation, it should, of course, be pointed out for all to see. Further, this creates the opportunity for all to contribute to an attempt to disrupt the offending pattern. In keeping with the tenet which says that mother cannot create or pursue a bad pattern of interaction alone, she need not be the sole protagonist in the effort to right the situation.

Sometimes families present themselves with a remarkably clear recognition of the interlocking pattern, but a lack of some crucial awareness, or fixed patterned responses, and/or an inability to experiment with fruitful alternatives, prevents them from altering their course without outside intervention. This was succinctly presented in a family, to be discussed shortly, in which the husband recognized the wife's incessant questioning of him as the source of his painful rage, yet they were unable to modify their interaction so that they could live together more peacefully.

What happens when one parent fights with one child in a family? Does the other parent intercede? Does this other parent take a side? Is it always the same side? Does the other parent use it as a vehicle to attack the spouse? Does the combatant-parent show weakness only when the spouse is available to come to the rescue? Do the spouses always join forces, thus demolishing the child's other emotional resource, because of a belief in the importance of presenting a unified front? These and many other thoughts occur as a family conflict evolves. No specific action by either parent can be in itself encounter-diminishing or encounter-enhancing. Which it is depends on the context—the total configuration of vectors in this family at that moment. How strong and capable is the fighting parent? How sturdy is the child? What are the values and merits involved in the actual subject of the fight? Is the fight over the daughter's use of mother's hair spray? Is it a matter of family policy, such as staying out late at night? Or, is it an issue of consequence, such as theft? Who does the therapist like best as he witnesses this encounter? With whom do his values most coincide?

All of these matters and much more contribute to the overall behavior of the intervening therapist. Rather than criticize or delete any factors, every aspect of the encounter, now extended to include the therapist in this family, albeit temporarily, needs to be appreciated and included as a vital part of a healthy encounter. Each of us has an inherent need to survive with and through others in preference to dying alone. During therapeutic encountering this need is sufficient incentive for each person to persevere through trying moments rather than flee, provided the therapist does not drive the person away with crass insensitivity. No other special protective devices are required. This cohesive power is always present. The therapist alone, through insensitivity or insincerity, can temporarily create enough doubt that the patient sees little difference between staying and going—choosing, wisely under such circumstances, to leave.

Regardless of the viewpoints brought to the interview by a family, by placing a high priority on the observable interaction, the therapist gives himself an opportunity to descend quickly and effectively to the central or core conflicts that are disrupting the family. The disrupting core conflicts are always manifested in the observable interactive behavior. By paying attention to the current interaction, the critical behavioral obstacles to growthful encountering are immediately in focus; time-consuming historical data-collecting (story-telling) is by-passed.

In the quest to discover which behavior in families is encounter-diminishing, the therapist's views, values and attitudes are a significant factor. Thus, a therapist's belief that children should never talk back to parents will certainly have its effect on what the therapist will perceive as encounter-diminishing. Hopefully, the therapist is willing to become aware also of his own current behavior and to welcome any explorations of his different attitudes that may be offered by family members. This applies equally to attitudes that differ from other family members as well as attitudes that may be pointed out as differing from the therapist's own behavior in the interview.

Just as no two families present their problems in exactly the same way, no two therapists can act or react in exactly the same fashion, even though they may subscribe to the same theoretical framework, and even though they may perceive a family pattern in a similar fashion. Psychotherapy, like prostitution, runs little risk of automation. Therapeutic interventions, particularly in an experiential approach to treatment, where the therapist is encouraged to respond more personally and wholly rather than as a representative of a theory, inevitably reveal the uniqueness of each therapist. There is no single "best" intervention for all therapists in a given therapeutic scene, for the intervention must be representative of the therapist, and each therapist is unique. Each family with the therapist makes a unique composite, and the best comments of any participant, whether therapist or not, cannot be prescribed.

The following material reveals not only encounter-diminishing tactics within families, but also how *this* therapist views the family problems presented. It includes prejudices, notions and bias that are a part of my perception of my encounters with families. Another therapist may experience a family scene quite differently, attend different aspects of their encounter and still be equally effective, providing the central premises for healthy encountering prevail.

A sample of differing viewpoints between the author, on the one hand, and a parent, on the other, occurred during an interview with a 15-year-old, hospitalized boy, diagnosed as schizophrenic, and his parents. The boy was communicating nonverbally. He had been known to say single words, usually requests for things that were important to him and that he wanted. However, in recent years he had been essentially nonverbal and communicated only by nonverbal cues.

At one point during the interview, he put his hand on his father's arm. The father smiled and put his own hand on the boy's arm in a comparable fashion. No words were spoken. One of the nurses in our meeting commented that this was a sign of affection that the boy demonstrated on the hospital ward also. The father did nothing with this information. I suggested to the father that he need not respond nonverbally merely because the boy was nonverbal. If he agreed that this was a gesture of affection, that the boy was saying in essence, "I like you," the father could respond verbally with a statement to the boy of his feelings towards him. The father acknowledged that he now understood the gesture, although he did not before.

The boy obviously also understood what we were talking about because he once again put his hand on his father's arm, seemingly with greater deliberateness. His father turned to him and said, "I like you, too," and momentarily touched the boy's arm. The boy responded by taking the father's hand and putting it back on his own arm. The father left his own hand on the boy's arm for a moment and then took it away again. The boy repeated this, putting the father's hand back on his arm. The father said, "I like you, too," and removed his arm again.

After the third time I asked the father what he thought was going on. He said, "Well, the boy put my hand on his arm three times." I responded, "That's not the way I see it. To me, he put your hand on his arm only one time, but you took it away three times." The boy, to me, obviously wanted more continued contact from the father. The father, for whatever reason, was unable to sustain this prolonged contact and so viewed the situation differently.

From this focus on the current interaction, and with slight encouragement, the father began to discuss his frustration in attempting to cope with the boy and his nonverbal mode of communication. He revealed how he himself was a rather silent person and came from a home where there was little talking. Also, he recognized that in his parent family as well as his own current family, anger and displeasure were expressed largely through silence. We were all immediately struck with the apparent connection to the boy who, in his nonverbal posture, was merely carrying on the family tradition, albeit in a ridiculously exaggerated fashion.

The father first acknowledged the relationship between his silence and his sense of frustration, then we discussed his anger and frustration with both himself and his son for their mutual failure to have a more satisfying relationship. All this was only at the level of discussion but it introduced significant awareness for this father to work with.

Another therapist in this conference, who was extremely sensitive to the boy during our meeting, constantly spoke to the boy, interpreting the boy's actions to him in the light of our discussion. Near the end of the interview, the boy began to speak and his wide-eyed staring, open-mouthed appearance, coupled with occasional idiotic appearing grins, changed. Now he looked at people with a much more sober and genuinely pleased appearance.

In adult-to-adult encountering within families, a significant source of conflict can be simply the different orientations and values brought to the marriage, intolerance for the specific differences, and the impact of such differences on the members' self-esteem. Let us consider for a moment the issue of silence. The charges leveled in families range from, "You talk too much" to "You never talk to me anymore." Both spouses may have some objections, or perhaps only one is irritated by this aspect of their relationship. How each behaves towards the other during interviews will reveal how important the issue is and what each does about it. In witnessing this negotiation, the therapist can observe much more than just what each has to say. The therapist can see how important this issue is to each, how this matches his or her behavior, and what each does in the negotiation for a better personal response.

The life-long experience of a wife, brought to her marriage, may be that silence is an expression of displeasure. In her original genetic family the silent treatment may have been used effectively by one parent (and taught to the children) to bring the other parent around to a conciliatory, genuflected posture. So now, when she is displeased with her spouse, regardless of the subject that provokes her displeasure, she pouts. Her husband, who was reared in an atmosphere where displeasure was expressed vocally and vigorously, and silence implied approval, feels at first that her pouting is best ignored. Later, as he becomes annoyed with her remoteness, he begins to protest and finally shouts angrily, "What the hell is the matter with you? You got something to say—say it." Of course, she won't. His behavior makes her angrier, so she becomes more silent. The cycle for the pouter-shouter combination is complete.

Sometimes the presentation of this awareness to both, showing them how each is functioning, is sufficient to inspire at least one of them to a search for a more fruitful mode of behavior. Attention may then focus on how the unyielding spouse attempts to continue the old pattern.

One family had more of a "crier-shrieker" pattern. When she cried, he yelled, and his yelling brought more tears. In this family, she moved out of the pattern first. Instead of crying, she ignored his shouting. This seriously frightened him and he became depressed. For him, yelling was tied to a sense of importance and control, which he now lost. In therapy, we spent many hours working at his depressive posture, which she viewed with alarm, playing the counterpart of her own past behavior which she knew so well. This was interrupted and she was eventually most helpful to him as an interested and loving standby without a need to manipulate. Gradually, through experiencing her in this way, and some soul-searching, he was able to relinquish his part in this painful interlocking pattern.

Between parents on the one hand and a child on the other, the generation of conflict is a different matter. Children, like parts in a puzzle, develop outcroppings or indentations which correspond and fit with parental contours.

The child may be learning a pattern that is unacceptable to the parent;

at the same time, he or she is learning it from that same parent. The worst behavior a child can manifest is something the parent does, but cannot accept in him/herself. A parent may give the shouting treatment and yet, when the child learns to shout back, the parent finds the child's temper totally unacceptable. If the parent is persistent, the child, as a psychological alternative, is likely to develop a motoric response like a tic, a restless behavior, etc., depending on the age of the child and the intensity of the onslaught. The presence of another parent can often be lifesaving. The other parent may offer, by example, other ways of negotiating with the raging parent, or may comfort the child, offering reassurance and a resource for ventilation. Or this other parent may intercede on the child's behalf.

In therapy, the therapist may also serve one of these functions. The therapist may leap into the fray as a principal or, if not emotionally charged, may participate by encouraging more direct encountering by all. Which path the therapist chooses depends on who he is at the time and what his needs are. The next chapter will focus on the therapist's interventions in such scenes. It is sufficient to say at this time that, in spite of important differences in the genesis of encountering conflicts such as occur between parents or between a parent and a child, the therapist functions essentially in the same manner. That is, the therapist may be reasonable when dealing with a reasonable parent or child and, at other times with the same family, may respond to a parent the same way he might to a child, insisting arbitrarily that some behavior be relinquished.

The descriptive material included here is composed largely of excerpts of the interlocking pattern which was most obvious at the time of the initial interview. Initial interviews are selected as examples because they give the reader an opportunity to join the author, in this ahistoric approach, in perceiving interlocking in its least complex form. In subsequent interviews one may find people exchanging old tactics for new tactics or perpetuating the same pattern with new devices. For instance, a couple may exchange a crying versus reasonable interlocking pattern for an angry versus silent pattern and, thus, still be interlocked. The objective is, naturally, encounter completion, not merely alteration of behavior patterns per se.

The term "interlocking pathology" frequently comes to my mind as I witness family interactions. This term identifies an observable family sequence in which each member behaves in a manner that perpetuates a painful pattern. Interlocking involves the use of, or at least the tolerance of, another person's behavior and is always a collaborative effort; there are no victims. If the interlocking is acceptable, desirable and useful to each person, it is called "friendship," "love," etc. If it is none of these and yet the relationship continues, it is called "pathological interlocking." This may be achieved by each person doing the same thing, or each behaving differently, yet serving equally to maintain a horrendous homeostasis.

Interlocking pathology may be sustained by use of individual encounter-diminishing tactics which become familial. Questioning, vagueness, interrupting, etc. may be acceptable familial modes for interactions. Each family member may bring unique behaviors that, when combined, contribute to the maintenance of a diminished or incomplete encounter. In still other families, both overt and covert operational premises such as, "Respect means never disagree" or "Children always come first" or "A show of anger means you lose," serve as contracts to which everyone subscribes and which, of course, can seriously impede the completion of an encounter. Evidence of all the aforementioned activities, and many others, may be found operating simultaneously in a single family. The following material is a sampling of interlocking familial pathology which conveys a flavor of intrafamilial dynamics as viewed in the framework of experiential encountering.

The husband is rocking on the rear legs of an upright chair.

Wife: Stop that rocking. It's annoying.

Husband: No.

W: You're making me nervous.

H: I'm comfortable rocking.

Therapist: (*To wife*) You rock.

W: The thought scares me. I can't. I remember falling over backwards once. I haven't thought of that for years. I hurt myself and I'm afraid he will fall and hurt himself.

Th: (*To wife*) Tell him this.

W: (*Sincerely*) That's right. That's what makes me nervous. I'm afraid you'll fall and hurt yourself.

H: I thought you were just nagging. When you put it that way it sounds like you're interested in me and I don't mind stopping.

W: Now that I've said it, I don't mind if you rock.

This example is elementary. In an uncomplicated fashion it reveals how reabsorbing one's projection ("You're rocking is the same as my rocking") and clarifying who "I" am (converting "I am annoyed" to "I am afraid") creates a comfortable separateness in a relationship where formerly there was an uncomfortable logjam. The interlocking lies in his seeing her comment as a demand when it is, in fact, concern, and her seeing his rocking as annoying when it is frightening.

The practice of constantly changing the subject under discussion has been observed as a serious impediment in some families. Sometimes this behavior is steeped in angry accusations and the therapist may be hard pressed to decide which aspect of the interaction to attack. As a general rule, focusing on the overall behavior takes precedence over paying attention merely to what people are saying. Which aspect to attack would depend on whether the therapist felt the subject-hopping or the accusations represented the more basically encounter-diminishing behavior. He may find himself focusing initially on the angry accusations, then vigorously defending himself from the family's concerted efforts to change the subject. This would inevitably lead to a discussion of their subject-hopping, and it is likely that the therapist would find this the crucial interlocking pathology that must be negotiated before therapy can proceed. Accusations can be momentarily ignored; changing the subject constantly cannot.

In the next two samples from initial family interviews, subject-hopping was a basic family pattern. No one in either family was aware of this action, nor was there the slightest objection to what I perceived as a serious interlocking pathology. In neither of these families, particularly the first where criticism was a contiguous phenomenon, was there evidence of what might be called psychotic behavior in anyone. Yet, this kind of familial behavior is reminiscent of the "flight of ideas," a term used to describe certain extremes of individual behavior. The essential difference here was, first, that it was shared, and second, that, at least superficially, it appeared to be purposeful. Presumably, everyone was negotiating with the other in a mutual effort to solve a problem.

In the first family, the mother begins with a complaint that the children need new shoes. Father reacts angrily, accusing her of being a spendthrift. She counters with the claim that he puts all his money in savings for someday in the future while the family is starving today. He responds with a claim that she has never respected him. This, of course, is denied with a counter claim by her: "All you want is a slave, not a wife." He responds vigorously against this slander by accusing her of constantly emasculating him by telling lies about him to the children. She says it is unnecessary, the kids can see for themselves—and so it went. This family did not even notice their subject-hopping and exchanges rife with accusations. What to me were the two most distressing aspects of their interaction was beyond their ken.

Another family used the same type of subject-hopping, but without accusations; they "hopped" calmly, almost aimlessly. In this latter family, frustration was manifested as an ever growing distancing and disinterest in each other. The calm varied from aimless comments to long, apathetic silences.

Initially, I try to find the range by listening, looking, sensing my own reactions—unthinkingly reaching for a clarification of my own discomfort and a means of injecting it. With the first family, I was rather slow in responding and did not speak for at least 15 minutes. I noticed they were both quite comfortable with their angry feelings, both fluent, both righteous, intelligent and evenly matched. The children appeared casual in this familiar scene, more interested in the furnishings than in this obvious rerun. "It's not an unfair fight—just an unproductive one," I thought to myself. There were lots of juicy topics, but the level of emotional investment seemed the same for all of them. There were even rare moments of intense reasoning without shouting. I did not like what was going on, but had nothing to offer. They did not ask, so I did not say.

Finally, however, I did intervene. I just wanted to stop this hopeless bickering and told them so. Not wanting to get enmeshed in their global content, I used some of the things they said to each other as starting points to share with them some of my feelings towards them, rather like free associating on my experience of them, to them. I frequently do this, and I usually strike something significant. As I spoke I found myself talking more to her than to him. I expressed an emerging awareness that she might be far more comfortable fighting than she would be with affection.

As I said it, I realized that this derived from her whole posture which was that of a gawky, unlovable, petulant thing. I say "thing" because she appeared quite neuter. Her legs were crossed in an ungainly fashion, one arm was flung over the back of the chair, and her expression kept changing from angry to quizzical to disdainful. I expressed all this to her and included some attempts her husband had made to bridge the gap, which had gone unremarked by her.

In my first impression of the two of them, I liked him better. He had looked more directly at me and appeared more willing to engage. Her voice was too shrill, rather cold and too casual. During their exchanges she would occasionally glance at me and give me a wink. I disliked her for that. He seemed so much more sincere and inclined to meaningful messages. Then, as they continued talking, my feelings turned. She became more pained, and he seemed to press more for victory than for understanding. She fought nobly, and then I liked her better than him. "She's right," I thought, "I don't know how she can stand this righteous tightwad." Then he became more convincing and my feelings flipped again.

All of these factors contributed to the opinions I was expressing to her at this time. As I continued to speak to her, her husband began to cry. She took her arm off the back of the chair, clasped her hands in her lap, uncrossed her legs and sat up, looking intensely and silently at me. She behaved as though she had been struck a sobering blow and pulled herself together. She glanced at her husband and she too began to weep. I offered him my awareness of his unwitting cooperation with her flight from attention. They both responded with interest and attention but offered nothing more active towards reconstruction. The hour ended as I shared with them my earlier feelings of hopelessness and my satisfaction that one link in their chain of discord had been exposed and, though not repaired, at least silently acknowledged by both of them. From this I felt slightly hopeful and said so.

In the second family the aimlessness was both their doing and undoing. I commented on it. They both responded with hopelessness. Often one partner will respond; her neither responded. Their overwhelming lifelessness irritated me. I told them. Still nothing. My choice was to become like them and run emotionally or to roll up my sleeves and become a counterpoint. I took over. "OK, let's start with the children's discipline. You will each mete out your own punishments. Mother, you will not save it for when father comes home and, father, you dish out yours directly to the children instead of complaining to your wife about her defective mothering." I demanded. I insisted. I focused on specifics until each was completed to my satisfaction. In my struggle for my own survival, I often unintentionally set a much needed example.

In other families or perhaps in the same family on another issue, there may be a recognition of the area of bad encountering but an inability to alter it. The bad encountering may be manifested locally in time and place or it may pervade the entire relationship. In the following example, the interlocking behavior was a characteristic of the entire relationship, and the inciting focal point was known and frequently debated by both of them, but remained unaltered. Previously, when I discussed individual encounter-diminishing tactics, the frequent use of questioning was explored as a serious impediment. In this family it was crucial.

The husband begins, "I can't stand my wife's incessant questioning of me. She questions everything I do, even when she knows the answer. If I'm driving down the street, she asks me why I took this street. If I take a glass of tea, she asks me why. If I take a second cup of tea, she will ask me if it is my second cup. If I tell my daughter to do something, she will ask me if I really want her to do it. If I'm driving down a particular street, she'll ask me why I didn't take another street. If I come in late, she asks me what took me so long, and if I come in early, she wants to know what I am doing home so early. She isn't asking anything. She is just criticizing. She looks for every opportunity to criticize."

The wife talks essentially in questions. She reports that the husband withdraws in the face of conflict and literally runs away, having abandoned the family countless times, the longest flight lasting 14 months. She tells this story with questions such as, "Isn't it unreasonable for a man to leave his family when he doesn't like what's going on?" It seems almost impossible for her to narrate. It is as easy for me to see the suggested criticism in the way she speaks as it is for me to see that this is the only way she knows how to communicate. In effect, and with sincerity, she says in her questioning way that she really does not mean anything by the questions and cannot see why her husband gets so upset about her simple inquiries. She readily agrees that, if he does not like her questions, she will not ask questions. To this he reports, "You've said that before and it means absolutely nothing." True to form she replies, "Don't you think I mean it?"

As we unraveled their interlocking behavior, it became acutely apparent that his interpretation of his wife's questions as criticism had little to do with his wife; it had to do with projections that belonged to a distant relationship from his past—with his mother. His mother was constantly critical of him and used questions as a means of belittling. At the age of 14, he ran away from home, never to return, because of his distress over this behavior. Questioning his behavior now elicited an enraged, irrational response which had little to do with his current life. Superficially at least, it would seem that his current wife was his mother revisited, but as we explored further, we found that this similarity was more superficial than actual.

In the initial phases of the interview it was rather comfortable for me to identify with his plausible displeasure over his incessantly questioning, guilt-inducing wife. At first her questioning behavior seemed to have corroborated his statements. Having them both present in the interview, however, and seeing their functioning from both sides was of immeasurable value in clarifying the nature of their interlocking.

I noticed that, in spite of her patterns of asking questions incessantly, the wife seemed relatively satisfied with the answers she got, regardless of what they were, even if they were criticisms of her questioning. She seemed ever ready and almost eager to participate in any kind of discussion or argument. Eventually the nature of her questioning became apparent. It fulfilled two important needs for her. First of all, it provided some kind of contact with another person which would tend to lock her into and perpetuate the conversation. The other, more unusual aspect was her use of a loved one as a signpost or a weather vane—as a relating or orienting device. Her emotional stability depended on using her husband as a compass to orient herself. The direction was unimportant, just so long as a direction was pointed. In our discussion, she revealed that she had related to her own father in this way, for he was a civilized man and would always answer any seemingly reasonable question posed by her. These historical roots are of peripheral interest only. It would not matter whether or not this material emerged verbally for us to hear. What is important is that this awareness emerged as a result of observing how she used the questioning in the interviews.

As long as her husband was saying something, and particularly if he was identifying clearly who he was and how he felt at any given moment, she felt reassured. He could express anger and criticism and this was reassuring to her. She didn't care where she stood in relation to him; she just had to know that she stood in *some* relation to him. It wasn't important whether the answers were accurate or whether they were meaningful to her, just as long as they contained some identifying data about her husband. Her questioning was not designed to be guilt inducing or hostile. This woman was quite capable of being vigorously and directly angry and seemed quite comfortable with her anger. When she first came to treatment, she was less capable of crying and particularly incapable of expressing any fearfulness. This seemed the most unsafe and unfamiliar territory for her. She could readily negotiate an argument that might be raised about her questions, but felt a terrifying sense of being lost if her husband should fail to respond to her.

The course of treatment consisted, first, of taking the sting of criticism out of the questioning pattern so that the husband did not need to flee. Then, by working on the husband's right to his identity as a man and by helping the wife to become more comfortable with her fears and dreaded sense of lostness, I helped bring them to a relationship that was quite compatible.

Areas for interlocking are numerous and range from conflicts over the children, money and sex to such things as what a family should do with their Sundays together. To every point at which a couple or family become deadlocked, each member has brought a very personal range of values, which is in itself natural and inevitable. The conflict arises, not in the uniqueness of the values that each brings, but rather in how much they are aware of the values and how capable they are at negotiating a discussion concerning these values.

For instance, one family constantly complains about the horrible weekends they spend together. On Sunday mornings, the husband shows marked agitation, restlessness. He expresses a wish for involvement with his wife, which manifests itself by his rising early and quickly becoming irritable because she prefers to sleep late. She expresses a wish to leave Sunday unplanned, unstructured. She would much rather have the family just "be together." She becomes irritated with his restlessness and they bicker.

As they begin to negotiate with each other over this issue, in a therapy session, it is obvious that the husband is becoming restless and nervous. His voice quivers and becomes inaudible. In response to this, the wife becomes increasingly angry. As she does, he falls into the posture of an ineffectual, frightened little boy. This nonnegotiable posture increases her anger and the interlocking is complete.

By calling attention to his behavior during this exchange and her responses to it, we discover something. Her confrontation arouses all of the dread and anxiety he felt as a child on Sunday mornings while waiting for his mother to visit him at the orphanage where he spent many years of his childhood. He had never verbalized the loneliness and anxiety that were a part of those Sunday visits. He had lived in constant fear that his behavior would not measure up to her expectations and that, therefore, she would not return the following Sunday. His wife's current anger on Sunday mornings reinstated in him the pattern of expressing his distress viscerally. His wife's experience, on the other hand, had taught her to react contemptuously to such obsequious behavior. Furthermore, because of her intense family involvement all week, Sundays were a welcome oasis in which each member of the family was allowed his or her own independence for the day.

Here we see two levels of interlocking conflict—one, social environmental, and the other, more personal and experiential. Awareness of their divergent backgrounds and attitudes in this instance was as important to the treatment as attention to and alteration of individual behavior characteristics.

Now let us consider another family in which the identified interlocking is expressed simply as a conflict over their home: He wants to sell it and she does not. As they discuss this, she reveals her reasons: Two years hence would be a better time because both of the children will have finished their particular school level and transfer would be less traumatic for them; they have moved 21 times in their 18 years of marriage; she feels the move will not settle their differences. His reasons for wishing to sell the house are: to locate slightly closer to their work, to reduce his mortgage payments, and to permit him to spend more time at home with his family. His not being at home enough has been identified by the wife as a major part of their conflict.

I see no behavioral components to pick up so I remain at content level for now. I respond by exploring my own view of the scene, which focuses on a discrepancy in his logic: In the name of having a better relationship with his wife and children he has chosen to do something which violates all of their wishes and, in my opinion, possibly even their best interests. I describe this to him as an attempt to hurt his wife in the name of improving their relationship. I further conclude that, if he wishes to hurt her, it must have something to do with expectations he has of her which she is failing to fulfill for him. So I ask him, "What do you want from her?" He responds, "I want an open, honest relationship with her, in which she does not intimidate me and in which she will not punish me by withdrawing from me."

As we explore these two elements, the intimidation refers to any strength that she shows in the form of a request for something from him, such as attention, more time, shared experiences other than the ones he chooses. The withdrawal punishment occurs in the following manner: She suggests or requests something, he gets angry and attacks her for "intimidating" him (for daring to be assertive), and she fearfully retreats to tears and silence. This is all she is able to do with her anger. He sees this as punishment of him. This is his misinterpretation and the crucial point. His concept that she is punishing him is in one sense true, that is, she would fight back more openly if she were able to, but since he experiences it as punishment, this part is a projection of his. This means that he expects punishment for his own assertiveness.

I ask him what he experiences when he is "punished" by her withdrawal. He replies "I get lonely after a few days of this treatment and get even angrier with her." Now I know what is happening. He will show her his anger but not his loneliness. I ask, "Do you tell her you are lonely?" He replies, "No, I only get angry with her." Since this communication has been left out until now, I suggest that he turn to his wife and share the part which he has always excluded, "Tell her about your loneliness." He looks at her, begins to cry and says, "That would be weak." He then reveals that he has always criticized her for crying and for her wish for him to comfort her in her loneliness—he has criticized her for being "weak." By doing this, he avoids revealing his own "weakness" (need for warmth, affection and love), since he is unable to ask her for help.

The interlocking pathological circuit at this level has to do with his fear of revealing himself as a needful person. As long as his wife was helpless and needful, he could feel superior and attack her for being weak. As she has now become more independent, he must embrace his own weakness, which makes him even more angry with her. The more angry he becomes towards her, the more she withdraws from him, seeking her own independence from him. The more she does this, the more he feels his loneliness, from which he must flee, and his own needfulness, from which he must also flee. This makes him angry, and so the circle is complete.

The next family to be discussed consists of a mother, father and only daughter, age 16. The mother is "upset" (depressed part of the time and petulant the remainder) and brings to therapy her husband, daughter, and the belief that her husband does not love her and, "in fact," prefers their daughter. She defends this attitude with the remark, "He pays much more attention to her, is interested in everything she does, and gives her his unqualified approval of whatever she does."

The daughter has no complaints and would like to be left alone by both of them. She does not agree with her mother, but is not terribly caught up in the situation and does not appear to be significantly partial to the father.

The husband-father has no complaints. He is cooperative, dutiful, modest, and most of all, a reasonable man. He can always "understand the reasonable importance of (anything)." Anything, of course, with the exception of the absurd unreasonableness of his own rigid posture. He is here because of the reasonable request of his wife, not because she is depressed or irritable or annoying to him. He is here because he can "understand the reasonable importance of helping" his wife with her reasonably important distress. He would never arbitrarily or even righteously insist upon anything.

The wife can insist. Not openly, not directly, but with her tears, her nagging, her incessant carping. Naturally, the obvious reasonableness of such behavior is readily acknowledged by her husband.

The essential theme expressed by mother to father is, "You don't really love me." His repeated and consistently ineffectual, though reasonable, response is, "But, of course I do." The daughter represents only one of the fields selected for this battle—selected partly because she is so conveniently available and partly because mother identifies with her daughter, who, like her, is an only child. The remarks "You love her more than you love me" and "Sometimes I wish I were your daughter instead of your wife" are versions of mother's main theme, "You don't really love me."

In this family this theme is manifested elsewhere and everywhere. For instance, in criticizing her spouse's social behavior, she may say: "You're always paying more attention to other women." Criticizing his job or profession, she will say, "You could take some time off your job occasionally and do something with me once in a while instead of giving all your attention to your work." When he goes out of town on a job and calls to say hello, she complains that he does not inquire about her backache. When he takes her on a business trip with him, she complains about having to use single beds despite the fact that he tried to accommodate her and that other reservations were unavailable.

She never acknowledges, much less appreciates, the fact that he takes her out, that he calls when he is out of town, that he takes her on trips with him. He does nothing but reasonably, ineffectually and reliably protest. His protest never focuses on her uncanny ability for finding flaws. He is unable to see unreasonableness. Instead, he merely insists that he loves her, which indeed seems true, and explains patiently, though not apologetically, his various behaviors.

As I witness this family's interaction, the daughter does not appear to be interlocked in this fruitless negotiation. What I hear is this wife saying to her husband, "I feel unlovable. I need you to convince me that I am lovable, but you could never do it with your reasonable explanations." The husband's statement is, "I love you and here is the reasonable proof." They are talking about different things and, in a sense, living in very different worlds. Neither of them is aware that her message is "I feel unlovable." This message represents some earlier, unfinished encountering, which she now imposes on their relationship by her impelling need to see him as the person who does not love her. Likewise, neither is aware that the emotional staff of his life is his reasonableness, that to be reasonable means to him that he is both loving and loved.

Merely offering such awareness could never be therapeutic. The therapeutic impact came from my fearless confrontation of the wife with her "unlovable" attitudes and behavior. Confronting her with the reality of her unlovableness was a welcome relief to her from the fearful myth that she might be unlovable. By telling her she was unlovable, by disliking her behavior, and by vigorously objecting to it, I was, in fact, telling her that she was worthy of being loved. Vigorous exposition of one's perspective and honest personal disclosure that risks retaliation are sound building blocks for stimulating durable relationships—and in this instance, a particularly valuable example for her husband, as well.

I stormed the husband's solid wall of reasonableness to the point of eliciting his abdominal distress. Pressing further, I evoked the deep-seated message, which I urged him to direct to his wife: "Abandoning my reasonableness is terrifying. I am afraid you will not love me were I to be without it." Gradually, he retrieved this projection also.

Although in this family much work was done essentially as individual therapy with each of them, having the other member present was at times crucial, such as when a truth that had to be ferreted out needed to be transmitted. At other times, such as when I confronted the wife with my "loving" behavior, it was valuable for the husband to witness such behavior as an alternative to his own.

Another family has no children, that is, none that anyone can see. Two people, a social worker and her engineer husband, both about 50, have long since sent their biological children off into the world and are now each other's only and last remaining child. Her constant complaint is, "He can never do anything right. He is a big baby; I have to tell him how to do every little thing, and still he can't do it correctly. He clings to me like an infant. I can't do anything without him. He can't think for himself, and when he does, it's wrong. He is selfish and never thinks in terms of what I may need." To this, he says to her tentatively, "I don't understand what you're saying. I spend all my time trying to please you, and I can't help it if sometimes I don't understand what it is you want from me. If you will just be clear about your needs, I will try to meet them."

In their negotiating I see a compulsive engineer whose behavior is supported by two planks: a wish to please his wife and a wish for structure and precision to help him to keep his bearings in the world. Underlying both wishes is terror. He expresses verbally his wishes and demonstrates nonverbally his fearfulness by obsequious, compliant attitudes and a constant look of fright. She, on the other hand, makes a cheery and glib plea for independence and freedom couched in persistent criticism of her husband.

Their deadly interlocking goes something like this: He needs to be a good boy or die (he is on the way to his fourth coronary). To be a "good boy" and earn his right to live he must 1) please his wife and 2) live an orderly life. She, on the other hand, thrives by opposing. She is compelled to push and challenge at every turn and must see everything as thwarting. I described her as the woman with the thwart-colored glasses, without which she could not see at all. Her content—clamoring for independence —is just a convenient vehicle since he wishes to be close to her. Were he to reverse field, she would reverse her argument, I am certain.

Not only are they at opposite poles, but they incite and aggravate each other at every turn. The more he tries to please, the more contemptuous and thwartive she becomes. The more thwarting she is, the harder he tries to please. Similarly, the more order he tries to create, the more disorderly she functions with him. When he tries to accept the disorder, she belittles him in her need to oppose. When terrorized sufficiently by his own mounting rage, which is always transformed into self-criticism, he has a coronary. She opposes his dying with the same vigor that she opposes his living (and everything else) and literally saves his life each time. Of course he is most grateful and manifests his gratitude by trying to please her . . . which of course she opposes. . . .

Again, the course of therapy is no mere exposition of these opinions of mine, but is rather a task of encouraging both to become aware of their behavior and make good use of such awareness. With the wife, I was vigorously thwarting, initially to her delight and later to her consternation. With him I found myself gently urging him to risk not pleasing her. At times I expressed to her, for him, the anguish that he must feel with her attacks and his inability to respond to them. At such times, he often cried as I spoke accurately for him. Gradually, he became better able to speak for himself.

When I first met this couple, I assumed that she would be much more responsive and negotiable. I based this on her obvious articulateness and readiness to engage and the fact that she was a social worker. However, although both changed significantly and their relationship improved, my impact on him was far greater, judging from the distance that each advanced emotionally during our six months of work together.

In still another family, everyone, including the three children, is brought in to help mother with her depression. The wife looks abject; the kids act as if they are walking on egg shells; and the father speaks softly and deferentially to his wife and considerately about her. Yet I notice that he chooses a seat far away from her and never once really looks at her. He begins stating that the entire family would like to help his wife, reporting that she dissolves into tears whenever they talk and interprets everything as a criticism. I ask him, "And what do you do then?" He replies, "Well, I try to be a gentleman. I comfort her and stop pressing the point. Maybe she needs hormones. She needs something." To his comment I immediately responded, "I agree she needs something, but I don't think it's hormones. She needs a husband who will not put up with that nonsense of turning everything into criticism—that's what she needs—a man who won't be washed away by a few tears."

This interlocked scene is such a familiar one, and this man seemed so ready to work, that I decided to press immediately. The interlocking goes something like this: They disagree. She dissolves into tears. He chivalrously backs off, converting his resentment into distant courtesy. The distancing depresses her further. The depression distances him further. Since he seemed ready, I demanded that he not back off. Subsequently, I demanded that she choose words rather than tears as negotiating tools.

With another couple, I call the shrew and the mouse combination, the wife was capable of only two postures of behavior: goading and pre-goading. The goading behavior was always couched in a smile and expressed with sarcastic comments such as, "The least you could do. . . ." or "After all. . . ." Her message was always conveyed with a raised eyebrow and a slightly turned head. She said in essence, "You're so stupid I don't know why I bother with you." Pre-goading occurred when there was no obvious material available for goading and took the form of questions designed to elicit from him a position or statement that she could then goad him about.

The mouse had his own devices for joining in this interaction. He had a tendency to appear reasonably cooperative and diverted his frustration into a gutteral grunt that was interspersed throughout his comments. He acted like a mouse inviting people to trap him. She always obliged him. This further diminished his self-esteem and he became mousier. The more devastated he became, the worse she felt, being disappointed that he did not stop her. The worse she felt about herself, the more carping she became. By focusing on each one's encounter-diminishing behavior—her sarcasm and gestures, his grunt and mousy reasonableness—their interlocking components were brought to their awareness and were made a part of their verbal exchange.

The reader, noting the previous samples of marital discord offered here, may wonder whether a contemporary characteristic of family life in this country is the depressed or critical wife coupled with the reasonable and ineffectual husband. This would seem to summarize more or less the families we have discussed. Perhaps, however, this is a distortion introduced by this therapist. I would not be the one to answer that question. From my viewpoint, much family difficulty is created by a father who chooses to be reasonable or distant in preference to being aggressively assertive and possibly wrong. I see the behavioral counterpart in the mother—the carping, shrewish, depressive patterns—as largely responses to these frustrating males. These women are clamoring, in the only way they know how, for a more involved, participating life together. It is also my notion that husbands would also like this more intense involvement but see it as unmanly. This is a pathetic twist, for it is in their very abdication that the unmanliness is manifested. Men don't seem to know that wanting, needing, and demanding, if necessary, from their wives are not only important to themselves but essential to the woman's feeling of femininity.

Although these and other notions and prejudices form the broader context in which my encountering occurs, I do not hold either the male or female solely responsible for the deadlocking that may occur in a marriage. Each couple brings a unique pattern of interlocking and each participant in that family has his or her own encounter-diminishing behavior that must be confronted and alerted. Who is confronted first and how vigorously he/she is faced depends upon what the therapist experiences at a particular moment during therapy. This is elaborated in the succeeding chapter.

Jimmy, age 12, is interviewed with his mother, father and three younger brothers at a residential facility where Jimmy has been incarcerated for two years. The children are neatly dressed and quiet; father, dressed as a worker, sits motionless, looking at no one. Mother speaks for the family in response to my invitation for commentary extended to the whole family, "We brought Jimmy here because the teachers at school couldn't handle him." My first thought was that perhaps the teachers should have been brought instead. My second thought, which quickly followed, noted the simplicity of her observation and her simple manner of presentation.

As I explored with this family, mother remained the only person to respond spontaneously. All of her comments found someone to blame for Jimmy's hospitalization. Teachers were at fault because they could not handle him; previous hospital personnel were responsible for his "not being well"; and discrimination, since Jimmy was black, was mentioned, placing the blame more broadly outside of the family. After repeated attempts to engage the father, he finally said, "Jimmy is a fine boy. If it weren't for what other people are doing to him, there'd be no problem, no how."

I moved into the here and now of our encounter and expressed interest and concern at the suspiciousness that I not only heard from them, but sensed even now as we sat together. I invited them to comment on my impression and the father responded, "You called us here. You ask the questions and I'll answer them." I suggested to the father that we search together for a better understanding of Jimmy's problem. I said that I did not have any particular questions in mind other than a wish to get better acquainted with how this family functioned together. The father turned away from me and I felt dismissed. I told him this and he again responded, "You ask the questions and I'll answer them." I told him that it was difficult for me to do it his way since I did not have any particular questions to ask. Then I thought of one and asked, "Do you see any things in your family that might be a problem for Jimmy?"

I knew it would be fruitless to focus the problem away from Jimmy and towards them since their position thoroughly exonerated themselves. A nonspecific focus towards the family would be a start, though. I wanted them involved in a discussion about their family. The father ignored my question. I decided against pushing him further, concluding it would only result in further antagonism and withdrawal. Instead, I turned to the wife, expressed how difficult I felt it was to talk with him and asked her for some assistance. At first she defended her husband by saying he never spoke much; then, as I encouraged her further participation, she revealed her husband's philosophy: "My family is right, no matter what." She went on to say that this did create some difficulty between the two of them, then she abruptly stopped, saying, "There's more that I could say, but I'd rather not."

Partly because of their suspiciousness, partly because of their simple, unsophisticated way of thinking, and partly because this family had never considered Jimmy as the problem, much less the family structure, I chose the softer path of discussion rather than a more abrasive confrontation. These factors tempered my annoyance and distilled my feelings into the simple lecture that I now gave. I told them both that the difficulty we were having in the interview was related to Jimmy's problem. At great length, I spelled out how I saw the cycle of events: If something occurred that the father did not like, he would become quiet, solemn and look to blame the situation outside of himself and his family members. Mother, although she knew better, chose not to oppose this. This would encourage Jimmy further to misbehave outside of the family, such as at school, which in turn led to more experiences that the father did not like, which of course, again, resulted in his becoming more quiet, more solemn and more accusative.

"Why did this occur with Jimmy and not with the other three children?" I asked. Mother explained that Jimmy was a slow learner and, therefore, was different from his siblings. Slow learners become more frustrated, more irritable, and begin to exhibit distress behavior signaling their discomfort. In this instance, and it is not unusual, Jimmy was examined at school, labeled as borderline retarded and hospitalized.

Actually, it was the secondary distress behavior that led to his hospitalization, and this, of course, was directly related to the central family pattern presented by the father and sustained by the mother. Father was able to discipline the other children, on occasion, and did not always say they were blameless. However, because of the diagnosis of retardation, he felt more protective of Jimmy and could never become angry with him directly. As the mother revealed, the father is a man determined to be fair to all of his children. In this situation, to be fair to Jimmy meant to overprotect him. The other children, being slightly more tractable than Jimmy, responded more readily to outside authority and, therefore, caused less frustration in the father.

As is often the case in families with a psychiatrically hospitalized child, the family's interactive patterns prevent the child from returning home, not the child's behavior as such. This has led to foster home placement for children such as Jimmy. The foster care program validates this observation, as many of these children adjust quite well in families other than their own. In spite of this, the significance of the genetic family has not been sufficiently acknowledged, and it is rare to find a hospital that insists on family therapy as the heart of treatment. Jimmy is no problem at the hospital. With the permission of the family, Jimmy will probably be placed in a foster home eventually. It is impossible for him to return to this home until the father's behavior and the mother's collaboration with it are modified. Otherwise, their posture coupled with Jimmy's behavior, which is not always the compliant behavior demanded in this family, will join together to create a conflict that would result in Jimmy's regression to the same maladaptive behavior patterns which would be likely to result in his rehospitalization.

In another family, the children have grown and departed, mother has been getting depressed and father has been attempting to rescue her for several years. Now he is tired. She has had several years of individual psychotherapy because it is obvious to both of them that she alone has the problem. Still believing this, but dissatisfied with the results of individual treatment, they decide to work together in therapy to see what he might do towards helping her. They are both well educated, bright, alert and verbal. He is a successful businessman, looks intent and a bit nervous in the initial interview. He is not aware of this nervousness but readily acknowledges it when the awareness is offered him. She looks terrible. She is obviously a very attractive woman who, in her depressed posture, has carefully avoided making herself up in any way.

Their interlocking goes something like this: She becomes depressed, and he responds with rescue activity—talking, cheering, complying, "loving." This, of course, makes her feel bad and she "tries to do better." She recognizes his need to be a rescuer and does not want to disappoint him. He, on the other hand, is not aware that his behavior meets a need within himself, but only sees it as being motivated out of his love for her. Actually, he is fulfilling his need to retain his self-image as a person who can always cope successfully with any crisis.

This is revealed early in the course of our work together. His mother's advice to him was, "If you put your mind to it, you can do anything." Her martyred, unspoken message was, "If you don't, you are letting your poor mother down." His mother had depressions, too. His wife, of course, cannot succeed, although she does "try to do better." Naturally, he gets frustrated at his own failures, becomes transiently and imperceptibly depressed, and then critical of her. "You'll feel better tomorrow, dear," becomes a veiled ultimatum in which he avoids adding, ". . . or else." Tomorrow comes and she feels more like a failure and, of course, is then worse. He becomes sullen and irritable.

She nags him with comments such as, "I don't know what to do," at times begging him to tell her. His attempts, of course, fail. Frustrated at his failure, he "loses his cool" and becomes violent, breaking windows, throwing telephones or putting his fist through the wall—then he sends her for therapy for her depressions. He is rather a perfectionist and she is not allowing him to be successful. In a sense, she too is a perfectionist and needs to feel she can be all things to her husband before she is acceptable to herself.

There are other aspects to their interlocking. For instance, she cannot tolerate his ability to remain calm for such long periods of time and is compelled to challenge him until he loses his temper and becomes ashamed of himself. His composure means so much to him that after his tantrums he becomes filled with remorse at his own behavior, so now she becomes the helpful one. She finds a job for herself (actually, for her self-image).

In terms of psychological awareness, this husband is a rock. As intelligent, sensitive, affable and capable of social intercourse as this man is, he is remarkably unfamiliar with nuances of behavior and their dynamic interactive significance. He is totally oblivious to the psychological games that he and his wife play or that he plays with himself. She, on the other hand, after several years of psychotherapy, coupled with her intelligent loquacity, has become the unchallenged interpreter of their behavior according to both of them.

We had been working for about two months (eight sessions) before the interlocking patterns were significantly interrupted. First, her constant threat of divorce or suicide was confronted and her husband was encouraged not to attempt to rescue her. These, coupled with his developing awareness of their relationship and some of the implications of his own behavior, were the initial steps taken to disrupt their interlocking. A turning point in therapy occurred when, after considerable pressure from me, he gave in to his sadness, crying as he relinquished his need to see himself as a man who could always cope. Recognizing his "incopability" permitted him to acknowledge much more about his own behavior and his own needs in his marriage. With this came a remarkable increase in his ability to comprehend nuances of behavior, especially in his relationship with his wife.

This had a remarkable effect upon her depression. When she realized that her husband's rescuing behavior had been dedicated largely to upholding his own image of "the man who could always cope" and when she significantly experienced the effect of his new awareness—that he no longer catered to her—she become furious. "You mean, I have always been feeling guilty for nothing?" she asked. She cried, screamed and raged at him through her tears, "I never realized that you were so selfish."

To me this indicated that we were approaching the final step. Now I had to help both convert the bad word "selfish" to the good word "selfish." They needed to learn that "selfishness" is a good, clean, honorable word; that she could say "no" to him and that this was good, clean, honorable selfishness; and that for him nonrescuing behavior (to be unable to cope) was not only permissible but admirable.

She continued with her rage at the unlocking, "It's so lonely just to be whatever we are. There's nothing romantic in it. Then, I can't look forward to his doing things for me. What do we need each other for then?" As she began to quiet down and became sober in considering her own questions, I responded, "When all your manipulations, couched in terms of romance, are abandoned, all that is left is today's experiences and the fullest possible participation in them. How do you feel now that you have raged at us?" To this she responded thoughtfully, "Great . . . (smiling) . . . I feel marvelous right now." After a few minutes of working silence, she added, "I understand what you are saying, but I'm not sure I want to give up my romantic anticipation. What you say sounds right but . . ."

Neither her husband nor I responded to her cortical objections with rescuing behavior. I was satisfied that this aspect of their interlocking had been sufficiently disturbed that her objections could not manipulate the awareness that both she and her husband had developed experientially in this and the preceding interview.

In this next family, there apparently is again an active, assertive, unhappy female with an ineffectual husband. Here the similarity ends, as we shall see, when we examine one part of their interlocking.

This couple, in their mid-forties, presented themselves neatly and modestly attired, socially proper, with the wife appearing somewhat more comfortable than her husband, who seemed shy. He followed her into the office more like a reluctant child than a courteous man. After a brief silence, the wife began by wailing, "Why do I always have to be the one to start things?" She was looking at the floor when she said this and I responded, "I am not sure what you are saying nor to whom you are speaking." Since she was looking at no one, her wailing question could have been a complaint to her husband or a request to the therapist.

Furthermore, her question was not a clear statement of what she wanted and was further distorted by the wail in her voice which seemed to exclude an important part of her message from her verbal expression. Pointing to her husband, she continued to wail, objecting to his silence and withdrawal from her and diagnosing it as a rejection. I urged her to direct her remarks to her husband, which she did. He responded with a stare and silence more reminiscent of catatonia than anger. He was sitting stiffly upright in his chair with a faint, blank smile, his hands held motionless in a mirrored position reminiscent of prayer. I didn't concur with her diagnosis but agreed that he was less than negotiable at this time, so I turned to him.

I began by attempting to explore with him his failure to respond to his wife. This met with an almost complete absence of response to me. I continued to speak softly to him and finally he was able to say that he felt blocked. I urged him to explore his block and he replied, "It feels like walls closing in on me." He continued, "I have disconnected thoughts in my head. I don't know what I am doing." At this point I decided to interrupt what could otherwise have been a spectacular demonstration of how to precipitate a psychosis, by saying, "Stop trying so hard to please me. You can't solve all your problems in one visit. I want to help you get over your compulsion to please people." It was as though the spring in his back was released and he visibly relaxed back into his chair. "But I must get better," he said. I replied, "You want to, you will, but it doesn't all have to be achieved today."

He smiled faintly for the first time and now began to look at each of us. His release relieved me. I now felt a twinge of sadness for his wife in recognition of her plight. I wanted to engage her and work with her loneliness and sadness for a while. I was not pleased with her wailing and wanted to convert it to crying. As we worked I realized how difficult it was for this woman to make this conversion. I began to feel that she preferred to retreat from me to her well of loneliness and sadness. Repeatedly, she would tell me of her sadness and her feelings of isolation and then would hide behind a veil of tears and a handkerchief. I struggled against her retreat, expressing at first my sense of abandonment and subsequently my irritation. From my experience with her, my feelings changed from empathy for her plight of having a husband who could not be involved with her, to irritation and an awareness that she too lived a remote existence; only her tactics were different from her husband's.

The collaborative interlocking of their behavior became apparent. She herself created interpersonal distance with resultant feelings of isolation and sadness and then used her husband's withdrawn behavior to explain her sad isolation. His objection to her criticism was, of course, expressed by further withdrawal; his withdrawal aggravated, in turn, her loneliness.

Despite the shared responsibility for the encounter, which always exists, my feelings for each of them (also, as always) were different. Towards him, I now felt protective; towards her, irritated. I chose to begin more intensive therapy by vigorously confronting the wife. This was because the feelings of irritation I had towards her were more uncomfortable for me and I needed to discharge them. Second, and as an afterthought, I believed that at this point in treatment, setting an example for him as to how to negotiate with her was one of the best things I could do for him.

Another couple, Ann and George, have a marital conflict. George characterizes the conflict as marital. He makes some vague reference to their dissatisfaction with each other, then quickly retreats into a refuge of ignorance. Since he identified the problem as localized between himself and his wife, the children were excluded from this initial interview. Ann identifies their problem differently. She sees conflict involving the children and identifies one problem as George's undercutting her in front of the children. Consequently the children do not pay attention to her requests, and she loses control over them.

Ann and George are in their mid-forties and the children are 16, 12 and 8. Ann claims the conflict around the children has been going on all of their married life and at this time she is struggling for greater identity of her own and a wish for self-respect. In my opinion, she is also fighting a personal battle against an impending depression. George, on the other hand, is "finding himself" in his work and says that he wants his wife to be independent if this is what she wants. He sees himself as a reasonable man, requesting only that she continue to assume her responsibilities as a wife and mother while she is seeking her independence.

Ann is clumsy about it and does things like going off for several days at a stretch to show herself and the world that she is independent. George accepts this in what she sees as bitter silence covered by a facade of tolerance and magnanimity.

Characteristic problems involving the children are sampled next. The 16-year-old ignores the mother, shouts at her and has, on occasion, hit her. Father feels that the 16-year-old is just looking for himself and that the mother does pick on him and is "treacherous" towards him. He admits that if he gets involved, he's always on the boy's side. The mother believes this is his way of attacking her, so he has decided to be generous and stay out of the fighting, allowing the boy to abuse mother in whatever way the boy sees fit. He now "stays out of it" and the mother also complains about this. She says there must be another alternative besides his either staying out of it or being on the boy's side. She sees the boy's lack of respect for her as the responsibility of the father.

Another sample involved the 12-year-old daughter. The daughter, as reported by the mother, turns to the father "because he will be easier with her, thereby involving himself in something that is none of his concern."

This is the scene: The daughter is found by the father in the morning crying in the kitchen softly to herself. He asks her what is wrong and she says that she has nothing to wear to school. He attempts to help her by suggesting that she iron a garment she likes. Mother enters and, without a word by her or anyone else, overhears the conversation, sees the daughter crying, turns and walks out of the room. She returns a few minutes later, saying, "There are plenty of clothes in your closet. You have no business making this big scene." She then accuses the father of playing up to the child in order to turn her against her mother. The father, in a very kindly and god-like fashion, reluctantly admits that he is trying to do all he can, that he cannot ignore his own children and that there have been occasions in which the mother's responsibility has been somewhat less than perfect.

As we cut through this in therapy, we find that the mother was provoked by nothing that was said to her but had flown off the handle when she observed the scene. She was provoked by her own guilt. Probably feeling that she was not an adequate mother, she had projected her resentment turned to guilt onto her husband and daughter and then became enraged at the fantasied negligence.

Father responds with what appears to be a patient, martyred emotional attitude which might be paraphrased by the statement, "It is so hard to be all things to all people, but that is the sad fate of us gods." George needs to see himself in this superior role. He does not really become incensed with his wife's inefficiency; he does not attempt to help her with it. Instead he maintains a posture which can only perpetuate it by telling her, in effect, that her behavior is the best she can do and that he will generously accept her as she is. All gods need followers.

As it turns out, his generosity (like everybody's) is steeped in his need to be seen as the superior one. As long as he can be seen by others in this light, he does not have to face his own feelings of inadequacy. In this family the mother reminds me of the beggar with the tin cup and a sign reading "Feel Superior!" Her husband has been a generous contributor to her cup. All charity contains this dynamic for the donor. If Ann should assert herself and become an equal, demanding respect from the children and from her husband, he abandons his posture and becomes terribly frightened.

Since he is not allowed to become fearful because gods cannot be fearful and dependent, he becomes enraged and intellectual. He tells her it's her own damn fault that she does not have the respect of the children. She fights back with two outmoded tools called "dignity" and "withdrawal." Sometimes she uses "tears." None of these things work. She may ultimately have to resort to self-assertion. Another weapon that both use is the threat of desertion by divorce. This is always good for arousing anxiety and bringing people into line. Regardless of how their "problem" is seen by either of them or the therapist, progress occurs by confronting each effectively with their encounter-diminishing tactics.

As we unfold the dynamics of their interlocking conflict, we find Ann struggling from the dependent side, striving for independence, maturity, growth or whatever you want to call it and thinking that the way to get there is by asking others for permission to be independent. The ultimate contradiction is expressed as "George should tell the children to respect me." George, on the other hand, struggles against his fears and dependent wishes, which until now Ann has "worn" for both of them. He struggles to keep them there. If they don't stay there, then they will be free-floating and may become identified as his own. To treat one of these people and not the other one at the same time is to make the burden doubly difficult. One individual, Ann, must struggle not only against her own inner conflict, but against the pressures from her confrere, George, who desperately fights her evolution in the name of helping. Here we see a spouse who cannot patiently stand by and be grateful for the development of his mate.

"Family, family, against the wall, which one of us is the fairest of all?" This chant came to me as I listened to a pair of parents "reasoning" with their 17-year-old son. He has learned to respond in kind, "reasoning" back in a similar manipulative fashion. The goal, as expressed by the father, is a meeting of minds in which everyone can understand things in the same fashion. Backed by the mother, the message which the father expresses to this lad is, "We must treat you as we do because you're only 17 years old, but we want you to understand as though you were an adult, which would then mean that you would see us as unquestionably fair."

Reasonableness was the vehicle used in this family to meet the parents' desperate need to be considered fair in their negotiations. Moreover, the parents often ignored their son's excesses of behavior in an attempt to prove their fairness. For instance, he had already been provided with a new car and four new transmissions within one year. The boy had learned well. He took advantage of every leniency and in return gave the parents what they gave him—a reasonable explanation—for his continued loose behavior. This was one phase.

There was also an alternate phase when the parents could no longer tolerate the situation. Then, they abruptly ended their permissiveness. Unfortunately, they would remain "reasonable," and the boy would confront them with the idea that it was unfair for them to suddenly become so strict when he was not used to restrictions. Of course, this approach, since it was "reasonable," reopened negotiation between the boy and the parents, which resulted in another cycle of excessive permissiveness.

To treat the boy alone, expecting him to change his behavior while still living in this home, would be an impossible task. Likewise, the parents could not be treated, either singly or as a couple, since they believed the "problem" was their son—after all, wasn't it the boy who burned out those transmissions?

Another family with two teen-agers, a boy and a girl, came in and I became painfully aware of how much these parents wished to express their affection to their children in a constructive, helpful and growth-productive fashion and yet how clumsily they functioned. These parents could not clearly, confidently oppose their children. The current conflict was over the question of how much autonomy these teen-agers, age 15 and 16 respectively, should have. Both parents struggled sincerely, wanting to permit their children the right to explore and experiment on their own. At the same time the parents felt a need to offer guidance to their awkward struggling adolescents. These were hesitant parents, reluctant to intervene in the children's lives and yet uncomfortable with their behavior. The points at issue had to do with extremes of clothing and hair styles and involved the girl particularly.

The children were bright and engaging but, as one might expect, a bit chaotic. There were no serious aberrations manifested by either of them, though I agreed with the parents that the daughter's blown hairdo looked ridiculous. As we talked everyone was responsive and negotiable.

Treatment consisted of four sessions during which the parents were encouraged to check out teen-age standards, temper them with their own, and then firmly set their rules. I had confidence that they would be just. As often occurs, they revealed interparental disagreement on some aspects of child rearing and were encouraged to debate their discord openly rather than agree to ignore the issues. The "right to fight" seemed all that was necessary in this family, whose prevailing philosophy had been "love is agreement." They all seemed eager to break this chain and broaden their behavioral horizon.

Rebellion is an underlying dynamic in every family with a teen-ager that comes to treatment, although it is manifested uniquely in each. It is not necessarily the only dynamic, but it is certainly a popular one. Parents of teen-agers generally fail to understand that it is the unalienable right if not a biological obligation for teen-agers to oppose their parents.

They must contest, manipulate, undermine and, in any way possible, attempt to unseat or destroy the parents. This is their testing ground for learning what the limits are to social negotiations. This is the age in which their own identity is finally shaped. The successful parent judiciously opposes the child. By judiciously I mean that the parent should first encourage the child's opposition rather than belittle it. And second, the parents must be loud and clear about their own limits. Parental limits are very different from parental action that is dedicated primarily to stopping all rebellious behavior.

Children should be encouraged to be rebellious. But at the same time, the parents must clearly define their own boundaries and prevent the child from overwhelming them. To achieve this, two things are required of the parents: 1) They must be sufficiently aware of their child's peer group values so that they do not consistently force the child do choose between friends and family; and, more important, 2) they must have enough self-esteem and self-respect to know they have a right to their own boundaries and values regardless of their child's transient anger towards them. This latter is the most crucial offering a parent can provide for a teen-age child, for it is only in the context of the parents' self-esteem, as expressed in opposing this child, that the child can develop his own sense of importance. This is a significant contribution to the child's capacity to develop his individuality and separateness from the tyrannical teenage pressures for conformity in the name of nonconformity.

The strength of the parental posture at this time significantly molds the child's personal and social behavior. One popular model is parents who permit the child the right to decide, then nag or criticize when he does not do what they wanted him to do. This produces a confident assertive individual quietly plagued, however, with self-doubts.

Another model is parents who are unsure of themselves and counteract these feelings by deciding everything for the teen-ager. This produces a helpless, dependent, bitter, usually quiet, passive and seemingly indecisive person (much like the parents themselves). I say "seemingly" as this indecisiveness is the posture which the child has decided upon for his relationship with the parents.

A third type of parents are those who, broadly speaking, are nonengaging. They produce children like themselves, whom we often call schizoid when we observe them behaving in a seemingly indecisive, affectless, disinterested fashion concerning their own lives.

To be helpful to a teen-age son or daughter, the parent must care enough to be interested and selectively decisive. They must care enough to respect the child's decisions, also selectively, which violate certain parental positions. The parents should clearly differentiate whether their position is motivated by the child's behavior violating the parents' integrity as persons or by a belief that it is "in the best interest of my child." Here it becomes necessary to love a child enough to release the child and, in a sense, not care which way he decides, thus giving the child an unburdened opportunity to begin making decisions for himself. This is an extremely difficult transaction for parent and child alike and a most critical aspect of the parent-teenage encounter.

"I have just remarried," an attractive 40-year-old woman reveals. "I have a 17-year-old son that I brought with me into this marriage and the three of us just aren't getting along. They bicker constantly and I don't know what to do about it." As their interaction unfolds, this woman reveals herself as a sensitive and loving person who, indeed, would like to assist her son and new husband overcome their differences, but is incapable of comprehending what is wrong or knowing what to do about it. The husband is interested in the boy but can't stand some of his behavior. The boy, likewise, seems to like the man, but is unable to accept him as a parent.

This aspect of their conflict is common in reconstructed families, and it is usually a fairly simple matter to modify the problem. It can often be accomplished by encouraging everyone to stop trying to be either a good parent or a dutiful child to someone who is, in reality, a relative stranger. In this situation, each person usually brings a strong desire to be acceptable and accepted. Each is very wary that he might not be. Each usually pretends that it is of no concern whether or not he is liked. Each becomes angry and frustrated at the failure to become something to the other that he is not, and most likely never could be, at least as completely as he might wish.

In this particular family, these matters were cleared away quickly. What emerged next is best exemplified by the following description of a point of conflict. The father claims that the boy has no manners and gives as an example the fact that, whenever the boy comes into a room where the new father is located, he "rudely" interrupts whatever father is doing by speaking to him. The father finds this most intrusive and objectionable. He has avoided mentioning this to the boy for fear of appearing cold and indifferent toward him. Instead, he harbors his thoughts and feelings until the frustration mounts and the only feeling left is anger. Then he bursts forth, leveling all sorts of charges at the boy, charges unrelated to this particular behavior. The boy, on the other hand, cannot understand why this new father is always so angry with him when he is making an effort to be friendly. He assumes that the father is just a man with a short temper and continues to try to be friends with him, responding to his mother's wish that they get along well.

The aforementioned behavior and attitudes emerge as they encounter one another more honestly. More specifically, a new awareness of the father's charge of "rudeness" emerges in the light of our open discourse. The father had been reared in a rather stringent family and taught that children are to be seen and not heard. Thus, when a child comes into the room, the appropriate social behavior is for him to stand silently until whoever is in that room acknowledges his presence and, in effect, gives him permission to speak. This boy's experience with his mother was quite different. She had taught him that whenever he entered a room and there were others present in the room, it was his social obligation to acknowledge their presence by speaking to them. To walk in and ignore them by remaining silent would be "rude." Awareness of these differing social attitudes made an enormous difference in this family's experiences together. This, coupled with their improved ability to be aware of themselves and share their awareness more, brought therapy to an end.

Secret agreements, articles of constitution, and covert contracts are all terms that have been used by therapists to describe operational premises that bind families in unrewarding behavior. Some of them are called covert because the premise is outside the awareness of any of the members in the family. Some of these are so absurd as to border on the un-believable. For instance, a couple in their mid-fifties, newlyweds of six weeks' duration, come for help with a problem in their new marriage. They are both employed, responsible and, by standard nomenclature, would be diagnosed in this interview as nonpsychotic character disorders. They are dressed conventionally and enter politely.

The husband begins sincerely, "You got to help us, Doc." With a word of encouragement he says that he personally needs help to overcome his fear of his wife, relating the onset as follows:

"I was home one evening and she called me from work, accusing me of having an affair with our neighbor. I was home alone and told her so. She wouldn't listen and for almost an hour kept cursing me. That was when I made my mistake; I hung up on her. I shouldn't have done it. I knew better than to hang up on her. I knew she'd be coming after me. So I decided that I had better get out of the house. She spotted me a few blocks away and chased me for several blocks. When she caught me, she beat me, pulled a gun on me, and threatened to kill me. I've been scared of her ever since. I've got to have some help getting over this fear or our marriage is headed for the rocks." I looked incredulously at her. She responded with great sympathy saying, "I'm here to help him in any way I can, Doc."

Of all the behaviors he recited, the only one they both found pathological was his fear. I felt like a stranger in my own office and still cannot think of this experience without a bewildered, uncontrollable chuckle.

Another couple's madness seems similar to the previous couple. Also a late remarriage, in this instance the husband is an attorney and his wife manages their varied properties. Their initial complaint, expressed by the husband, is as follows: "I bought my wife a new car for Christmas and when she saw that it didn't have air conditioning, she refused it. I apologized and told her I'd take it back and have air conditioning put into it, but she called me a 'cheap bastard,' packed her things and left. It took me a week to find her and she has finally agreed to come with me to help me get over being so stingy. Perhaps with your help and hers, things could be different."

Most family agreements, secret or not, are far less obtuse and absurd than those just cited, yet they can be equally binding and almost as crippling. A family should be a retreat, a vacationland, a resource for emotional refueling. Often, however, the family structure itself inadvertently contributes the most painful experience to its members as the result of some unseen operating premise.

Each family has certain values it imposes on every member, the magnitude being similar to the ten commandments. Beyond these are premises, sometimes seemingly quite trivial, that subtly, casually, unwittingly and lovingly can be quite crippling to a child. For instance, in one family where physical prowess for the boys was highly valued, the younger, smaller lads were in constant competition with their older siblings.

Furthermore, one frail boy was automatically placed in the girls' camp within this family. I say "automatically" as there seemed to be no malicious intent nor awareness of what was developing as this boy took on secondary female traits and identifications. There was no room in this family for neutrality—or should I say "neuterality." Each boy had to be muscularly male or he was clearly not "one of the boys."

In some families all behavior is either good or bad, right or wrong; there can be no neutral behavior. In other families this is never discussed but children are simply either allowed certain behavior or not. In the former instance, where all behavior is judged as good or bad, each child manifests his life based on which side of the ledger he scores best. His self worth, attitudes, occupation all revolve around the central score keeping. All of the children in one family, for instance, chose careers in keeping with their side of the ledger, and we see, of five children, one minister, two police officers and two with criminal records, one of whom is alcoholic.

In another family "service to humanity justifies your existence" was a predominant premise which influenced the children's choice of careers. As long as each child was in public service his self-esteem was retained; if not, depression emerged.

"Don't just sit there, do something" was the fearful plea of parents in one family where idleness literally represented the devil's workshop. Here, a contemplative or passive child was in trouble. Not to be "doing something" was to be either sick or lazy. These parents knew of no other alternatives.

One familiar characteristic of family life is the tendency for cohesion, despite profound discord. To "keep peace in the family" is often offered as an explanation for sustaining a painful premise. Of course, the motives for such compromises are far more complex than suggested by this explanation. "Keeping peace" is something all of us must support some of the time. Among teen-agers, this phenomenon seems acutely exaggerated. It can be readily observed in their conforming attire and what they can or cannot say to each other. Mother to daughter: "Why don't you just tell your friend that you would like to talk about something else for a while besides sports?" Daughter (obviously exasperated): "Oh, Mother, you don't say things like *that*."

To go along quietly with something that is not objectionable cannot be called "keeping the peace"; it *is* peaceful. Going along quietly with something that is objectionable is "keeping the peace." It also places a brick in the wall between the individuals that can usually be removed only by revenge or some other type of emotional payoff. What the retaliation will be depends on the extent of the bitterness and the individual personality. The peace-keeping individual may just "forget" about the discomfort, concluding, "I guess, we just aren't as close as we used to be...."

It is sufficient to acknowledge the tendency towards cohesion, or what some might call "loyalty," in family life. This tendency may arise from the infant's correct premise that survival depends on submission to the ways of mother, the source of all things. Mothers, of necessity, teach this to their children, for their own survival. To the degree that mother and father fail to help the child to remain loyal also to his own physiological organism—to that degree are the seeds sown for later self-defeating submission to painful family premises. Further theoretical pursuit in search of the answer to "why" is unnecessary. Time is better spent in discovering how each person manifests his/her learned methods for submitting to unrewarding agreements. To be "unaware" of such painful agreements is often part of what is learned in families.

An alert but very nervous 10-year-old boy accompanied by his mother, father and sister, who is slightly older, is brought in for treatment. Mother has been in individual therapy for two years. Father had never conceived of therapy for himself but agrees to come in for the sake of his son, who ran away from home rather than present his family with his poor report card. Father always demands a cheerful and successful performance. Mother is aware that father pressures his son beyond the child's capabilities and then condemns and criticizes the child. Mother has also learned that father becomes enraged if his authority is questioned. The behavior she sets as an example for her children involved a perennial capricious smile and vaguely sarcastic comments. What the children did not know was that she was in psychotherapy for a sanctuary, an escape from her painful home life. The boy, unable to identify with his father or comply with his demands, chews his smiling lips and blinks constantly. The daughter looks frightened, clings to mother, remains silent and smiles. The father's attitude is, "I am reasonable. All you have to do is confirm it by agreeing with me." He supports this image by interrupting others, not hearing or understanding what they say and by repeatedly asking guilt-encouraging questions, also with a broad smile.

The painful unspoken premise or presumption is that the father cannot have his behavior questioned. Father fears questioning and insists on accord with his views by his rage (seen only at home) and the devices mentioned earlier. Mother acquiesces and the children submit. Since I was not a member of this family and therefore had not had the opportunity to learn how to accept the premise, I violated it by confronting them all with it. I did not consider the father as the culprit. I considered the entire family the culprit because of everyone's collaboration in sustaining this premise. Father has the right to be imperfect just as does anyone else in the family.

The premise that to confront him would end in chaos was actually unfounded as we learned from our experience in this interview. Each person had created his own behavior around the painful premise that any feelings towards father that he might not find palatable must never be acknowledged openly. Not only did each individual have his own individual encounter-diminishing behavior, but each also collaborated conversationally by subject hopping in an attempt to prevent a serious confrontation.

A segment of the interview went something like this: When I pointed out to the mother that she was looking away and grimacing distastefully in response to a comment made by the father, the son answered, "Oh, she does that all the time and it really doesn't mean anything. I don't think that's a problem." As I called the boy's attention to his interruption, which prevented his mother's responding to me, the father interrupted, questioning the boy with a smile, "Do you think I'm the problem?" The boy blinked at his father. His sister came to the rescue, saying to her father, "He doesn't mean anything by that. Maybe he just gets upset because you yell at him so much." Father turned to his daughter, questioning smilingly, "Do I really yell at him a lot?" The daughter cringed closer to mother, smiled, and looked at her mother. Father silently continued to smile at her, and I commented to the father, "You smile and ask questions and never seem to comment on how you feel about things." He responded, "Well, yes. . . ." But before he could finish, mother defended him, "That's just the way he is." Her smile became a grimace. I pointed to her grimace and asked her how she felt about him being this way, and before she could answer, her daughter, who was silent when confronted directly by the father, came to the rescue saying, "We all know that Daddy is like that, but it doesn't bother us." We had now come full circle.

I shared my awareness and my discomfort with all of them and my conclusions about what had been revealed above. The mother responded by expressing some fear and hopelessness about confronting father directly. This was the opening wedge into a serious familial agreement that had remained subtle and powerful by being kept out of everyone's view.

In another family, composed of a psychologist mother, slightly older than her new husband, and her two teen-age boys by a previous marriage, we find an unspoken contractual message which might go something like this: Whereas the mother is a psychologist and the oldest member of the family, be is resolved that mother's interpretations are never to be questioned. The identified patient was the oldest son who was rather inarticulate, subject to outbursts of temper and criticized by his family for his offbeat qualities. He was the one who found this impossible rule the most difficult to live with and reacted most violently to it. However, since he was outvoted and only 19, he did not have a chance, especially since age was a significant criterion of mature judgment. The other three members managed around this family rule concerning mother's behavior with socially acceptable pathology (pathological because of its roots): Mother got needed personal acknowledgment and appreciation vicariously through her career; her new husband (still a student working towards a Ph.D.) abdicated his function as an adult partner by pleasantly, and without further contribution, accepting his wife as the sole breadwinner, manager and decision maker, in exchange for being left alone to complete his studies without further demands upon him; and the third member, the younger teenager, rarely at home, met his personal needs through a compelling interest in sports. Social achievement could work for three out of four—for now.

In therapy, the identified patient initially became my most valuable ally in disrupting this encounter-diminishing rule. This does not imply that my ally was free of any need for sustaining this rule. As we worked and searched, it became evident that he, too, profited by receiving mother's appreciation and interest as payment for his submission. Again, it should be emphasized that mother was not the prime offender. It required all four family members to sustain this shackling arrangement, each using a method consonant with his or her own personality.

In discussing familial encounter-diminishing behavior I have purposely attempted to avoid generalizing about intrafamilial dynamics. Too much attention to such matters deflects attention that rightfully belongs to the ongoing observable phenomena in the current encounter. Also, thinking about intrafamilial dynamics in general encourages the therapist to squeeze current interactions into previously conceptualized patterns, impairing his ability for fresh awareness found in the uniqueness of each family's interaction. Therefore, the examples of familial encounter-diminishing activities have been presented in a way that hopefully encourages attention to the encounter rather than stimulates thoughtful probing of the inherent implications. Intellectual browsing will occur inevitably and spontaneously anyway and, though it is interesting, generalizing is a very common pitfall of therapists that impairs their vision for the ongoing and the obvious.

7

Intervening

A therapist is a person being. A therapist is a person being, skillfully. A therapist is not a person being skillful. The "experiential I" is the verbal expression of a person being.

Discussion begets more discussion, interpretations produce understanding, and "experiential 'I'ness" elicits responsible and responsive behavior. What is "experiential 'I'ness"? Have you ever known and said with conviction, "I mean what I say and I'm saying what I mean." This is what I mean by the "experiential I." It is an expression that reflects the certain knowledge that what I represent at that moment is accurately and thoroughly all of me: I am in concert. Furthermore it is conveyed in every manifestation of my person: my look, my stride, my attitude, as well as my words. It is the "experiential I" that has the greatest impact on others.

The expression of one's "being" is not always dramatic. Its credentials are a profound certainty and a quiet conviction that require no justification. It may emerge lightheartedly but without frivolity or silliness. It may emerge slowly, yet without hesitation. It may be spontaneous but is never impulsive. It may come out as a truthful, tearful, "I am sorry." It may be seen in a teary-eyed smile and sigh of relief when what one has hoped would be comes to pass. It may be obvious in a tender, wordless, lingering embrace. It may be expressed as unabashed and uncontrolled laughter. It may come out with fang-flashing fury.

In therapy, "I am interested in knowing what you want" is the baseline opening statement of the therapist regardless of how it is conveyed. Hopefully, this is the "experiential I" of the therapist at that moment. If not, hopefully the therapist will still present himself accurately, even if he must begin, "I am preoccupied and need your indulgence for a few moments. . . ." This is in contrast to feigned interest or asking a patient "why" he or she has come. Such questions obscure the therapist, inviting the patient into a personal, yet not intimate, discussion. The foregoing may seem a picayune difference; yet when it reflects accurately the overall orientation of the therapist and is not merely an exchange of words (such as saying, "I felt . . ." instead of "I think . . ." as one continues "thinking . . ."), the entire atmosphere of the therapeutic interview changes from discursive to experiential. The expressed experiential "I"ness of the therapist is the epitome of the experiential intervention.

For the patient of the experiential psychotherapist nothing is "too advanced." The therapist knows that each patient is always ready, if not eager, for what he needs; it is only necessary for the therapist to develop and convey his person sufficiently to match his patient's receptiveness. No more labeling patients as "resistant" instead of the therapist expressing frustration or disappointment in his own current inability to cope. No more pretending that the label "therapist" is a precious private possession, instead of recognizing that who the "patient" is at any given moment circulates through all members present, including the labeled therapist. "I don't know what to do right now" can become a stimulating intervention by the therapist who is willing to be more than a mere "therapist" in his therapeutic encounters. Let the therapist clearly accept the responsibility, if not entirely for the therapy, at least for his own part in the encounter.

Other approaches have been criticized for having a built in, airtight system for making the therapist always appear correct. If the patient does not accept the therapist's position, the patient is labeled "resistant." One might argue that in the experiential approach the therapist is also "covered" since whatever he says or does can be justified with the claim that he is being himself. The difference is an important one. In the experiential approach, since everyone is responsible for his own behavior, there is no one to blame or label as deficient. It is not a closed system. No one is required to fit into the model of another at the risk of being called a name if he does not. Whatever the therapist may believe is incomplete in his encounter with a patient, he can complete for himself. He may need to express his anger towards the patient or cry with a family over his sense of loss or failure, but he need never resort to the accusation "resistance."

There is no prescribed formula for greeting families coming into therapy. I greet them as I experience them. I do not attempt to be anything but what I am. Sometimes I feel like smiling and do. Other times this may not be my mood. At first glance, one person may arouse my suspicion by his manner while another evokes a smile. There is no introductory discussion "about" what we are going to do. They will know soon enough as we begin doing it. Sometimes I begin speaking with someone immediately, other times I am silent.

You might well ask if this is not an anxiety-provoking situation in which a stranger comes in and sits down, expecting the therapist to do something and the therapist just sits there doing nothing. First of all, there is no such thing as "doing nothing." I am sitting silently, diligently being myself. Sometimes, this is anxiety-provoking for me and I may begin by observing that aloud. Should I become aware of someone else's anxiety, I am likely to respond to it verbally if the anxiety affects me. I am not aware that I "always" do anything. I respond as I am in each particular setting and, since the setting is never identical with any other previous setting, whether I am dealing with the same family or not, my exploration in each hour begins afresh. My patients and I are different each time we meet.

The assumption that anyone can remain unchanged is untenable. At best we might claim that changes are unobservable. It is an existential fact that no moment can ever be identical with any other moment and, likewise, no person can remain the same. In this atmosphere, not only is each family interesting as we differentiate ourselves, but each experience within each therapeutic session with the same family takes on a delightfully exciting air as we explore and experiment.

As I consider the often silent opening moments of a family therapy session, I think of the poetic observation that the blank canvas is a most perfect bit of art. In therapy, each comment or gesture is, of course, a part of the representation of the underlying needs and conflicts within each of us in the group. At the conclusion of therapy, when we no longer have to talk or gesture at each other in this setting, the quiet beauty of the blank canvas is restored—hopefully, though, now ready for a different picture. The time between the initial and concluding canvases is filled with lines, erasings, more lines, and more erasings. The initial moments of silence are tension filled; the concluding moments of silence are satisfying. The initial facade of courtesy and pretense is exchanged for an active involvement with the imperfections of reality. The underlying turmoil is becalmed.

Usually after some courteous introductions, I fall silent. Such initial silence seems appropriate to me; it is a working silence in which each person begins to fill our time and space together. Some fill it with anxiety, some with curiosity, some with suspicion, while others fill it with patience and play a waiting game. I do not feel that I am withholding intentionally, for the purpose, let us say, of creating anxiety. If I become aware of anxiety in the silent behavior of others, the silence is no longer comfortable for me and I will usually respond with words. Such behavior creates the first lines or sketches on our canvas. Initial comments or actions draw my attention, but I am uncertain as to where these lines are being placed on our canvas. At any moment when initial action draws my attention, it becomes the center of our canvas for me. As we proceed, from moment to moment, these lines or sketches are continually displaced as others become central. For me, therapy becomes a constant search for the proper location of each gesture or comment by any of us. This is not something I think about or speak of, but something that I am aware happens to me during my encounters. To comprehend the location, stability and importance of each marking on our canvas often requires that I tease it out to fuller view or position it against a previous daub for a clarifying contrast. Endorsements or objections to my behavior are also daubs that command my attention. Such is the nature of experiential intervention. In practical terms, interventions, whether casual catalytic observations or vigorous, heated confrontations, are geared to a clarifying exposition and appreciation of our differences —who each of us is in relation to one another in the current moment.

When a persistent, relatively silent, inarticulate and inert family presents themselves, I probe initially to see if there is anyone in this family who objects to living this way. This can be done with an open invitation such as, "I find the atmosphere in this family oppressive and dull and I wonder how each of you feels about living in this family." If this is unproductive, the therapist may next select someone who looks like a possible ally, but seems afraid to open his/her mouth. This fantasy may have grown out of a knowing glance or a smile following the invitation, for example.

However sparse the verbal participation may be, someone presents the complaint and everyone looks (or doesn't look), moves (or sits motionless) and responds (or fails to respond) in each moment. The therapist will have some feelings about each of these items. From this rich field of observable behavior (active or not, verbal or not) there are a multitude of interventions possible, varying from provocative observation of what each is not doing to personal remarks by the therapist about his own frustrations in relation to such behavior. It is usually not long before someone is displeased with this insipid activity and will take heart from the therapist's antithetical behavior to join him.

Sometimes an active response is long in coming. Then it behooves the therapist to continue speaking, even lecturing, should he feel the inarticulateness is genuine and pervasive. Teasing out topics of concern, he may continue to invite commentary, freely offering his own opinions on any topic raised. If comfortable with this behavior, the therapist can be a "dutch uncle" in the family, serving them usefully and also enjoying his own expressiveness.

Before discussing more intimate details of intervening, it would be well to explore some of the reluctances or objections the therapist may have to experiential encountering and to look at some of the devices used by therapists to escape from the here-and-now experience. Two of the most common resistances used by therapists are: 1) to lean toward historical data; and 2) to raise "why" questions, which send both patient and therapist into the world of abstract thoughts and encourage the exploration of circumstances which are not immediate and of questionable theoretical pertinence.

The experiential approach is an ahistoric approach. Taking histories is a time-tested, professionally reliable method for allaying the anxiety of the therapist. It is, for instance, unnecessary to know that an individual has been hospitalized psychiatrically four times in the past 10 years when there is such a simple, direct and up-to-date avenue for information, such as tossing a bit of one's own person towards the individual and observing what he does with it. This causes data to be furnished immediately by direct observation, data which the therapist can now use in preparation for his next sally.

Not only is the individual's immediate behavior of more significance than last year's, but attention to the way in which he or she responds to other family members and the therapist provides immediate information on whether this person should be hospitalized today or tomorrow. This also seems more valuable than the knowledge of yesteryear's hospitalization potentials. Therapists have trained themselves to use histories, psychological test material and other once-removed data; it is equally possible and far more valuable for them to learn to read directly the data provided by the person's immediate behavior. With experience we can reverse the pattern to our advantage and come to know our patients' incidental past history through their current behavior rather than vice versa.

Should the therapist become anxious at not having a retreat to the past available as a buffer, I would suggest that he explore this anxiety with his patients. Not only may the patients be helpful, but they are likely to also benefit from such honest, personal exposure from the therapist. Certainly, the atmosphere will become more exciting and realistic.

Introducing the question of "why" is another popular therapist's retreat from encountering. Asking the question "why" can serve no profoundly beneficial function. Regardless of whether the patient knows or does not know the answer to the question, and regardless of whether or not the therapist gives the patient the answer, it is still an intellectual game that is fundamentally nontherapeutic. I say fundamentally because there can be some secondary benefit from using question-and-answer activity as a way of each becoming more comfortable with the other when neither patient nor therapist knows a more effective or direct means of safely becoming engaged with another person.

Asking "why" in therapy serves three functions, none of which are encounter-enhancing. First, it serves to structure the time-space between the therapist and patient, permitting the therapist to introduce his training or theoretical framework into the encounter, like a foreign body. Second, it permits, even encourages, an escape from the explorations or awareness of the current experiences. Third, it sets up an interactive game in which the patient is the student and the therapist the knowledgeable one. When the therapist asks why, it is assumed that he has the answer "because . . ." For example, let us consider what happens when a patient says to the therapist, "I feel anger towards you." I suggest anger as the emotion to consider since, when a patient expresses appreciation or affection, the therapist is less inclined to ask "why?" To the statement of anger, the therapist *is* likely to inquire "why?" The patient has three possible responses: not to know why, to know why, or not to care why.

The usual answer is "I don't know why," which takes many forms, such as, "If I knew why I wouldn't be here," "How should I know, you're the doctor," "Yes, there must be a reason. Can you give me a hint?" All of these depend on the interest the patient has both in playing the game of "why-because" and in being a good patient. In responding to a patient the therapist probably believes his action is based on thoughtful theoretical considerations. Actually, his like or dislike of the patient and his needs from that patient at that time are the critical determinants. Therapists will never become machines.

The important goal of experiential therapy is to alter behavior, not to "understand."

Now, depending upon how much the therapist likes the patient, he decides whether he wants to tease the patient by not responding at all, offering a hint, or if he thinks he can sell it (the patient is ready) making an interpretive answer.

If the patient thinks he knows the answer and tells it to the doctor, there are two possibilities: 1) The analysis may be wrong. Wrong means that it does not conform with the therapist's particular discipline, such as giving a Jungian therapist a Freudian explanation. 2) The analysis may be correct. Correct means it is capable of fitting into the therapist's frame of reference, such as a cultural explanation to a neo-Freudian.

Patients are rarely so healthy that they are able to say, "Who cares?" I do not wish to belabor this presentation. It is obvious that in such encounters the emotional impact of the individuals on each other is thwarted by maneuvering around the question "why?" It is also obvious that a hierarchical structure is established in order to play an intellectual game which bears little relationship to therapy. Any therapy that occurs during such intercourse, that is, any changes that occur in these individuals, is fortuitous and results as a consequence of their prolonged relationship and appreciation of each other for their fine capacity to play the game. When intellectual compromises based on the patient-therapist relationship cannot be made, the patient calls the therapist a bad therapist and the therapist calls the patient resistant. Labels are an essential part of any intellectual game.

The uses of countertransference fears as encounter-diminishing operations have been discussed previously and will not be elaborated here. Suffice it to say that elaborate, intellectual and theoretical discourse lies resplendently throughout the professional literature effectively admonishing and frightening therapists for many years. The therapists' fear of encountering is neatly cloaked under the intellectual and professional concern over matters of countertransference.

Any individual encounter-diminishing tactic used by a patient can also be a part of a therapist's encounter-diminishing behavior. Questioning, for example, is a therapeutic tool, often valuable and sometimes necessary during encounters with patients. It is essential for the therapist to be reasonably certain of what he experiences, and asking a direct question in such instances is naturally encounter-enhancing. Questions geared to increasing current awareness such as, "What are you aware of at this moment?" "How do you like me right now?" "What are you doing to me?" or "What do you want from me now?" are also particularly valuable for encouraging awareness of a participant's encountering behavior. Beyond these categories, however, the therapist would do well to avoid questions as a form for intervening. Also, it would be well to keep in mind that even such seemingly encounter-enhancing questions can serve to mask a therapist's momentary discomfort and be actually encounter-diminishing.

Working with families offers a special setting where I find that revealing myself and engaging vigorously is facilitated. In my parents' home, we were taught that home is a haven where we are most likely to find a friendly reception for our behavior. This was not to say our behavior would always be acceptable nor that it would always be received without anger, but there was no question of an underlying and unfaltering acceptability, coupled with a relative openness and readiness for discussion. I do not deny that "unacceptable parts" were also installed in my parents' home. But by and large, by example, they encouraged open, emotion-laden exchange. One result is that working with families has a freeing quality for me. I have found that amongst my colleagues this is not always true. One therapist revealed after his first family interview, "It was positively alarming. So many things started to happen at once. I wanted to run away. It felt just like returning to my home when I was a child. I didn't know what to do (just as I didn't know what to do when a child)." The only recourse a therapist has in this situation, or in any other for that matter, is to retreat to who he is in the here and now and share himself as fully and richly as he is able.

"But I don't want to be partial" is a frequent cry of the new family therapist. I am not afraid to be partial. I am partial, I know I am partial, and the best I can do is to be as clear as possible about my partiality at any moment. I also know that my partiality is whimsical and changes from time to time. I must also be clear about this.

For me, absurd partiality is diminished when I can witness an interaction first hand. In such a setting, I become less concerned that I am siding with a woman because she is attractive or with her husband because of my identification with him. The "other" parties become real and their viewpoints more comprehensible. I take sides—loudly and vigorously sometimes, gently at others. I side with one, two, three, everyone, or at times I stand firmly alone. I change from moment to moment. I see little point in pretending to be objective. As stated earlier, and it bears repetition, objectivity, the concept of the immaculate perception, is an absurd notion. To side with one's own person as honestly as possible at every moment is to side ultimately and thoroughly with everyone.

Sometimes, while I am vigorously confronting one family member, another family member will join me, taking heart from my assault. If I feel this second person can benefit from a much needed ventilation, I am likely to encourage it. However, if I suspect he is joining my bandwagon for a sneak attack rather than an honest confrontation, I am likely to turn on him and demand that he wage his own battle. I do not like all people equally, I do not appreciate all kinds of behavior to the same extent. My task is not to deny this, but rather to incorporate this into the most effective presentation of who I am.

As the therapist relinquishes old encounter-diminishing tactics endorsed by old encounter-diminishing psychological theories, he is likely to feel excitement. One therapist, returning from an initial interview with a family in which he attempted the experiential approach, described his anxiety in the following remarks, "The mother began by telling me how terrible her son was, and when her son tried to intercede in his own behalf, the mother just ignored him. Immediately, I found myself involved with many emotions of my own which had never occurred to me before in an initial session of individual therapy using a more conventional approach. I pointed out to her how she had ignored the boy, and she ignored me in the same way. I didn't like what she was doing. I felt sorry for the boy. She wanted to be blameless. I wanted to do something further to stop it, but wasn't sure just what. I was afraid to get involved with my own feelings as perhaps it was all just countertransference problems. I didn't want to bring my problems into it."

This therapist had allowed himself the luxury of becoming aware of some of the feelings that are elicited in such a situation. He was as yet unable to overcome his personal and professional prejudices to allow these feelings to serve him and his working family. There is little point in questioning whether or not he should bring his "problems" into it. They *are* in it. They are *always* in it. The issue is not whether or not to introduce them but how one can most effectively use one's feelings as a person. Attempting to keep them out diverts much of the therapist's energy and attention. Hiding one's own person is also a bad example.

Let us consider at this time some of the "what ifs" that have been asked at conferences where experiential psychotherapy was being discussed.

"What if the family comes in, is rather unsophisticated, and after one of them describes the problem in the family they all become silent?" In asking my colleague to rephrase the question to a statement he said, "I'm fearful that I might be faced with a group of people who would be silent, expecting me to take responsibility and I wouldn't know what to do." I urged my colleague to pursue his fantasy using a projective approach. I suggested he visualize the scene and begin by telling his family of his newness in the field and his associated anxiety. He replied to me, "I don't think I could do that." Rather than ask "why," I suggested that we bypass his obstruction for the moment and assume that he had said this. I then inquired what the family's response might be. He thought awhile and replied, "They would think I'm incompetent. They would expect me to know what I am doing."

Not wishing to pursue further at this time the exploration of this therapist's projection, I suggested that he view this as his own projection and consider the possibility of discussing his feelings of incompetence with his family should this situation ever arise.

What you have just witnessed in the dialogue between my colleague and myself is a sample of experiential psychotherapy at the first or catalytic level. In an actual treatment session I would have pursued this further, urging the therapist-patient to utilize a projective technique, which will be discussed later, for attempting to reintegrate this unacceptable part of himself labeled "incompetent."

To answer the question more directly requires some comment on silence. As mentioned earlier, silences can be working silences or nonworking silences (cf. encounter-diminishing tactics). Eventually, prolonged silences become uncomfortable for me and motivate me into action. I may explore who I am, expressed as what I perceive or what I am experiencing. I may "poke around" different individuals in an attempt to tease out some discomfort worthy of our consideration. If someone has spoken as was suggested in the initial question, there are innumerable avenues which can be tapped to further the encounter. The speaker can be encouraged to direct his comments to someone specifically. If he is looking to the therapist, the silence might elicit from the therapist, "And what is it you want from me?" This might lead to some complaint about another member of the family, and this other member might now be invited to respond. The silence may merely be verbally noted as a minimal stimulus to see what they will do with it. The entire family can be asked to comment on the silence. Any member may be invited by the therapist to comment on the original speaker's description of the family problem. Last, but far from least, the therapist can respond directly to the speaker with his opinion of the speaker's description or of the speaker's manner of presentation.

The possibilities for intervention are infinite. The direction the therapist chooses should be based on his most immediate concern—not on some pre-set formulation or theory that he has learned from reading material such as this. When in session, be with the family, not with the book you've just finished.

"What if the family seems to be saying the same things over and over again and there doesn't seem to be any movement? Nothing changes. It's rather frustrating and I don't know what to do." "It" is not frustrated, the therapist is. When the therapist was asked if he confronted the family with his feelings of frustration, his reply was, "No." When asked what his feelings were towards this family, the therapist replied, "I was fed up with the constant repetition. All of my attempts to stop them failed. I was frustrated with this impossible situation and didn't know where to go with it."

At that moment in therapy it is likely that the feelings of both the therapist and the family are identical. Neither of them knew what to do that might alter their impasse. They may have differed in their degree of frustration about the matter, but at the moment when neither knows what to do they are essentially identical. When this occurs there can be no movement. The seer and the seen are one; the family and therapist are alike. This oneness or homeostasis paralyzes treatment. The impasse is defined as: the moment when neither patient nor therapist knows what to do; the moment when neither one knows what to do or say differently; when each has, like a scratched record, recited his responsive part valiantly without, however, the wished-for impact. Likely both are frustrated.

This is not to say that there is no motivation for movement or that there will be no movement. Hopefully, it will be the therapist's dynamics that will initiate movement, but this is not necessarily so, nor is it a requirement for a good therapeutic experience.

The way out of this dilemma lies in the exploration of the impasse itself. It is when the therapist ceases to play at being the therapist and begins to respond as a person, or as the patient if necessary, that therapy resumes. It is when the therapist expresses his frustration, disappointment, irritation or whatever he may feel that movement is initiated. It is when the therapist knows what he is experiencing at the moment and is able effectively to introduce these feelings that therapy is resumed. This is not only a valuable technical device for the therapist, but also a living example to the patient of how he might also respond.

What immediately precedes any impasse is an exchange in which the patient is behaving in an ineffective (neurotic, sick, inefficient, self-defeating, etc.) manner; the therapist has, without success, done everything he can to disrupt this behavior and now both are frustrated and angry— the patient, because he has failed the therapist; the therapist because he has failed the patient.

What the therapist needs to know at this moment is that his frustration now is identical to frustration the patient experienced many times during his childhood evolution. And further, that the behavior of the patient now is *identical to the parental frustrating behavior he once experienced as the child.* So now, unwittingly, the therapist is the frustrated child and the patient is the frustrating parent in a weird reconstruction of an historical scene. At this moment the therapist has two courses he may follow: 1) to persevere, combat, experiment, challenge, pursue and defeat this child-now-turned-parent, as a long overdue example; or 2) to withdraw, defeated, as the patient did in original scenes during his growing years. If he follows the latter, the therapist has failed to see the starving, longing child, locked inside the frustrating creature before him, strong enough only to come feebly for help yet not strong enough to do more. When the therapist recognizes the nature of the impasse, he can struggle vigorously, knowing from the experiences of his own internal child that his patient's inner child will take heart from his endeavors despite any protest of the child-turned-parent presenting personality facet.

A stony, intelligent 40-year-old professional man, disturbed with his ineffectuality, presents himself always smiling, reasonable and analytic.

The more I talk with him the more irritated I become, for every offering of mine is lost amidst a reasonable, analytic torrent of words comfortably couched in a hollow smile. Every action is blunted and I reach the moment of truth—the impasse—where I feel I must chose between killing him or abandoning him. Then I know what he did: He abandoned his child rather than defy or threaten to kill his mother. He "identified with the aggressor" and has become the frustrating parent. I will not. I defy him. I tell him how I feel towards him. I speak to him (without realizing it as I began) as the frustrated child that *he once was*, only I am more powerful and more eloquent. After several minutes during which I refuse to let him swamp me with reasonable words, he begins crying and says, "I'm blank. I don't even know what I'm crying about. I must be crazy."

I knew what he was crying about. His incarcerated child had looked out the dungeon window and saw help coming. Now we were ready to work. I persevered while he failingly tried to reconstruct his child-now-turned-parent self-image. As his child (self) cried gratefully, he became stronger. Then he was encouraged to "try on" being the child-now-stronger against the image of the smiling, analytic, reasonable parent.

I shall not pursue this further as the purpose of these comments was to explore the impasse, not the course of therapy. Suffice it to say that the path of therapy was for the child (self) and the parents (self-images—for his ineffectual father also is an integral part of his disability) to engage in a mortal struggle out of which an integrated being emerges. This was only the beginning.

In the supervision of psychotherapists doing family therapy, I am impressed with how frequently the best possible interventions are excluded from the therapy and saved for a supervisory meeting (or for discussion with colleagues). One therapist reports, "All the family seemed interested in talking about were minutiae and superficialities. They all seemed comfortable and interested enough, but it bored me. I saw nothing to be gained by the discussion. I tried to join in for awhile and then gently suggested we change the subject. This didn't work and I became frustrated as my boredom grew." These comments would have been valuable to the progress of therapy had the therapist fully mobilized his feelings of frustration and boredom and then introduced them heartily during the interview.

Another therapist reports, "I have a group of several patients who for some reason I do not seem to enjoy. I am not sure whether it is that I do not like them or just don't seem to know how to work with them. I'm not sure what it is. I noticed that they are all of Mexican descent and suspect that my discomfort may be related to this. However, I don't recognize any particular prejudice in myself since I have friends who have a Mexican heritage and with them it doesn't seem to make any difference. These patients all speak English sufficiently well so I can understand them and this does not seem to be a barrier. They appear to be of average intelligence and don't seem to be particularly dull to me. As I am talking with you about this I recall a patient of Mexican descent whom I enjoyed very much, with whom I was able to work quite comfortably and successfully. The only difference that I can think of between her and these other patients is, first of all that she is female, and they are male. Also, (laughing) she was very attractive and I can't say the same for these men. (Blushing) it's embarrassing to think that I might want my patients to be appealing to me or else I will find fault with them. I feel better having said this and also feel more comfortable about working with these men."

This monologue reveals the therapist's search and at least partial resolution of his conflict. Now what is the difference that makes him able to do this with me, his supervisor, rather than with his patients? I suspect this has to do with role expectations. With me he is expected to explore himself and to be rewarded for being introspective and insightful. With his patients he expects himself to maintain a posture that would deny his need for introspection or gratification. This posture or image of a therapist becomes the obstacle to further elaboration of his therapeutic experience with his patients. To have made these remarks to his patients would have opened the possibility for even greater personal awareness and, at the same time, would have been a therapeutic experience for his group members.

It seems that all questions of therapists regarding what they should do in difficult or uncertain situations during the treatment of families can be summarized in the question, "What do I do when I don't know what to do?" This question becomes particularly pressing when the therapist is denied the possibility of retreat to historical data, to asking why, or to labeling his patients as "resistant." In general terms, the answer is quite simple. When in doubt, retreat to yourself in the here and now. As best you can, become aware of what you are experiencing and introduce this into the treatment situation, directing your expression as accurately as possible to the person who seems most related to the declared feelings.

A therapist, who was beginning work with families, reported, "I seem so much more comfortable with individuals. With families, we seem to get into things in the very first visit. I'm emotionally involved right from the beginning and it's a little frightening. For instance, recently, a mother, father and their son who was identified as a delinquent came in to see me. At the very beginning mother wants to read me a letter she wrote a relative listing all of the boy's delinquent behavior. I asked the boy how he felt about it, and he admitted that he did not like the idea of her reading him off in this way, and she proceeded to do it anyway. I pointed out that she was ignoring the boy's interest at this time because she was ignoring me in the same way that she ignored the boy. I felt badly that I had become so angry with her. I didn't know what to do so I just told her I didn't want to hear the letter. It was kind of a strained session."

Family therapy is more vitally interactive right from the beginning. The conflict is on the surface, and we don't have to wait for conflicts to develop or spend our initial time talking about conflicts that are elsewhere—that is, other than in the session itself. But let's look at the concern of the therapist. His disturbance lies in the fact that he is aroused emotionally by what occurs. To me, this is an advantage, not a disadvantage. The disadvantage felt by the therapist has to do with his concern about revealing his discomfort. His "image" of the calm, all-understanding, wise, emotionally flat guru will be shattered. Furthermore, he will not fit the unspoken middle class ethic, which tells us exactly how each human being is to behave or "perform" in any given situation. Perform is a better word because that is what it is—a performance.

On the issue of effective alternatives in this situation, two paths can be followed: 1) to act as a catalyst or 2) to become a principal. The path chosen is decided by one's own level of involvement. In some situations I am less emotionally involved than in others. In the kind of situation just mentioned, I may not be eminently involved emotionally and, therefore, would not necessarily become a principal, at least early in the session. I might urge the boy to repeat his statement to his mother of his discomfort and perhaps request directly that she not read the letter of condemnation. I would also suggest to the mother that she attempt to listen to the boy. Thus, I would remain an observer-participant, encouraging each of them to reconcile their differences with suggested behavior that I believe would be helpful. Should both of them ignore me, my frustration would rise, my interventions would become more vigorous and be directed towards each of them, perhaps with an emotional description of how I see each ignoring my offerings. The other alternative is to become a principal myself earlier. This would occur if my feelings ran high from the start (although until such time as the mother actually ignores me I would be responding via identification with the boy rather than because I am personally being ignored. So be it). When I become a principal, I am a participant-observer instead of observer-participant. This is rewarding behavior. It teaches everyone in this family to fight back at the primary source of pain, and it teaches by example, not by description. This is a most important benefit. In addition, it saves the therapist from having to divert some of his attention to controlling his own emotional world and, thus, reducing his effectiveness and reducing his involvement with the family. Again, it creates a healthy working atmosphere for the actual resolution of the conflicts.

Where might all this lead? At this point I am always impressed with how other therapists who witness this moment "of truth" become fearful of disaster. The assumption that forthrightness and anger mean disastrous retaliation is our own fantasy. It does not happen. The mother in this situation, for instance, may respond either with further combativeness, and we will fight it out on the spot. She may retreat, feel misunderstood, and we can work from that point, again, by staying in the here and now and observing the way in which she responds to my forthrightness. She may claim that she is misunderstood, that I am wrong and that her interests are primarily to help the boy. If she can be so insightfully verbal, we will explore this on a verbal content level. If she just sits back silently, I will point this out, and perhaps even invite her to share her thoughts and feelings at the moment with us. This moment is not an end point. It is a beginning point.

"With such an approach as is suggested here, there is a high risk of saying the wrong thing sometimes. What happens then?" There is only one "wrong" or "mistake" possible—that is to refuse to acknowledge errors. There is nothing "wrong" with an incorrect or inaccurate observation, there is nothing "wrong" with a misguided outburst. There is a great deal wrong with denying such errors when the therapist becomes aware of them.

Good therapeutic results are generally attributed to good therapeutic technique—proper interpretations, sound analyses, appropriate interventions or meaningful encounters. It all depends on the doctrine to which one subscribes. Occasionally, in more magnanimous mood, we admit the beneficial impact is inexplicable. The following is an explicable sample of what can happen from saying "the wrong thing."

Mr. came in, as he often did, looking sullen. Mrs. came in, as she often did, trying to look small and sweet. As usual when they came in like this, they had been fighting, and she makes the overtures towards reconciliation.

Mrs. Do you want me to start dear, or do you want to?

Mr. (*Refusing to answer straight, angrily*) You always dictate anyway —why ask me?

Mrs. (*Retreating further into sweetness*) You seem so uncomfortable. I thought you might like to share it.

Mr. (*Same pose*) You're so damn helpful!

Mrs. Well, if you won't start, can I start?

Mr. (*Still refusing to answer*) You act like I'm stopping you—it's always my fault isn't it?

Mrs. (*Defending, smile gone*) I didn't say it was your fault. (*pause*) It's just that this always happens and we never get to talk things over. For weeks now I've had these things to discuss.

And so it went for several minutes. I pointed up his push-back attitude and he balked further. I mentioned her intimidated sweet retreat, and she expressed difficulty in coping with this wall of his. I sided with her and knew from past experience she could not break into his wall so I decided to intercede. I had become angry with him and told him so. I vigorously attacked his inpenetrable pose of "I dare you to reach me" and then I got global. In my anger I charged him with doing this elsewhere in their marriage. For example, his wife had been pleading for years to have him attend to some much needed repairs around the house, yet he always petulantly expressed some excuse for doing nothing: He did not like the way she asked . . . and why in the hell did he always have to be asked. . . .

He turned on me in a righteous rage, shaking his finger at me, "Now you listen here a damn minute. You always listen to her as though she's telling the whole truth and then you assume that's the story. Well, let me tell you, Mister, I've done plenty around there." He began to list all that he had done and it was considerable. True, he had never mentioned it in the sessions and I never bothered to inquire. I do not work with content generally, but when I am responding, I sometimes use content from previous meetings as the vehicle to express my feelings, as I did in this instance. He raved on and gradually he slowed down, but by his furrowed look I saw he was not finished so I goaded him, "So, am I supposed to be a mind reader? You never said anything." And off he went again, "You're supposed to be a therapist and know better than to believe everything you hear from one side—especially from her—you should know by now she exaggerates. I've been telling you that." Then as the cloud of anger cleared away, he saw himself and began to chuckle.

"Listen to me tell you off—I've never done that before. That's pretty good for a guy who usually just sulks. Thanks for being so wrong. (thoughtfully) I never could have done it otherwise. I felt so righteous. It's a shame that I have to be so sure I'm right before I can get angry. That sulking is inpenetrable, I know. (turning to his wife and smiling) Okay, let's get at it now. What are some of those things you've been wanting to talk over with me?"

He is not "cured" and she will still retreat into useless sweetness. The interlocking problem was not touched, but the air was cleared so they could work this hour. His explosion at me was a valuable experience for him and will have a useful effect on their life together.

As it turned out, his explosion at me did more than clear the air for this session. This explosion signaled the beginning of his self-assertion as was borne out during the remaining treatment sessions.

A greater danger than saying the "wrong" thing, for therapists new to the experiential approach, is not following through with one's personal investment. Often, in their eagerness to learn, therapists will make initial attempts at forthright interactions but may become quickly blunted by some patient's distressed response. A patient may retaliate by crying, having hurt feelings, becoming crazy, or simply telling the therapist to get back into his therapeutic garb and stop using behavior that should remain exclusively for the privileged class—the patient. Whatever the gambit, an inexperienced therapist may become frightened and/ or embarrassed, and decide to retreat. The utilization of one's total personality in the therapeutic encounter is not something to be worn like a garment. It is only valuable when the therapist incorporates these principles into himself and can thereby sustain his behavior in therapy. When the therapist becomes frightened or embarrassed, it behooves the therapist to continue to include such feelings. Effectiveness lies in the therapist becoming and remaining a person, not in his intermittently using his person. Remember: A therapist is a person being, skillfully—not being skillful.

I had been working several months with a couple. The content of recent sessions hovered about the husband's sexual impotence, which was infuriating to the wife, terrifying to him, provocative and interesting to me—at least till this session. I had been confronting his total groveling attitude, which I held accountable, his sexual impotence being merely one local manifestation of an inhibited posture with which he tried to extract friendliness and jolly good fellowship from the world. Effectiveness was secondary to him. He was a capable, reasonably successful man in the world and did not know it yet.

On this particular day, I had lost my awareness that I too was a reasonably successful man in the world. I felt quite inadequate on this morning. As we worked I became increasingly aware of being ineffective and, with it, increasingly uncomfortable. I was going through a personal reevaluation generated by criticism of my work by some colleagues. My resentment towards them for their unkindly gossip, and particularly their failure to confront me directly, was converted into self-doubt. I had such experiences before, knew what was happening to me, but was helpless to alter my course. Knowing—understanding the "whys" of my behavior—was of no value. I did not dare share all this with this couple for I decided "it" was not pertinent. I had decided that I was not pertinent. It was a terrible session.

Immediately after the session I called a colleague-friend and bawled and babbled at her, confessing my incompetence as a therapist, exploring my inadequacy as a person. She listened well as I rambled through a briery path of self-criticism and remorse. For the first time, I risked feeling the painful sting of a respected colleague's disapproval, adding my own resonating self-criticism. It was almost too much to bear. As I rambled on I began to feel some relief and dared to ask her opinion of me. "Is there truth in what they say? Am I losing my touch?" She's a good therapist-person and replied, "It's about time you let yourself feel that pain. Frankly, I'm relieved."

I too felt relief, then gratitude; then, rather surprised, I felt like running outside to play. In the secret safety of this friend ("mother" for those of you who must!), I opened and grew. "*That* mother-wife in the session was too risky for me," I thought, chuckling to myself, or rather at my self-image.

Yet in the session, though I could see and speak vaguely of my discomfort and hint at its relationship to this couple, I could not be competent. The wife, a therapist herself, expressed her disappointment in me and a wish to discontinue our sessions. I pointed up the similarity of her response to her husband and to me, yet I could not be competent. I knew better, but couldn't *be* better. I expressed my disappointment at her decision and secretly suppressed my concurrence with her decision. I felt depressed.

Her husband decided to continue.

That evening she called and expressed concern over the session and wanted to return to explore it further. I had planned to call her. I was feeling much better since my phone call to my friend and was delighted to hear from her. She sounded depressed and I suggested she not take it all so seriously since I felt better and more confident (see, I'm still potent, nothing to fear . . .). I told her that I too had many afterthoughts and feelings which would be available to me on the next session.

All this is a preamble to the description of the next session which follows.

Three people met, all quite dedicated to searching for a way in. She took the initiative, expressing first her sadness, telling of her affection for me and her wish to bridge a gap, though not knowing how. I responded with the story of my phone call, my inability to share with her any feelings of inadequacy and my realization that I still could not share such feelings with her for fear she would respond to me as she does towards her husband. I expressed the realization that this very revelation was made in the safety of my self-confidence today.

Her husband responded, "What I saw last week and today has touched me more than all our previous work together. I somehow now know what has been said before is true. I can accept myself more as I continue to respect you. I'm sorry about your discomfort but grateful for the opportunity to share it with you." He turned to his wife and said, "I hope someday you'll be able to accept me as I am. I cannot try to be all things to you any longer and I no longer feel either the guilt or the resentment to you for your expectations of me." He truly had experienced something in those sessions.

The wife began to cry again, "I love you both and suspect that it's my own fear of my own failure that has been so frightening to me. I feel angry still with you (to me) for failing to see my strength and affection for you."

I began to cry as I became aware and expressed my need for her appreciation of me. I had formerly criticized her for idealizing me as a distancing operation, which I still felt. I now saw how I also used her idealization to deny my own need for appreciation.

I now know that, had I dared, sharing my pertinent self in the earlier session would have rewardingly deepened our growthful experience together.

Suggesting intensive commitment of the therapist often arouses the therapist's concern for his patients' ability to cope with it. Though it is often a smoke screen to hide his own anxiety, a reasonable question which occurs to every responsible therapist is, "What is the psychotic potential of this person?" or "How much can I push, dig, explore, confront a patient with my own behavior and still safely avoid eliciting psychotic ideation or behavior as a response to me?" The powerful effect inherent in this approach makes this question most reasonable and pertinent. The safety lies in the therapist's astute awareness of himself and what he is experiencing. This approach often rapidly denudes the patient of psychological protective coverings by circumventing old, stock defense patterns before the patient (perceiving ego) has the opportunity to devise new methods of remaining cloaked.

The terms "cloaked" and "denuded" are most appropriate since the responses of patients to confrontation are often suggestive of what they might experience if suddenly they were publicly unclothed. Embarrassment, embarrassed laughter, blushing, confusion, anxiety, a sense of shame, sometimes a feeling of depersonalization, and often a sense of being lost may all appear. It is incumbent upon the therapist to know how much of the response represents a genuine internal struggle for the patient and what portion of such behavior is manipulative and being directed externally to deter further interpersonal interacting.

When a patient's behavior represents a true struggle within him/herself, there is little attention to or energy expended in the direction of other people. This is not to imply that there is no awareness of the presence of others, but refers only to the use of this awareness for manipulating others. When a patient has been uncloaked and is now struggling within himself with his awareness, there is no need for the therapist to intervene further at this time. Interpretations become interruptions. No assistance or support should be given at this moment unless the therapist has evidence that the patient is incapable of coping at this point. This should be derived from a perceptive awareness of what the patient is doing from moment to moment.

Unnecessary assistance impedes therapy by not permitting patients to experience this primitive state of crisis from which, hopefully, they will begin to find their own resources instead of stuffing this moment from an outside source. This was part of the original dilemma and should not be repeated by the therapist if possible. If the therapist observes that the patient is unable to proceed without help, then the least possible assistance should be given, to encourage the patient's own maximal efforts at self-development. Any excessive assistance at this point is detrimental, since it directs the patient away from internal reorganization in favor of an interpersonal interaction. This can become a prototype for future interpersonal manipulative behavior. Whenever possible, permit the person the opportunity to reintegrate his personality alone. The therapist is merely scaffolding around the reconstruction, to be used as needed by the person.

In recent years, as I have permitted myself greater latitude as a person within my therapeutic interviews, I have on some occasions had the experience of breaking down (what an unfortunate expression) and crying helplessly over some internal matter, those instances having been sparked by something that a family member had said to another person in our group. On these occasions I found that I was able to speak through my sobbing and merely shared out loud what I was experiencing and the thoughts that were associated with it. Afterwards, I was impressed by how unimportant anyone else's supportive responses were. It made little difference that they comforted me, cried with me or came over and put an arm around me. On both occasions, immediately afterwards, I felt a glow of affection towards all persons present, regardless of their response to me. I felt at peace and, after a brief few moments of further interest in my own person, I became aware of and interested in the others.

There are three criteria by which I judge the mental health or ego-strength of a person that I encounter in therapy. The first is the degree to which the person can clearly state who he is and what he wants from our encounter. For example, contrast the person who enters, introduces himself by name, sits down and begins speaking, "I need some help. In recent months I've been unable to cope with . . ." with another person who enters by standing at the doorway saying nothing. When invited to sit down, he sees several choices and asks, "Anywhere in particular?" When finally seated he either remains silent or asks hesitantly, "What do you want me to say?" When encouraged to speak about anything he wishes, he searches silently awhile and begins, "I don't know what's the matter . . . It seems . . . maybe this isn't even where I should be . . . you sure have a nice office."

The second criterion is a more dynamic one, derived from further encountering, and concerns persons' capacity for and comfort with an identity apart from the therapist. Are they rigid and impenetrable? Do they readily attack, criticize and/or "not understand" everything offered? As I become distressed at our failure to make contact and share this with them, do they persevere in their containment or is there some attempt on their part at a rapprochement? In such instances the price of the separateness is no encounter.

Seemingly, at the other extreme are those who are eager to absorb the therapist without question. Whatever the therapist says is swallowed without chewing, without evidence of digestion to any degree. They agree with everything and their severest objection is, "Yes, that's probably right." They are really not at the other extreme at all. They too cannot openly accept an identity apart from the therapist and the price of their nonseparateness is the same—no encounter.

The healthier the individual, the greater his capacity to openly appreciate differences. The healthier the individual, the greater his capacity to openly appreciate sameness. The healthier the individual, the greater his capacity to openly acknowledge and negotiate those differences or likenesses that are displeasing to him. This, of course, applies equally to patient and therapist.

The third criterion considers how ably the person can remain in the here and now. This not only means physically staying in the room or being socially conversant, but refers most pertinently to the person's ability to remain with a current topic that may be psychologically painful to him—here and now. For instance, should the current encounter become painful, how readily does this person flee the here and now— "That reminds me of . . ."—in preference to some expression of his current discomfort? And, again, when this is pointed out, can he become aware of and discuss his discomfort or is this confrontation met with a similar or more removed response, such as silence or a change of topic? Also, should the subject matter reach beyond our current encounter to some painful recollection, I am interested in just how profoundly the person loses perspective in our current encounter and how much stimulus was required for his departure. An adult person who spontaneously begins to speak to a deceased parent, as though he or she were present, is quite different from the person who does this in response to an experiment suggested by the therapist.

No single criterion by itself is pathognomonic of ego-strength or impending psychosis. An extreme of any aspect of the aforementioned, by itself, may be found in most of us at various times. Even combinations may be exhibited simultaneously without implying serious mental disorder. However, a persistent posture relatively unresponsive to outside manipulation is suggestive of a brittleness or what familiarly has been called the "psychotic potential" for that individual.

The amount and quality of "I"ness a person uses, the first criterion, can be detected early not only from how clearly an individual states who he is and what he wants from the therapist, but also by noting how much of his expression is verbal and how much is tied up in nonverbal gestures. If gesticulating is prominent, I am interested in evaluating whether the mannerisms are rather commonplace or unusual. The presence of good eye contact denotes relative strength, but the absence of eye contact alone does not necessarily signal danger.

Many persons with a fairly sound mental structure are unable to look at a person while they are talking with him, but as soon as they stop talking and start listening, eye contact becomes possible for them. There are many variations on eye contact: Furtive glancing at the other person for cues, for instance, is a popular behavior. Each behavior in itself must be evaluated in the broader context of the person's total behavior.

The amount of "I"ness, i.e., how often the person is able to say, "I like . . ." or "I am . . ." or, especially, "I don't like . . ." serves as a valuable index of personal worth. And, of course, personal worth is related to personality strength. Sometimes this is a social facade when the person has been raised to pretend selflessness by avoiding the use of the word "I." "Never start a sentence with the word 'I' " is the strongest admonition I can recall from my first grammar school composition class. This social avoidance is of negligible consequence and generally quite responsive to a simple suggestion that the person say "I" when he means "I," instead of using such terms as "you" or "one." This is an elementary communication-improving (encounter-enhancing) activity. However, when suggesting this, we may detect a more profound or qualitative significance of the person's "I"ness by his readiness to alter such behavior.

A pertinent qualitative aspect of "I"ness has to do with how much of the "I" is identified with the person's total being and how much of it is in the service of maintaining an image of himself, thereby representing just a small portion of the total person.

Let us consider the two statements, "I think people should not be demanding" and "I want what I want when I want it and will do everything that I consider reasonable to obtain what I want." In the first statement the individual generalizes. The subject is "people," thus obscuring a more personal "I" statement. Furthermore, by couching the statement in terms of a "should" he is, in effect, admitting that the statement represents only a small part of his total being. By contrast, the other statement clearly identifies the "I" of the person and represents more an expression of the total person by considering both what the person wants and acknowledging also the need to be reasonable.

Though admittedly sketchy, this comparison should show the qualitative differences of "I"ness detectable at the verbal level. The person's total behavior and expression which surrounds these statements are best incorporated into the therapist's total perception of this individual.

The distance between the subject (the person) and the subject matter under discussion is often an indicator of psychotic potential and our second criterion. In a couples group one member, whom I shall call Art, murmured softly and almost inaudibly, "People seem to talk in such deep tones." This statement had no clear "I" representation and was presented in such a manner that there was no clear object person to receive the message. The almost inaudible quality of the message was a pertinent part of this individual's need for distance.

Someone responded saying, "Your high voice sounds feminine and weak to me." This remark was not exactly a clear "I" statement, such as, "I don't like your high voice . . ." but it was more committed and involved than Art's statement. Art responded, "Your voice sounds friendly." By paying attention to the person's voice and to the subject of voices, and ignoring the personal message, this man in effect was saying, "Let's not talk about us but rather let's talk about our voices." That Art carefully chose to ignore the clearly negative implication speaks of his fragility. The other person aggressively said, "You aren't talking to the subject I raised. If you don't want to talk about yourself in relation to weakness and femininity, why don't you just say so." Art again replied, "Your voice has a nice quality to it." Art was not psychotic at this time.

I intervened and said, "Talking *about* people's voices is important to you." To this he became visibly more interested and responsive and began talking remotely about the voices of people. He was still unable to talk about his own voice and found this distance operation the only way in which he could discuss himself at this time. This difficulty with his "I"ness and his inability to contend with the conversation except in a most peripheral manner readily provided everyone with the awareness of this man's psychological fragility and his psychotic potential. I concluded our interaction with Art, and our session, since the time was up, saying to him, "Since there isn't time to pursue this further, I just want to tell you that I would be afraid to argue with you with any vigor. I'm afraid you would go crazy rather than fight back with me. I don't like that so I'm going to try to teach you how to fight better, another time." He smiled with obvious relief and *didn't comment on my voice.*

This was an "I" statement by the therapist. Later in this chapter, when interventions are reviewed more closely, the "Royal 'I'ness" intervention will be discussed as the optimal intervention. This was an example.

So far what has been discussed is largely observational in terms of the "what" and "how" of a person's messages. The third criterion of psychotic potential, as hinted at above, is the interaction: What happens to a person's "I"ness when he is pushed, challenged or confronted. In the foregoing example, as Art was pushed, he persevered even more strongly in his original position. Though not crazy at this time, his response to the stimulus of other group members revealed his potential for what we would call psychosis. He was unable to negotiate freely with the subject at hand. Let us compare this behavior with another member in the same group whose behavior consisted of angrily throwing back, often in a clumsy fashion, whatever was offered. The other group members were irritated with him. His "I"ness seemed as remote as Art's, though his pertinence to content was somewhat better.

For instance, someone said to him, "George, you look angry all the time and you hardly ever say anything to us." He just glared back. Someone else said to him, "Oh, come on George, why don't you say something?" To this George responded, "What's the matter? You got a problem?"

he replied, "What are you sore about?" Another tried, "I want to talk with you about your obvious discomfort and would like to help you with it." George said, "When I get ready to talk, I'll talk, and if you have something to say, why don't you just go ahead and do your own talking."

Then someone made an "I" statement, saying to him, "I'm frightened by your behavior." George replied with a sardonic smile, "Why don't you tell me about it." The other person said, "I don't know what to say other than that I am afraid to talk with you because you always bat answers back at me." George visibly warmed, his hard expression softened as he responded, "I feel nervous talking to you but I have felt pushed around all my life, and at this point I have decided to take a chance and say what I damn well please, and I don't care whether you or anyone else likes it or not." This last stimulus led to a weakening of his posture and to a strengthening both of his pertinence to content and his "I"ness. Pushing the encounter, as this last person did, led to a strengthening rather than a diminution of his "I"ness. Following this, with slight encouragement, he continued to volunteer information about himself. He revealed an inability to eat in recent weeks as accompanied with continuous abdominal pain. When he finished he reported that his abdominal pain had abated.

How ably an individual remains in the here and now in the face of vigorous encountering aids in evaluating ego-strength. Many persons can speak comfortably in "I" terms and even be pertinent to the content of the subject matter as long as the subject matter is related to their remote past or potential future. For instance, persons can often discuss quite intimately their memories or past experience, yet be particularly inarticulate when it is suggested that they discuss their obvious anxiety in the current encounter.

Patients with previous experience in therapy are often able to speak with great aplomb on subjects such as their sexual behavior and their hatred of their mothers. They may even appear to feel strongly on such matters. Yet when it comes to speaking of their affectionate or angry feelings towards a current and present family member—or perhaps, the therapist—they psychologically resign from the encounter.

Let us compare the opening presentation of two depressed patients. The first comes in, sits down, looks sad and begins his conversation, saying, "I don't know what's the matter. I've been overwhelmed with sadness and I know I need some help. I don't know whether you or anybody can really help me." He begins to cry. Immediately, I know that this individual is in relatively good shape. He speaks in terms of "I" in the context of his present moment. Another individual comes in, sits down and begins to cry. After a period of crying, with or without an invitation from the therapist to share the words that go with the tears, he begins, "There is no sense in living. Nobody is interested in anybody else. It's always been this way. Things will never change." Here, there is no "I" statement. Further, there is no direct acknowledgment of the presence of the therapist (but this is still a better sign than if he didn't speak spontaneously), nor is there any attempt at a critical evaluation of the immediate situation. Nowness is quite peripheral to his awareness. Comparing these two presentations, the second individual is far less negotiable.

The psychotic potential of the individual cannot be determined directly by these features alone since the precipitating circumstances surrounding onset of the depression and the duration of the depression have not been clarified. However, it isn't necessary to have this information to evaluate the individual's psychotic potential. The historical data are unnecessary if the therapist is willing to become engaged with the individual in the immediate situation. By confronting the individual, the therapist can immediately test, without risk, the power and tractability of the individual's depressive posture and the therapist's capacity to cope with it. In my experience, the more remote presentation as suggested by the second individual requires a far heavier therapeutic hand, a more vigorous attack, in order to first get this person into the here and now where a greater therapeutic impact can be felt.

The willingness and ability to participate in the here and now are urgent clues of psychic vitality. *It is always astonishing to see how much time people spend away from their existence in the current moment.* In itself, avoidance of the here and now does not imply psychotic behavior or a strong psychotic potential since it is so prevalent. However, the persistent inability to function in the here and now and the absence of "I"ness become the definition for the label psychotic.

Therapists often have a tendency to flee emotionally from so-called borderline or psychotic individuals and respond to them gingerly, if not squeamishly. In my experience patients languish with such mawkish attitudes. Crazy people dramatically improve with vigorous yet sensitive involvement. The example below is submitted in evidence.

Mrs. S. was a 35-year-old, married, Spanish-speaking mother of three children, who was hospitalized for a psychotic episode about two years before our interview. The predominant features, then as now, were depression and paranoia, and included crying, hopelessness, self-deprecation, delusions of men watching her, accusing her of being in love with them, and suspiciousness concerning her husband's fidelity. She elaborated on these by animating such objects as her refrigerator, which would now watch her hoping to catch her in some unacceptable behavior.

After several months of hospitalization, some psychotherapy and considerable medication, the patient improved. As long as she was maintained on tranquilizers, she seemed able to function and could keep some objectivity about her delusional material, which never completely disappeared, however. Therapy stopped and the patient went to work. She was not seen for about a year and a half. Several weeks before our interview her symptoms became exacerbated and she returned to treatment. Since I spoke no Spanish we worked with a female interpreter, a middle-aged, married office worker who was employed at the hospital where Mrs. S. had been incarcerated two years before.

On the latest visit the patient complained that I was rather difficult to see and appeared fuzzy to her and that she was uncomfortable about the movement of my hands. I was unable to engage her in interaction with her fantasies about my hands and so sought to explore her visual difficulty. I suggested that she close her eyes and experience wearing the most powerful and clarifying glasses in the world and that she could see everything clearly.

I asked her to look around and tell me what she saw. At first the glasses were obviously rose-colored because she offered her idealized wishes about the world around her: conflict-free and pleasurable. I was not pictured among her visions. I suggested she look for me in the scene. After a moment's silence she clouded up to cry and said, "It gives me feelings to look at you."

Her not wanting to see me and her concern about my hands led me to assume she was fearful of a more intimate contact with me of either an affectionate or an aggressive nature. I remembered her history and her need to project onto others her fantasies of close affectionate relations. I asked her what feelings she had, but she just shook her head silently in a negative fashion. With individuals who have healthier ego structures, I will often share a fantasy of mine with them for their consideration. With individuals who have had psychotic episodes or whose ego structure, for

Someone else said, "What are you so sore about all the time?" To this whatever reason, appears to be more fragile, I become more and more direct, as I was in this instance when I said, "You have ideas and feelings about making love with me which you find intolerable." She burst into tears, nodded affirmatively and said, "I feel like an animal now."

Again, considering the psychotically constructed ego, I leaped into her psychic structure, attacking her conscience, and said, "Now I am angry. I will not tolerate the kind of conscience that will not permit a person to have fantasies. I will not tolerate a conscience that cannot tell the difference between fact and fantasy. I hate that kind of conscience."

The patient stopped crying and looked up at me and the translator and explained that it was true that she had these fantasies and that according to her religion she was being sinful and that she could not understand what I was saying. This statement led me to feel that she was beginning to understand what I was saying. I went on, "Fantasies are the food of the mind, and without them the mind starves. All of us have many kinds of fantasies. All of us have had fantasies such as you have. I have had fantasies of making love with you as well as Mrs. . . . . . . (the translator). I am not afraid of these fantasies. I know the difference between fantasy and fact. I will not condemn myself for having such fantasies. I can only condemn the conscience that is so mean it will not tolerate such fantasy."

The translator, who is a religious, middle-aged, married mother of several children who presents herself as a neat, clean, matronly figure, and who has been extremely reliable and accurate in her translations, repeated this last statement in Spanish and then added on her own volition, "And even I have fantasies like this, too." The patient looked surprised and somewhat bewildered at both of us. She spoke lucidly about her conflict with the church, some of her childhood experiences, and the difficulties encountered in her cultural transition to the United States. After about three or four minutes of this, the patient concluded, "I see you clear doctor, and I am not afraid of your hands moving." The hour ended.

Interventions are fundamentally of two types: catalytic observation and active participation.

Catalytic observation represents the relatively uninvolved, encounter-enhancing service the therapist renders. This is baseline therapeutic activity and consists of urging family members to confront one another directly and then, based on direct observation, suggesting a modification of their encounters that will enhance them—such as looking at one another when they speak or perhaps urging that a gesture be converted to words and included in verbal exchange. The therapist is largely an observer, participating minimally.

As work proceeds there will inevitably be times when the therapist is aroused above the catalytic level. Then, rather than maintaining a posture of indifference while inserting interpretations and labels like "resistant," the therapist becomes more richly engaged in the encounter, becoming a principal in the fray. In such cases the therapist is largely a participant and only peripherally an observer. Interventions reflect the level of the therapist's involvement and range from calm simple directions, such as, "Rather than tell me, I suggest you tell it to your wife," to profound personal expressions made with great affect, such as, "I can't stand the way you constantly bombard your wife with questions. If that's all you can do then just shut up." Though offerings may be made simply or loquaciously, said softly or shouted, gesticulated or with deadly stillness, the character of the optimal intervention at all times, which pervades the entire range of therapeutic intervening, is the "I" statement.

I call this affectionately the concept of our "royal" "I"ness. The optimal intervention will convey, with full resonance, the total person of the therapist at that moment, made in the context of an "I" statement. This is not to say that the word "I" is necessary. It is not always possible. Sometimes I suspect it is not even always desirable, as in the heat of battle it may even be rather stilted.

The "all meat and no potatoes" (purist) level of experiential psychotherapy is an incisive, constant confrontation of what each person is now doing that is encounter-diminishing, and how each does it. As we continue, the confrontations include rigorous attention to what is done with each confrontation and the therapist's personal reaction to each one's behavior. In order to be effective, interventions must include an awareness of the patient's tolerance for the intensity of this interaction and must be coupled with a flexibility for modifying such intensity when indicated by the other person's inability to cope with this level of encountering.

The optimal level of therapy is not necessarily the purest level of therapy. The speed and efficiency of the therapeutic process depend, not on what the therapist alone is able to do, but on what the family group, including the therapist, are able to do together. The purest or most intense level of therapy must be reserved exclusively for those— and at moments may be used with anyone—who are capable of a driving, intense look at themselves in relation to another person, with no support from that other person. Silence often serves such a function at this level of interaction.

Any variation from this intense approach is considered a dilution. This is not to imply that a modification of the intensity is "less good" since the "goodness" is determined by the effectiveness of the treatment, not the purity of the treatment approach. Whenever an individual in an encounter cannot beneficially work further at this intense level, which requires his integrating his current experience without outside assistance, dilution must be introduced.

One means of introducing dilution without losing continuity is by directing attention or awareness to what the person is experiencing at this moment. Such awareness may permit a breaking through to some affect which the person has been struggling to exclude and which may now serve to deepen or concentrate the experience, rather than dilute it, should the person succeed in expanding his awareness and experiencing his associated affect.

This type of intervention may serve as a direct invitation for the individual to change from active participant to observer, providing him with the opportunity to "talk about" what is happening, thus permitting him a more gradual integration by allowing a preparatory intellectual awareness. Such awareness must not be misperceived as a personality-altering therapeutic intervention. It merely serves to strengthen the individual's capacity for persevering to a future encounter that will, in fact, be personality altering.

Distancing can be accomplished by introducing intellectual pap, discussion, "talking about." This often seeds the interaction by building up respect and trust in the therapist. This is not therapy, but as a preamble to therapy it is helpful.

There are other, less valuable, forms of dilution. Any behavior that may be considered encounter-diminishing in a pure sense may be used to diminish the intensity of an encounter, permitting a participant to continue in the encounter, who might otherwise have fled, either by withdrawing from therapy or by resorting to less negotiable behavior.

For instance, it may be necessary to ask a patient who is having too much difficulty coping with the current encounter, "Is what you are experiencing now something that has happened to you on previous occasions?" This permits the individual to flee from the here and now and yet still stay close to the subject. Hopefully, the therapist will again return from "talking about" in other times and places to an actual experience in the here and now. How to determine whether an individual is coping adequately in a current encounter has been discussed in the preceding pages. Essentially, should patients' responses deteriorate by becoming less effective on their behalf, dilution must be considered.

Another means of distancing from an intense encounter with one individual without discontinuing working is to momentarily abandon the individual and turn to other members of the family and invite them to explore their current feelings in relation to what they are witnessing.

The following example demonstrates both the intense confronting engagement and the selective use of distancing. This was the sixth visit. The teenage daughter had, by general agreement, been permitted to withdraw from the treatment. Since then, mother and father had worked alone, with the mother sparking the sessions. A prevailing attitude, shared by the entire family and unaltered so far, was that mother was the problem and father was coming along to assist her. Until now her obvious distress—her depression, her open conflict with the daughter —stood in glaring contrast to his calm, yet seemingly interested attitude. At no time had his calm behavior—uninvolved, one might say—been questioned. He was for all practical purposes asymptomatic. In accusative jargon, he was a typical "character disorder," no pain, just painful. To date, this had not even been suggested.

This husband, a professor, was quite intellectual and proper. Superficially he appeared casual, rarely said much and, then, only when spoken to. He seemed most attentive to his wife and his pipe. His attitude had been that of the sincere outsider. He had remained superficial and affectless. By contrast, his wife was volatile, almost scatterbrained, as she hopped glibly from subject to subject. Tangentially, with derisive humor, she complained about her husband's inactivity. This was an improvement since the initial visit in which she had presented herself in a state of depression which had continued for several months. In this session, for the first time, the husband initiated the verbal interaction.

Husband: I must not want to come here, because I sure tend to forget. Last time I completely forgot about it and scheduled a meeting at this hour, and this time I almost forgot about it.

Wife: Last time when we left you said you thought it was a good idea that we were coming here.

H: (*Increasing his smile*) Did I really say that?

W: Yes, you sounded very enthusiastic about the whole thing.

H: I don't recall anything like that.

W: You said it. I remember.

(I recalled that it was the wife who had urged the therapy originally. She always became anxious when he showed any reluctance for therapy. After a brief silence which signified to me that neither of them knew where to go with it from there, I commented.)

Therapist: (*To the wife*) Today he shares a part of himself with us that does not want to be here and you seem impelled to "accentuate the positive." (*turning to husband*) I find myself more curious about the part of you that does not wish to be here today.

W: (*Laughingly*) I get kind of tired of that part that doesn't want to do things.

Th: (*To wife—preferring to engage the husband directly based on past experience with them*) I suspect it bothers you more than your smile would indicate, but at this moment I would prefer to take a better look at this reluctant part of him that he seems prepared to share with us today.

H: (*To therapist*) Well, I know I have some anxiety about being here. I don't look forward to coming. (*long pause*) I guess the completely unstructured nature of it is threatening.

Th: (*To husband*) Could you speak of this in terms of you and me? (*I know he is speaking to me and I wish to intensify our encounter.*)

H: (*To therapist*) Well, I don't know—I know I sort of panic at meetings when I'm called on to comment on something I haven't prepared for—you know—no previous warning—to be called on to perform spontaneously, like giving my opinion on something. It sort of frightens me.

(I had suggested that he talk about his discomfort in the here and now in relation to him and me and he responds by talking about it in the there and then in relation to someone else. So I simply observe.)

Th: What you say is removed from us.

H: (*To therapist, responding quickly and with raised voice*) Well, all right, this situation is one where I walk in the door and I haven't the slightest idea what we're going to talk about—I haven't thought of it —I haven't done any planning of it and I know we're going to try to do something like open up some areas or something but I don't know beforehand what it will be. Before when I was in therapy I could talk about whatever came into my mind and I could plan to talk about a dream or an incident that happened at work and I could go along without any particular anxiety. (*This man had some seven years of individual psychotherapy prior to this.*)

Th: (*To husband*) Are you aware of how you are still distancing yourself from me? Now you are talking about the comfort of your previous therapy in preference to talking about your discomfort at this moment.

H: I don't know if I see it in terms of you, I don't have any particular feelings one way or the other. I'm just aware that you seem rather capable and you are focusing pretty well on blind spots—that you play the role of the therapist capably. As far as feeling toward you, I don't know. I can't put my finger on any.

Th: (*still functioning as a catalyst*) The anxiety you speak of, I feel, has to do with me.

H: Oh, with you and with the situation and it seems also with my wife.

Th: The "situation" is a vague object. As far as you are concerned here, I am the situation for you. And as far as your wife is concerned I disqualify her since you do not have this feeling merely in her presence.

(Now we see how he directs his emotions towards an inanimate object —the situation—where there is safety from any possible encountering retaliation. Others will do the same thing with time. "It makes me so mad that I don't have the time to . . ." How much safer it is to be angry with time, fate, circumstance, or a situation!)

H: I feel like I can't react spontaneously here and in other places. I play a role. (*pause*) I'd like to have less control and be more spontaneous. (*long pause, one and a half minutes*) I don't know how I feel here. I'm not real sure but I think I know how I feel toward my wife's last therapist.

(I become acutely aware of his pervasive uncertainty. I feel that uncertainty is an underlying element, more obstructing than his discussing other people and other places—that keeps him from participating with me, so I suggest)

Th: You associate your anxiety or discomfort with uncertainty and at the same time I see you being uncertain. (*in an attempt to explore or tease out what is going on, I suggest*) Could you objectify uncertainty? Could you create some object that would represent uncertainty to you. It seems that I am such an object but it is difficult for you to talk directly to me. What would uncertainty represent to you if it could take form?

(This has been effective occasionally when a patient picks this up and identifies this uncertainty with a particular experience or a particular person in his historical life. When this occurs I have worked with it, using a projective technique which is discussed subsequently.)

H: I think I know what you mean but I'm not sure.
Th: More uncertainty.
H: (*after a long pause*) I know I'm more comfortable with certainty than I am with uncertainty. If I would have to go to an interview or something like that I would become very tense although I am not so tense in those situations anymore.
Th: Are you aware of how you left me again for another time and place?
H: Oh, you mean how I left this situation.
Th: Yes, you ran out again.
H: (*After another pause*) You asked me to deal with the uncertainty of this situation and I'm stymied. I don't know what I feel anxious about here except the uncertainty of it. (*He is still talking about uncertainty in preference to experiencing it.*) The worst thing that could happen, I suppose, is that I could get very emotional, break down and cry and get very upset, but that's so very far removed—it seems very unlikely.
Th: (*To himself, in silence, "Oh, yeah?" And to the patient*) I'm not so sure of that, but I am certain of your avoiding me.
H: Yes, I know. Particularly in my dealings with men, I'm that way, not so much with women.
Th: I call your attention again to how every sentence is a moving away

from me. You have now generalized to the subject of men. You avoid talking directly to me about you and me.

H: It's very difficult for me to talk with you. (*His smile is now gone.*) I don't know what it is I'm afraid of or how to go about finding out or doing anything about it.

Th: Now at least you stay here with me. But as you stay here with me you become vague and speculative. But at least you do try to stay with me. (*I say this to both clarify and encourage. I am not uncertain. This projection is in the process of being confronted.*)

H: (*After another long silence*) Well, I tried to focus on this thing but I don't seem to get anywhere.

Th: On this "thing"?

H: Focus on what I think you're getting at—on relating to you. I don't get anywhere.

Th: Even this statement is in the service of avoiding me. You focus on this "thing" as though you are isolating the subject and looking at it as an observer from the outside.

H: It *is* rather amorphous.

Th: "It" is me that I am suggesting you focus on. Who am I? And you remove yourself in favor of talking about a "thing" as though there were some subject matter between us that we could look at with distance and objectivity. I am interested in what happens to you as you look at me. I am interested in you and me right here.

H: Well, nothing seems to come through directly.

(To me, this is saying nothing so I wait, and then I feel that he is unable to proceed, so I suggest an alternative.)

Th: I wonder if you experience anything within yourself other than ideas and words as you sit here with me?

H: No, except a certain amount of anxiety.

Th: Could you please look directly at me and describe this anxiety?

H: Describe it?

Th: Yes, describe what you feel, where you feel it and how it feels to you as you feel it.

H: I feel a tightening in the stomach area. (*pause*) My mind is sort of jumping around—it isn't performing quietly, it's sort of looking this way and that—it seems like I'm not particularly concerned about

what you think of me—I have a block against participating any
further.

Th: Can you see this block?

H: It's a white wall.

Th: Could you see yourself as this white wall standing between us?

H: Yes, I can do that. When I am the wall, I see myself as a very small
thing behind it. Remarkably small.

(He suggests the subject is the wall and the object is himself—so I
suggest they encounter to find the predicate.)

Th: What can this wall say to this small person?

H: (*Silent awhile, begins to cry*) You are so small and helpless. I am
ashamed of you.

(The patient has now made an important statement about himself that
he has been unable to share either with himself or with anyone else. Is
it any wonder that this diminished self is fearful and uncertain. The
beginning of therapy is to be able to share this concern and embarrassment.)

Th: I would like you to tell me now in the first person what you have
just said as the wall. Could you make this statement to me?

H: It is embarrassing. I feel so small and helpless. (*His weeping deepens.*)
He is so small he just really can't do anything. (*The husband has
again distanced himself by referring to himself as "he." This way he
again becomes the observer rather than the participant.*)

Th: (*Softly and gently*) Could you tell me these things in the first person.
I would like to know this part of you also.

H: (*Trying to turn away from becoming aware of this part of himself*) I
don't feel this way at all levels.

Th: I'm sure you don't. But I am interested in you at this level at this
time. I would prefer not to abandon this helpless part of you. This
part of you seems lonely and cries not to be abandoned.

H: (*Wiping his tears and pulling himself together*) I can't seem to get in
touch with that little figure helplessly running around with his arms
outstretched.

Th: Talk to him. What can you say to him?

(He obviously must distance himself from this other inner part of himself and so I must go with him. If he cannot be this part, perhaps at least he might be able to become less afraid to befriend it from a distance. This also would be a step forward. What has occurred so far is already a significant step—that he has let anyone go behind the wall at all.)

H: He is so incredibly small. About one-thousandth the size of the wall.
Th: Can you talk to him? (*Again urging an interaction between these two parts rather than a talking about.*)
H: I try to say, "What do you want?" But he doesn't answer. He just runs around in circles helplessly with his arm outstretched. (*a long pause*) He turned into a tomato (*he smiles*).
Th: And what is it like to be a tomato?
H: (*Responding quickly*) It would spoil, decay.
Th: Seems very painful to be in touch with this part of yourself that feels so helpless and decayed. (*This is said after a long silence in which the patient could not work further. After another silence I offer more assistance.*) This part seems so isolated and somehow cannot ask for help.

After a long silence he agreed and left the scene to describe other times and places where he felt his helplessness and inferiority. His crying stopped and he again became the wall, although he was not the same wall that he was before. Until this interview he had remained rather silent, but now he described in great detail many things about himself with which he was dissatisfied. He spent the remainder of our time together freely talking about himself. True, he was in the world of "aboutness." However, viewed somewhat more broadly, he was sharing himself in a much more profound way than he had done until now. At one other time before our interview terminated he wept again as he recalled and associated this experience today with a moment from his remote past which he reported as the only other time that he felt completely (for him) acceptable in a relationship with another person.

At the conclusion of this interview I invited the wife's participation. I noticed that during the interview she sat calmly and seemed interested in what was going on. At no time did I sense any need for her active participation. This was confirmed at the conclusion of the session when she said simply and seriously, "I don't know what to say except that I wish I could help him." To this I responded, "Tell him."

Essentially this entire session was spent with one family member. It is unusual to spend an entire session with one family member. However, attention is frequently directed during a session exclusively to one or another member of the family to assist him/her in overcoming some intrapsychically determined behavior that obstructs his/her encountering. Wherever one individual is attended for any length of time, when the experience is completed, it is helpful to encourage other members to comment on what they are experiencing in relation to the work that has just been done. This serves a dual purpose. It offers the others an opportunity, should they not spontaneously take it, to learn something about themselves in relation to what has occurred, and secondly, it is always reassuring to working members to find that their revelations are received with so much understanding.

The question is frequently asked, "With all of the possible observations that can be made about interactions in the here and now, are there any guidelines for selecting the optimal point for intervening?" The therapist is a finely tuned sensing device that functions on many levels. During an encounter, each person, including the therapist, brings needs to be fulfilled. These are in a constant state of change, and it is the therapist's task to maximize the awareness of such needs.

The therapist is constantly tapping and sounding, first the entire situation, then a specific configuration or interaction. His attention moves, perhaps to another person who seems to have become restless, now back to the therapist's own discomforts. From all that the therapist perceives and experiences, he searches for a specific common denominator: the obstacle in this encounter that, more than any other, seems to prevent the interaction from developing.

One person's sadness may require attention before the interaction can proceed, but then someone else threatens to walk out and this becomes the crucial obstacle requiring our attention. Each behavior that the therapist is capable of observing becomes part of the total gestalt which helps him to determine what now is the obstacle to be assaulted. Sometimes a member chimes in and it is welcome, another time he will be deflected, "Be quiet a minute and let me finish." Sometimes the restlessness of children requires our concerted attention, other times the children are asked to wait outside in the reception room. It is extremely difficult to spell out the mechanism for what may truthfully be called the therapist's intuitive behavior. For me, it is a combination of what I perceive as the most significant obstacle in a family at a given moment and what I am experiencing about our time together.

As I sat with a family of five in an initial interview, the mother spoke first and I became aware of her depression. Since there was nothing else to go on, this became the most significant obstacle to be attended. As this family interaction began, a teen-age child began to cry and woefully complained that neither of his parents understood him. This displaced mother's depression as the central theme to be attended. As we worked together, the boy charged the father with the greatest negligence, so the father's indifferent behavior within his family became the most obvious obstacle to the evolution within this family. For the next three hours, because of my conviction that father's distance from this family was crucial in the boy's depression as well as his mother's, I chose to engage the father predominantly. With the help of the rest of the family, father was reintegrated into the family, and the behavior of the others changed for the better.

Should I find that I am losing interest in the interaction of a family, I am likely to introduce my boredom for all of us to scrutinize. Perhaps I am the greatest obstacle at this moment, and if so, we should all know it. It may, however, turn out that my boredom accurately signals a superficiality of which everyone was slightly aware, yet not sufficiently to do something about it.

On occasion I select some level of the family interaction to focus upon and find myself being challenged by a family member who may say emphatically, "That's just your opinion." To this, my response is, "Of course, that's all I ever have to offer." I will neither simply submit nor stubbornly stand my ground. I am negotiable, much of the time. It may be that this challenge will become the most crucial level for our continued interaction and I may encourage further exploration. On one occasion it felt as if a family member were interrupting when he said, "That's just your opinion." I angrily retorted with, "And that's just yours" as I continued my interaction with another member. Regardless of the character of my response at any given moment, which I have learned is usually pertinent to the other person's emotional whereabouts, my intention is to have a maximal impact on the development of our encounter.

This experiential approach urges capturing the essence of the therapist's feelings at the moment and introducing it as part of the encounter. Somehow this facilitates the therapist's ability to select the more appropriate levels for interaction. Should certain feelings arise within me and were I to attempt to exclude them, a part of my energy and awareness would be diverted to handling these feelings. To the degree that such awareness is diverted and to the degree that parts of myself must be excluded, to that degree my capacity for freely and sensitively selecting a level for interacting will be hampered.

It is not *whether* we include our self-awareness that matters, but *how* we include it. Keeping our self-awareness as part of the foreground, constantly integrating it into our current behavior, our experiences are enriched and our vision remains unblurred. An example of how unexpressed feelings on the part of the therapist can distort the therapeutic impact will be discussed.

A colleague expressed his dissatisfaction with the course of an interview. The identified patient was a boy, an only child in his early teens, who was accused of "antisocial behavior." He was brought in by his mother and father, who immediately began condemning the boy's behavior to the doctor. As they spoke the lad gradually shrank in his chair and turned away from the group. The therapist, astute in his observation, failed to utilize this awareness. Instead, he allowed the parents to continue on a while longer and then finally turned to the boy and said hopefully, "Son, I'd like to hear your side of it. What do you think of your behavior?" The boy refused to talk to him. The therapist spent the remaining time talking with the parents, attempting to diminish their angry attitude towards the boy. He was as unsuccessful with them as he had been with the boy. What a tragedy.

As the therapist described his experience, the first thing that he became aware of was his antagonism toward the parents at the very outset of the hour. He did not like their insensitive and righteous criticism of their son. He didn't say this. He next became aware of his wish to appear to be fair to them. From this point forward the session reveals the effect of this sensitive therapist's attempt to exclude a significant part of his own person from the encounter.

By contrast I shall explore one fantasy as to what might have happened had the therapist not been blocked by his attempt to curb his own feelings and had, instead, responded to the boy's shrinking under the parental onslaught. The therapist, speaking for the lad might say, "I feel hurt by your remarks and attitude. Please stop." More than this, he might also say, "I am unable (for whatever reason which we need not speculate on here) to tell you how painful it is to listen to your criticism of me. The only thing I can do is to move away from you as I have done in the past. I hope I won't end up with more bad behavior but I am afraid that I might. I don't understand about these things." Whether he is aware of it or not we know that as he becomes more uncomfortable with himself, and feels more alone and more resentful, he will end up with more antisocial behavior.

In some way this message needed to become a part of the verbal exchange. Whether the therapist encouraged the lad to speak his mind or whether the therapist would have to speak for him makes no difference in the situation. It is of course better to have the boy make his own statements, if possible. Regardless of how the statement is made, as long as it is made, there is an opportunity for the parents to react, possibly in a different manner. At least the door would have been open to negotiations, and the child would not have been ostracized.

By paying attention to the content of the interview as presented by the parents, rather than to what was going on in the interview as the parents were speaking, the therapist inadvertently defeated his own wish to encourage the boy's participation. By his question to the lad he confirmed to the boy that he was in fact the patient and that his "bad" behavior was truly the subject of the interview. Unwittingly, in his attempt to invite the boy's participation, the therapist aligned himself with the parents, identifying the boy's behavior as the issue. So, of course, the therapist received the same treatment as the parents.

The pathological encountering in this family, in glowing evidence during this interview, revealed parents who could not accept any responsibility for their child's behavior and a child who was pained at being labeled "bad" and, at the same time, was unable to speak about it in this same family where he was so insensitively received. By turning his head down and withdrawing from the group the boy expressed his feeling about his current encounter. This is the subject matter for the therapist's attention. At that moment the therapist could have invited the boy to speak. If the boy was unable to speak on his own behalf, the therapist had the alternative either of expressing how he suspected the boy might have been feeling or of voicing his own negative feelings to the parents.

Unfortunately, the therapist felt unreasonable about expressing his own negative feelings and therefore had to deny the boy that opportunity.

Had he been able, he might have spoken to the boy saying, "If I were you right now I'd feel very unhappy about the way they are placing all the blame on me when I already feel so badly about it. I wonder if you feel anything like that?" He would be telling the boy that he thought he knew how the boy felt and at the same time offering him an invitation to talk with him. I would not ask the boy a direct question in a way that would burden him with the requirement of an answer, for he obviously was feeling so remorseful. I would not wish to add another failure to his already obvious overwhelming sense of failure. Should he fail to respond to me I would listen to what emerged next in myself and continue to share myself with him.

As I explored some of my thoughts with my colleague, he said, "When I asked the boy to tell me his side I was thinking that his parents had been very hard on him. I wanted him to fight back and say it wasn't all his fault." The therapist obviously had messages for both the boy and his parents. The first part of his message should have been made to the parents and the second part to the boy. The anger towards the parents, as expressed in the first part of this statement, was unfortunately included in the message to the boy. Had the message been expressed candidly to each of them, the therapist would have said to the parents, "I feel you are being hard on him," and to the boy, "I'd like you to be able to fight back and tell them how they hurt you with their blaming."

The angry condemning of the parents was the first obstacle observed in this encounter. The boy's inability to respond verbally to their attack became the next significant obstacle. Finally, the therapist's need to exclude his resentment for the parents became the most significant obstacle in this therapeutic (?) interview.

As an exercise let us consider the possibilities for intervening in an encounter when the therapist feels that the grimacing of one member is diminishing their encounter. The therapist wishes to have the grimace converted into words so that the grimacing person can more fully participate in the encounter. First of all, the therapist has decided that this grimacing, at this time, is the most important obstacle to further illumination of this encounter. The gesture may or may not be important to the recipient, who is, therefore, in no position to struggle vigorously against it. Thus, it becomes the task of the therapist to create a new encounter with the grimacer, temporarily, until the grimacing can be eliminated. Then, the former grimacer can return to the original encounter.

It is likely that the therapist has learned something about the grimacer. From his own behavioral bag of tricks he will try to interrupt the grimacing in whatever way he feels can be done with the least pain for all concerned. The simplest comment would be, "You grimaced." If this should fail, the therapist may choose merely to continue repeating the observation whenever the person grimaces during the encounter. Should this fail the therapist may wish to impinge more rigorously and may comment, "Pay attention to your grimace and try to put the words with it each time you notice it" The therapist may offer constant and hopefully annoying reminders to the grimacer. Should this fail, the therapist may suggest a "try on," putting fantasied words to the grimace, such as, "Everytime you grimace just try saying, 'Ouch, that remark hurt me.'" Should the therapist continue to fail, he may wish to take up the issue of his own feebleness or the patient's stubbornness depending on how he views the situation. If the combatant of the moment is a rather uncomplicated person, open readily to reasonableness, the therapist would do well to "explain" "why" the grimacing should be abandoned. This may provide the necessary incentive for the patient to acquiesce.

It is unimportant how the therapist achieves the goal of eliminating encounter-diminishing behavior. It is only important that it be achieved and, in the course of this achievement, that the significance of the behavior become more flexibly available to the patient. For instance, if the grimace means, "I don't like what you're saying," making it verbal also makes it far more useful to the person, permitting him to explore what he does not like if he should now choose to do so. The behavior is more flexible. The goal is not to abandon the behavior but to make behavior more functional. Then the patient will be free to decide if, how, when and for how long he chooses to abandon it.

Regardless of whether an encounter is intrapsychic or interpersonal at any given moment, the therapeutic encounter-enhancing activities of the therapist are the same. The goal is to clarify the subject and object of each encounter in the here and now so that a situation may be completed.

When one member confounds the current experience by contaminating it with material from a previous unfinished situation, it is necessary to separate the two situations, current from ancient, before the current encounter can continue successfully.

This is achieved by temporarily interrupting the current interpersonal encounter and encouraging one member to return, in fantasy, to the scene of the unfinished situation and to speak to the person with whom he has the unfinished business. This creates a new "nowness" as the person is encouraged to move *into* an old situation, not merely to talk *about* it. This is the start. Then, when he has completed his monologue, he must take the other person's part and respond to his own original position.

The unfinished nature of the problem exists only in the person's head now, as an incompleted or unintegrated aspect of his own psychic structure. It has little to do with the remembered person. It is sometimes necessary to remind patients that the feelings they have today towards, for instance, their mother, with whom they were angry in some childhood experience, no longer have anything to do with the old woman who lives a few miles away and who at one time served as their mothering figure. Occasionally objections are raised such as, "I don't know what she would say" or "How can I finish with her, she died three years ago." No, she is very much alive in this person's head, or else the confusion would not exist. "Never mind what she would say—make up something—anything," I reply.

Anything this person constructs is derived from the leftover materials remaining in this individual's storehouse of unfinished situations. Objections to trying this type of experiment are expressed in many ways. Sometimes in response to a suggestion of "Put your mother in that empty chair and talk with her" the person will respond, "I can't talk to an empty chair." "Of course not," I reply, "I suggested you talk to your mother, not to the empty chair. Are you saying that you must keep the chair empty?" At other times it may be advisable to suggest modifications of the experiment, such as having the person close his/her eyes as a means of more readily transposing him/herself into another "nowness."

As the interaction begins, the therapist needs to note carefully whether the person is negotiating with an intrapsychic "other" or whether he/she is in fact negotiating with the therapist primarily in an attempt to please. What are the detectable differences? When genuinely immersed in the experiment, the person begins slowly, often with a moment of silence as he or she transpose him/herself into the new set. Then, body posture and movements are consonant with remarks. At the close of each commentary of dialogue the person does not turn to the therapist with a smile that says, "See how well I have done" or a quizzical look that might inquire, "Is this correct, teacher?" If such *is* the case, this must be confronted and clarified before further work can be done intrapsychically.

In such an instance, the patient is, in fact, encountering with the therapist in preference to conducting the experiment suggested by the therapist. Initially, the therapist may merely mention behavior that signals the patient's engagement with the therapist, and wait. If this fails to be productive, the therapist can urge the person to explore the objection to the experiment by suggesting the patient openly "be" the objection. This approach can and should be pursued until the person is either aided to complete the experiment or can willfully and openly refuse to comply with the therapist's suggested projective experiment. When the latter is achieved, the experiment can be considered a partial success, since in this current encounter the individual has assumed responsibility for his or her unwillingness, not as a confession but as an assertion.

It is also valuable to shift from an interpersonal encounter to an intrapsychic one, as when a person becomes, for instance, blocked. At this moment his encounter shifts from being with the other person with whom he is engaged to an encounter within his own psyche: One part saying "I want to continue negotiating" and the other part that is the block, saying, "I won't let you." Now it is necessary to tease up into clear view these two parts and then urge them to encounter one another.

How this is teased up or presented varies. The simplest method is to offer the person an experiment urging him/her to personify the part of him/herself with which he/she has not yet identified, in this instance, the "block," attempting to speak as (not for!) the block. Again, the encounter is completed only when the individual fully engages with both parts to some conclusion, as in the previous example of the man who saw his block as a white wall. Using this vitalizing, projective technique, the catalyzing therapist can assist a patient to cope with intrapsychic obstacles to further encountering in the here and now. In addition, this technique can be used fruitfully to explore memories and dream material. By fitting such material into an active encountering framework, rather than "talking about" such material, resolution and integrations inevitably ensue.

Another method of activating an intrapsychic encounter, particularly useful when the individual needs the safety of passive behavior, is to suggest that he close his eyes and become a viewer, as in a theater, and simply observe quietly what happens to him as he stands outside of his fantasied encounter. This is a method for instigating a working silence. As mentioned previously, when there is evidence that the working silence is at a point of change, the therapist can invite the person to describe what he has witnessed. Such a distancing operation can be particularly valuable as an initial uncovering activity. It will still be necessary for the individual to more actively engage in that fantasy before today's behavior can become significantly modified.

While some patients prefer to exclude everything in the here and now in their transition into a fantasy, there are others who choose to utilize the therapist or a family member as though they were the fantasied other person.

When the patient is using the therapist to talk through to some figure from his past history, the therapist must consider what his behavior must be during this contrived encounter. Should the therapist remain in the here and now as himself or would it be more beneficial for the therapist to assume the role of the historical figure? For myself, once I have agreed to be used as the object through which this person will work, I attempt to remain obscure. This is accomplished by sitting still, looking directly into the eyes of the other person and avoiding all comments, except those necessary to structure the encounter. For instance, I may suggest that he turn his chair so that he can see me more comfortably; I usually suggest that he look at me directly.

In one such intrapsychic encounter during a family interview I was serving as this woman's brother. As she became more intensely and emotionally involved, she burst into a critical crying, condemning me (as her brother) for having developed a serious paranoid illness which finally ended in suicide. I became caught up in the encounter and found myself saying what I might have said as her brother had I been able to speak knowledgeably. "Can't you see that I am as desperate as you are in this family? You criticize me for not being more than I was to you and yet you also were unable to be more to me." She responded to this with more sadness, more criticism and increasing interest in who I was, as her brother. It was a stirring experience for me as she concluded through her tears, "It would have helped so if we could have talked like this sooner. I understand so much more now."

Following our encounter I encouraged her to explore with her current family members, all of whom were present, and myself how she saw each of us in relation to her. This began her sifting out who each of us was, as apart from her brother, and further assisted her in clarifying many feelings associated with her brother. Now she spoke to her family about his death for the first time.

Such intrapsychic work as may be required with individual family members from time to time during our family sessions must always be retained in the context of the here and now of the existing family during our therapy interviews. The individual intrapsychic work may require a few minutes or it may take an entire session. In some instances it has taken the better part of several sessions.

Regardless of the time required, it is appropriate as long as there is unfinished business that is an obstacle to more efficient current encountering. It is appropriate as long as no other critical obstacles arise in another family member during this time. At the conclusion of any intrapsychic work, whether it be momentary or carried on over a period of several sessions, the other family members are invited to respond. It is most helpful to encourage both the working member and the other family members to integrate whatever experience they witnessed during this incident. This is a valuable "working through" operation that encourages the final differentiation and separation of the figures in our current existence.

Here is a brief example. During an interview a father tells his daughter to speak up and feel free to say anything she wishes when it is quite apparent that the daughter is speaking up quite clearly and articulately. He continually reiterates, "You must talk up. A child has to have the opportunity to speak. Please dear, say whatever you want. I want you to feel free to talk. . . ." It is eminently clear that his plea has little to do with his daughter. I point this out to him. Thoughtfully, he concludes that it must be a reference to himself in his own original family. I suggest that he return now, in fantasy, to his original family and make his plea to them for his right to speak. As he begins to do this, all of the feelings attendant on this long thwarted birthright become evident. He clenches his fists and tears come to his eyes as he speaks to them. I encourage him to include the words in his fists and in his tears. Rage and remorse reign for several minutes. When he finishes, he chooses to go no further at this time. However, he is now much better able to see himself apart from his daughter.

The remainder of this chapter consists of a sampling of catalytic and principled interventions, intended to convey spirit rather than specific, precise, therapeutic sallies.

"What do you want from me right now?" is the essence of the catalytic intervention. Examples are: "That was last year. What would you like right now?" or "Tell him," when the person is gossiping to the therapist about someone else in the room. Perseverance is often valuable. Should the person respond, "I can't tell him," suggest, "Tell him that!" Should he say, "He wouldn't understand," rejoin, "Tell him that!" ("Tell him why" can be used as a starter for a laconic patient, but whenever possible it is better to avoid "Why" explanations.)

If the point is reached where the person flatly states, "No!" a positive assertion has been made and the encounter is completed unless the therapist is aware of unfinished feelings in himself or the patient. If so, these should be enticed to a verbal level. Of the patient, the therapist might ask, "How do you feel right now?" For himself he might remark, "I don't like you coming here asking for help and then refusing something helpful that I offer."

Should there be no evidence of emotional residues following the patient's flat, "No!", awareness is likely to expand to the entire group and the therapist can now wait for subsequent phenomena—a comment from a family member on what has happened or a shifting of the focus of attention to some other matter. It would be easy to yield to temptation to utilize this opportunity for explanations and interpretations such as: This individual has placed the therapist in the same position as other family members, of being unable to understand him, because the therapist does not comply with his request; or, this person has had a verbal battle and, in the process of asking for help, has chosen instead a posture of stubbornness in order to win the battle of the moment. But such interpretations not only would be fruitless, but would also thwart his opportunity to evaluate the exchange on his own terms, at his own speed, and would interfere with the opportunity of other members of the family to respond to what they saw.

Also at the catalytic level, when the therapist is confronted with a rather untalkative, close-mouthed family, the phrase "Tell me about . . ." is a helpful launching device. Any invitation to engage in an intellectual discussion should be clearly recognized for what it is—an expedient to initiate an interaction. Hopefully, it will be abandoned as quickly as possible for a face-to-face encounter. For a negotiable encounter, it is necessary to be more than "tellers and listeners" to one another. "Talking about" must be exchanged for being and doing with one another.

Therapist: (*When observing some unspoken emotional response during*

a conversation) What are you aware of about yourself at this moment?
Patient: That's a good question.
Th: That's a poor answer.

Here the therapist has invited a deepening of awareness, and the patient
has leaped to content as a shallowing device, which is then parried by
the therapist.

Frequently an observation can be made, "I noticed that you criticize but
you do not ask for what you want," to which the patient may respond
sincerely, "I'm sorry." The person has moved to content rather than
make the effort to utilize the intervention to further his/her own awareness. This can simply be pointed out by the therapist or he may prefer to
pursue this obstacle with the remark, "To whom do you apologize?"
Another possibility, of course, is for the therapist to simply state, "I don't
want your apology. I prefer that you merely use what I have said." The
precise intervention will depend upon how the therapist experiences
this person.

The therapist is encouraged to utilize his imagination. Frequently
during an exchange I am struck with a phrase which seems to summarize
what someone is trying to say. When this occurs, I offer it as a "try on."
This can bypass, without doing harm, many obstacles to the awareness
contained in the "try on" and, when complied with, will elicit a profound
response, if it is in fact accurate. The obstacles to having arrived at an
awareness on one's own need not be analyzed or even discussed. Frequently, however, immediately following an awareness offered by the
therapist, the individual becomes aware of the obstacles. Often, reversing
the subject and object of a statement has a remarkably clarifying effect
and may also be introduced as a "try on."

The "try on" is a valuable means of introducing various experiments
designed to develop the interactions during encounters. They apply
equally well to patient and therapist alike, serving to tease out important
emotional components that may seem frivolous initially.

"I feel so tired I can't keep my eyes open," a wife seriously observed
as she began the session. We explored fruitlessly for several minutes. She
then said, "I could probably just fall asleep," to which I responded, "Then
go to sleep." Smiling with a halfhearted wish, I added, "Perchance to
dream a dream that will help us." She leaned back, closed her eyes, and
I turned to her husband.

For several minutes he and I ruminated about her fatigue, comparing our feelings about it. She remained motionless for several minutes, then began crying in her sleep. We waited silently awhile and, when she opened her eyes, I invited her to speak. "I can't reach the mountain and it's so beautiful . . ." she said through her tears. "Describe it," I suggested. "It's beautiful. It's cold and impervious. It is so strong that it cannot be hurt." She was accurately and poetically describing the image of herself that she had tried to create. I did not say this to her; instead, I encouraged her to continue this intrapsychic encounter, first by changing the "it" to "I"—to "try on" being the mountain. As we pursued this dream, the current "hurt" that she felt came to the fore. At the conclusion of this exploration, her fatigue disappeared and she became far less "cold and impervious."

Catalytic observations apply equally well to intrapsychic and intrafamilial encounters. In one family the father's deadness became the prevailing obstacle in the family. He looked gray, his face was always expressionless, his voice monotonous and his body movements reduced to bare necessity. According to his wife, he had been this way as long as she knew him, although it seemed to progress gradually.

I decided to poke around as one might with a stick when finding what appeared to be a dead bird alongside the road, just to see if it were really dead. I was surprised to see that he seemed to welcome the stimulation—at least he croaked out an occasional "Yes" or "I agree" or "You're probably right." Though I poked more vigorously, he remained at death's door, but he did say that he wanted to change. "And what if you became like me," I shouted at him, slamming my hand on the table, "What's so damned terrible about that?" He croaked out in his monotonous voice, "It's all right for you. You know what you are doing. When I was a kid I was hostile and loud mouthed, and I hurt lots of people."

Therapist: For instance?
Patient: I told one kid his ears were too big.
Th: What else? (*He looks at the floor in silence for several minutes and then I noticed a sudden change in body position and ephemeral facial grimace*) What were you just thinking?
P: I saw the eyes of a sparrow I shot. (*pause*) I was paralyzed . . . (*pause*) lucky a friend was there . . . (*another pause of several seconds*) killed him for me (*long silence*).

Th: Talk to that sparrow.

P: (*Welling up with tears and after a moment's silence*) I can't talk.

Th: What stops you?

P: (*Grabs his throat*) All choked up tight.

Th: Tell the sparrow how badly you felt.

P: No.

Th: (*I was recalling how difficult it is for people to speak in their own behalf and I thought to myself that he has given up his life for the sparrow. In a sense, he was living as the dead sparrow. With these thoughts I now spoke*) Could you be the sparrow? The bird needs to speak. . . .

P: (*Pause*) I'll try. (*after several moments of silence*) Why did you do this to me? What did I ever do to you? (*He now begins to cry.*)

Th: (*As the crying subsides*) And who could you say that to?

P: (*After another several moments of silence*) Mother, why did you let me be so cruel? Why didn't you stop me? Why did you always excuse me? (*His crying interrupts his talking.*)

At this point I chose not to interrupt his feeling by, for instance, suggesting that he convert his questions into statements. This would have been a gross interruption of his encounter with his mother. When the crying subsided I invited him to continue talking with his mother. He sat up in his chair as though a weight had been removed, looked directly at me, smiling slightly and said, "I've had enough for today." I agreed.

The following excerpt from a family session shows a number of catalytic interventions during a family encounter.

Often, a family member will say something to the therapist that is changed when it is redirected to a family member.

Wife: (*Speaking to therapist*) I want to be more helpful to him (husband) but I don't know what I can do. I feel so incompetent.

Therapist: (*She is gossiping to me about her husband so I suggest*) Share that with him.

W: (*She turns to him, composes herself and after a moment of silence speaks coldly*) If only you knew what you wanted and were able to be clear. If only you. . . .

Th: (*Interrupting*) That's not what you were telling me. To me you were speaking of yourself—your helplessness, your sense of incompetence and your sadness. To him you complain about *his* behavior.

W: I guess I'm afraid to admit those things to him.

Th: (*She is still gossiping*) Tell him that.

W: That frightens me, he won't—I expect him not to like me if I am incompetent.

Th: Could you tell him that?

Husband: I wish you could talk to me that way. The other makes me defensive and I want to fight with you. When I hear you talk this way I feel very friendly.

W: (*Looking at her husband*) It's a crazy thing but now that I look at you I know you would accept my talking to you this way.

(I thought this could possibly have been a dodge—an attempt to talk about rather than do the thing I suggested, namely tell him of her helplessness. But there was something in the slow thoughtful way in which she spoke that suggested sincere searching, not manipulation. Armed with this conclusion, I urged her to continue down this path.)

Th: Then, if it is not him, to whom might you wish to say these things?

W: (*After a thoughtful moment of silence*) I guess my mother.

Th: Put her in that empty chair, look at her and talk to her.

(On another occasion, I might have first demanded that she eliminate the uncertainty by confronting her with, "You guess?" This would have been done to sharpen her own identity or to test whether this was merely a "pat" answer. In this instance, she seemed quite ready to work, and I took the "I guess" as a figure of speech that had little significance. As she stared at the chair and began crying, my assumption was confirmed.)

W: (*After several moments of crying*) You never did trust me. You always assumed I'd do things wrong. It seemed like then I had to do them wrong. Oh how I wish you could have had confidence in me. I needed that from you so much and all you did was pick and complain.

(I was delighted that she was describing her own behavior in her criticism of her mother. Somehow this portended success in the work that she had to do to resolve this conflict with her mother. This pattern lived on in her head, interfering in her current relationship with her husband, long after her mother had physically died.)

Th: Now be your mother and respond.
W: She wouldn't understand. She'd just pick some more.
Th: You're gossiping; either do it or refuse me.
W: (Mimicking her mother) Well if you did things right the first time I wouldn't pick at you.
Th: (After several moments of silence during which she just stared) Answer her.
W: (First with great anger, then tearfully) I'm not perfect. I'm not perfect. I'm not perfect. Why can't you understand that? (shouting) I can't do everything right the first time. You weren't that perfect either, why did you demand it of me? (Then, like she had been hit, she suddenly stopped her crying) That's why! You wanted me to be perfect for you because you weren't. I won't. I'm not and I won't. I don't have to be perfect all of the time. I won't. (Then after a brief silence she turns to her husband saying) I feel so ashamed. That's why I pick at you, just like she picked at me. And you never really asked me to be perfect. I'm sorry (She weeps softly).
H: (Lovingly) You needn't be.
Th: (I appreciated his loving support but I did not like her apology. To me it meant she was not finished). You're sorry? Why, because you're not perfect right now?

(I could have let her work, rather than give her the answer, by saying for instance, "Could you explain to your husband what you are apologizing for?" Or, dishonestly yet invitingly, "I don't understand your apology." But I did understand it, and she had done a lot of work. As I think back on it I believe she could have worked more, but I wanted to give her something as a recognition of my appreciation of her diligent effort. This is unfinished business of mine which occurs to me only as I make these notes. I was unaware of this aspect of my actions at that time.)

W: (Laughing and blushing) It doesn't just all go away at once, does it? But I feel different. I also believe it is all right to feel sorry when you needlessly hurt someone.

(She is talking back to me now as an assertive woman, not a tearful child. This pleases me and is more important than engaging in an intellectual debate on whether or not it is all right to feel "sorry." I found myself smiling and searching her comment for a point of closure as our time for ending the interview had passed sometime before.)

Th: How do you feel different?
W: I don't feel so picked on. I feel loving towards my husband.
Th: (*Getting up*) You're gossiping again.

She looked warmly at her husband, and he responded as he had throughout the meeting, affectionately. I felt good.

Humor can be therapeutic as well as diversionary. Here are examples of each.

A young lady, recently married and recently divorced, moves back into the home of her parents. I should say apartment, for with daughter's marriage mother and father sold their home and took a small one-bedroom apartment for themselves. Now daughter sleeps inconveniently in the living room. All three agree that the daughter needs therapy and all three agree to join in this project. On this occasion mother begins by gently pushing daughter out of the apartment, saying, "You came in late again last night and woke me when you turned the bathroom light on."

Apparently this had been previously debated and now daughter, infuriated, screams at mother, "How could I? I was so damn careful. I purposely closed the door before I turned the light on and then snapped it off before opening the door to leave. How could turning the light on possibly wake you?" "The noise of the switch wakes me," mother innocently replies. Exasperated and angry, daughter replies, "Oh for goodness sake," and everyone falls into a painful silence. I offer daughter an interpretation, "It's just a simple misunderstanding. You thought your mother was a light sleeper when in reality she is a sound sleeper." Daughter laughs and replies, "Oh, go to hell—I'm getting out of there."

In the next example, the patient, a vigorous abounding 50-year-old man has just finished reading a poem in strict compliance with a casual suggestion made at the end of the previous session by the therapist. Following this, he loosely examines the poem. The only comment the therapist makes is to the effect that he has complied with the suggestion of last visit and that he has not touched his subject matter intimately, but has only referred to it. He accepts this as a meaningful comment and observes that he will not ask for further help in exploring this, as he knows that it must come from himself. All this is said with a broad smile.

He then reports almost laughingly that he has spoken to his mother's attorney who reported that, since the death of her husband (the patient's father) three weeks ago, his mother has made a remarkable recovery from a previously chronic bedridden, almost stuporous, state to an alert, intelligent, healthy woman who is now leaving the sanitarium to resume an active life. On previous visits to me the patient has complained bitterly about his wife's insensitivity and dependency on him. Both of these things have been suggested as projections which the patient has considered intellectually but has never touched.

He smiles, acknowledging that he must do the work himself, citing the joke of the reverend who observed to the farmer who had just bought a dilapidated farm and done a tremendous amount of work improving it, "You and the Good Lord have done an excellent job in revamping the old place." The farmer replied, "When the Lord had the place to himself it didn't look like this, did it?"

My response is, "I sense a note of unexpressed resentment." For a moment my patient looks sober, saying, "I guess that's a good possibility," and quickly returns to a smiling state, commenting, "I guess that's your business, to know more about those things than I."

I feel he is resentful, he senses it, and neither of us is able to generate his expression. I suddenly have the fantasy of his confronting not just me, but his mother and his wife simultaneously, and having us serve as a more forceful stimulus than I am alone. I say to the patient, "I suddenly envision your mother as your past frustrator, your wife as your present frustrator, and you are setting me up as your future frustrator. I wonder if you could visualize the three of us here in front of you, not just me alone. What might you say if your mother and wife were also here with me at this point in front of you?" The patient looks very serious and with genuine anger says, "I don't need any of you. I can get along without all of you. None of you are essential to me. I can survive without all of you." I reply, "That's an easy one for you. The difficult one is to survive *with* us." "Touché," the patient replies with a thoughtful, sobering look.

At this point I failed. His "touché" was a way of joining forces with me, acknowledging my intellectual victory in this gambit without pursuing further his much-needed reconciliation on an affect level. I was seduced and sat back comfortably, accepting his applause. It would have been more meaningful for him had I rejected his becoming an observer of our interaction instead of remaining an active participant. Silence or "Go on" as a suggestion might have allowed him to reach his own statement of "I *can't* survive with you but am afraid to know it."

Later in that same interview the patient seemed to be floundering and observed, "I'm not sure that what I am doing right now has any meaning for me. Do you have any ideas, Doc?" I replied, "At this moment I'm not sure either just what you are doing." He responded angrily, "I can understand my not knowing, but how do you explain your not knowing what I'm doing?" I replied, "Now I do." The patient again responded, "Touché," laughing and redfaced. And once again I succumbed to the flattery and allowed him to move away from his awareness of his laughing embarrassment.

When he said with anger, "I don't need you," a better observation might have been to suggest that he try saying to the three of us, "I don't *want* to need you because you hurt me." To reinforce this, I might have suggested that he continue to repeat this phrase in a louder voice. This might serve to touch the core of what I felt he was trying to say, "I want to contact you or feel *with* you, but you make me so angry I can't." This is what I might feel as a little boy responding to a demanding critical mother. I might also want to say, "Please love me and help me to gain confidence. You don't do it by eternally criticizing me. It makes it harder for me and confusing. I can make it without you, yes, but I would rather not, because it's harder that way."

I imagine that the patient's resistances evolved this way:

I need you.

I need you; you don't fulfill my needs, so I am angry with you.

I am so angry with you I will try not to need you.

I am so angry with you I *won't* need you.

I *don't* need you.

You need me. (This is the conclusion he has come to in marrying his chronically ill wife.)

This technique bypasses all the resistances to the core statement (the core feeling that has been dis-integrated) and leads the patient to it on the premise that experiencing that part of himself which he has rejected is a direct path towards reintegration. He can intellectually play with the reasoning process of "understanding" how his resistances evolved, but this is not a necessary part of the reintegration.

At the end of the hour, I became aware of the deep satisfaction that both of us derived from playing this intellectual game of upmanship. I commented on this satisfaction, pointing intellectually to it as a formidable difficulty we had. I am not sure what the value of this is. I explain it to myself as seeing the difficulty, wanting to attack it, but knowing of no way other than by sharing my recognition of it with the patient. I am not sure that it has any value. I say to myself that I am attacking from both ends this way: urging the part of self that is not integrated to come forth, and at the same time, urging the patient to use the same weapon he uses for his defense (thinking logically) in the service of attacking the defense. Thus, I urge him to use his intellect to look critically at his old "gratifying" intellectual diversionary tactics of laughter and charming quips.

The therapist's functioning as an active, identifiable person in the therapeutic encounter has long been debated. Advocacy of involvement is becoming more popular. Often, advocacy of participation exceeds participation at the interview level. Some therapists dare reveal personal matters, such as dreams, and report to patients something about their sex lives. Some audacious therapists now even acknowledge physiological aspects of themselves by interrupting interviews and going to the bathroom. A few are so crass that they dare to tell the patients what they do not like about them, usually explaining to the patient that it is in the interest of creating a more open and, therefore, therapeutic atmosphere.

Most therapists, however, would not dare to explore and examine a dream they had that is pertinent to a patient, with that patient. Most therapists would not negotiate and debate, if necessary, all of their negative feelings to a patient as they emerge, merely because they are there. In doing such "terrible" things, it has been my experience that patients have benefited along with me as I cleared my own emotional tracks of debris that developed in our time together. The following dialogue from my first interview with Molly is offered in evidence.

Molly was a 40-year-old, crippled woman who had been abandoned by her husband. She was led in, hobbling on crutches, for she was also blind. Once attractive, she looked as if she had just returned from the Inquisition. I was repelled. I expressed my disgust. She smiled sweetly. I hated the sardonic grin and angrily told her so. She immediately tried to turn it off. Such selflessness sickened me and I told her so. The entire hour was spent expressing my revulsion to almost everything about her. I hated her for what she had done to herself. At the end of the hour, she sweetly asked how I knew she was not the victim of an accident. I did not know exactly, but my reaction had to do with her total gestalt—with every sickeningly sweet, selfless response she made. I knew that someone is charged for each frustration in life and that she obviously charged only herself. I do not yet clearly know how I knew, but experientially, I knew.

The second session was not much different. By the third session, she began to fight back and I began to appreciate her. I do not know which came first. In the fifth session she revealed that a nightmare, which occurred three times before in the past 10 years, had recurred and she was eager to report it. It was a tactile experience, not a visual image. "He came in again, put the pillow over my head and tried to smother me again. I've known all along that he will kill—this is how I will die—but this time it was different. This time I fought back and stopped him. I fought dirty—I bit his arm (smiles sheepishly) but I stopped him. I actually stopped him. And when I awoke, instead of being in absolute terror, I felt strong and pleased with myself and thought 'maybe someday you'll kill me—just maybe.'" She was talking to me, too, of course. Now she could tackle something (someone) tangible, and maybe, yes, maybe there was a way up. She had begun to take back her power.

Therapists' fear of harming the patient, in keeping with the famous medical dictum "First, do no harm," is most admirable. However, too often it is interpreted, "First do no harm to your own reputation." Translated into action this means, "Do only what every other therapist does and remember that doing something is always potentially more reprehensible than doing nothing." To sit with a patient in therapy for five years, gently befriending him in the name of therapy, carries far less hazard of criticism from colleagues than, for instance, charging a patient angrily, risking his anger or eliciting tears to achieve altered behavior in five months. To stand by and watch a patient suffer timidly, offering comparably timid, hollow interpretations, is clearly acceptable. Demanding altered behavior and a cessation to suffering is considered by some therapists as an imposition. In the eyes of some colleagues, I take too many risks. Granted, it is more important for me to be effective than it is to be safe. However, what they call a risk, my own life experiences have proven clearly to be not a risk. I am not a particularly courageous man. I do have a need to be effective.

To have my patient leave untouched is the most painful thing that can occur during therapy. So I must impose. I must be clearly and demonstrably felt—not tomorrow, not next year, not after five years, but now. Each session must justify its own existence; each moment must carry its own importance. I do not ask for immediate, unconditional change. I do demand involvement in this, each moment of our time together. The harvest is gratifying behavioral change.

Make no mistake, I do not wish to suffer ostracism or desertion by my patients or colleagues, though I've discovered some is inevitable. This pains me and sometimes temporarily paralyzes me in my work as I attempt to become a likeable fellow. But, I seem hopelessly recidivistic, and am constantly lured back into my old irascible ways.

Sometimes therapists become aware of feelings that are elicited by and within the therapeutic interview that are felt to be nonpertinent. The therapist would reasonably be concerned that such feelings might distort his perceptions and thereby diminish his effectiveness as a therapist. I have had several experiences which would tend to contradict this idea, one of which is now included.

As the couple sat down, both obviously distressed, she said, "I feel it's useless to continue this marriage." He said nothing. I gently poked around, first with her, then with him and got nowhere. She stood increasingly firm, refusing to convert her threat to an overt angry harangue, which I thought might clear the air a bit. He remained sullen and also firm. He wouldn't get out and she threatened to have him forcibly removed if necessary, adding that she would, of course, keep the house, the kids and, if he did not go quietly, one-half of his business, concluding, "and besides I'll make a big stink." He remained deadly firm, stating, "I'm not moving out and leaving my kids."

I began to think of my divorce of a few years back and the terrible rage I felt when threatened similarly. It was easier now. I also saw that she hoped he would fight her and stay—but be involved with her. I urged him to respond, but he was too threatened. He could barely mutter, "I won't move out." I urged her to tell him of her recent loneliness and concern, clearly connected with his sudden increased work commitment. She denied this. I was afraid to push further for fear of being partial, but I was seething at her for what seemed to be an unjust attack. I was angry with him only for not fighting back.

They were deadlocked. We were deadlocked. The silence was broken only by occasional caustic remarks from her and the sound of his teeth on his pipe tightly locked between his fist and his jaws. I thought, "to hell with my partiality," and off I went. I denounced her vigorously and painlessly, calling her ultimatum and high-handedness for what it was. I told her if she were my wife I would paddle the hell out of her. I accused her of charging her husband with all her misdirected venom, probably meant for her father. I interpreted. I analyzed. I accused. Any vehicle to express my anger. When I finished, I fully expected a ready counterattack. Instead she glared at me and said, "Why can't he talk like that to me? Why does he have to use you to do it for him?"

"Because he's scared silly, that's why."

"Well, that's too bad. I don't want to live with a scared man. I need someone to be involved with."

My anger gone I laughingly said, "Sorry, I'm not available, you'll have to remodel the one you've got."

"It's not funny and I don't feel any different," she said in a much softer tone.

"You're a liar," I said seriously.

She laughed, "Well, I do feel better, but I still feel it's hopeless, and I think that I'll leave."

Husband took heart from what he witnessed and said stoutly, "I not only won't move out, I won't let you leave."

"Oh yeah," she snarled, "just try to stop me. Anyway, don't you have any self-respect? Why do you want someone who doesn't want you?"

"I want my family and that's that," he answered firmly. And to me he said, "We'll be in for our next appointment."

She said, "I may not be here."

I said, sincerely, "I'll miss you if you aren't."

She—misunderstanding—thinking I was sarcastic, said in the doorway, "Drop dead."

They returned.

On occasion feelings will emerge in a therapist which are clearly not elicited by the interview and clearly have no bearing on the current experience. In such situations, it is far better for the therapist to acknowledge the distraction immediately. If at all possible, the therapy time should be used for a brief exposition of how the therapist is feeling. This may be sufficient to abate if not complete an unfinished situation for the therapist, thus freeing him for fuller attention to his current interview. Of course, if the therapist feels unable to share himself with his patient family, then this should at least be announced, along with the therapist's decision of whether or not he will attempt to complete the current interview.

A family therapist, a woman working with lower-income families through a public agency of social work, once commented to me during a conversation about family therapy, "I have only one cardinal rule—no hitting, no kicking, no biting and no spitting." I inquired, "Is that for the therapist or the family?" Actually, although I believe in the good fight, I abhor physical violence. For negotiating with children, where it is relatively safe, I may find myself leaning toward physical assault. But it is always a tragedy, for I know it is my own defective encountering that has elicited the impasse, and the punishment should at least be shared.

But this is not my main rationale for the abhorrence. Short of physical violence, each of us has the privilege of learning new ways to negotiate and paying the consequences born only of our own behavior. Therefore I always have an incentive to assume responsibility for myself. The moment violence creeps in, the issue becomes one of brute strength and there is no chance for a resolution based on my having learned to cope and negotiate. As may be expected, such feelings apply widely—to war, to capital punishment, to hitting a child. Regardless of the issues in the conflict, the moment violence is launched against another human being, the greater battle has been lost. This is not to say that I have never felt like killing. I have, many, many times. To think it, say it, shout it—not about but *to* a person—is perfectly acceptable to me. I am certain that no one can muster more murderous feelings in his/her heart than those which I have felt. What has saved me, for I am the one who would have been lost, is the inalienable right to know and to express the feelings verbally. To gain my soul, I must, at times, lose my temper.

When families are first seen, at least one and perhaps all of the family members are stalemated in non-negotiable poses. The impact required to alleviate this logjam varies. As they begin to encounter, my attention often gravitates to the least negotiable posture. At this point I direct a stimulus: perhaps an invitation to look at some aspect of the person's behavior not considered; perhaps a suggestion to "try on" a phrase; perhaps a simple observation. When such attempts fail, my tendency usually is to become more vigorous rather than retreat from the encounter. To become more vigorous is to assault. To assault is to abandon social courtesies and use whatever device my person is capable of, short of mayhem, to disrupt the obstacle and bring the person to the point of negotiation. The person need not agree nor submit; he need only seriously engage.

Pseudopostures of apparent negotiability are unacceptable. The words "I am willing" or "Just tell me," of themselves, signify nothing. Action alone counts. Willingness must be visible, cooperation must be in evidence. "But if I could do that I wouldn't be here." That's partially correct and I respond, "And I intend to alter you so you won't spend the rest of your life here." I range through soft, loving offerings, casual observations, sarcasm and rage, to ridicule and outrage, if necessary. "No human behavior of which I am capable will be denied you" is my active response.

A father brings his wife and four children (usually it is the mother that brings) and starts loquaciously and confidently to describe his "impossible but basically good" children. Everyone laughs to his cue and seems cheerful but wary. I urge him not to gossip but rather confront each of them with what he wants. He starts with his oldest, 17-year-old, anti-loquacious lad and confronts the boy with his "impossible" behavior.

Father: Since you and I get into it so often, Ted I'm going to choose you first. How come yesterday you denied putting your laundry in my hamper? How can you deny it? They were your socks, weren't they?

Ted: Bill (*younger brother*) and I use the same socks. I don't recall putting them in there. You kept insisting it was me and backed me into a corner.

F: You're a liar. I didn't back you into any corner. We were in the hallway. How can a person not remember? Either you did it or you didn't. You've done it before, so I know you did it. Nobody ever forgets. (*Now trying to appear reasonable to me he lets up a bit*) How can you say I cornered you?

Ted: You were shouting at me and shaking your finger at me.

F: You're just putting on this story for the doctor. (*turning to me*) This is how he is at home. Vague, doesn't remember things and won't be truthful about what happens.

Previously, I had pointed out, to no avail, the striking polarity of father's loquacity and specificity and his children's vagueness and inarticulateness. My implied criticism of father at that time seemed to have given the kids more of an incentive to fight back verbally but I am not

certain of this. I had also pointed out father's questions, which seemed
to cover his despotic attitude, also to no avail. Now, I was angered. I felt
Ted had done well, but I could not hold back. I was not finished. Angrily,
I turned to father.

Therapist: (*To father*) You've just done it again. You've wiped him out
—or as he accurately puts it "cornered him." There's no room for
him to have a position of his own. There's only *your* position—and
wrong ones. He can't move. Anything he says or does other than what
you want gets criticized.

F: Don't you agree that no one forgets? Especially something as basic as
what you do with your socks when you take them off? What do you
mean I wipe him out? He can answer. I'm not telling him what to
say, but at least he can be logical. He's not stupid.

Th: (*Still angry*) Now you're doing it to me. I feel just like I'm sure Ted
feels. You don't listen to me, you just try to convince me you're
right. You don't ask questions sincerely in search of answers. You're
a faker. It's taking a pseudo-reasonable position. (*My anger spent, I
stopped "you-ing" him.*) I agree Ted isn't stupid. He's figured out the
best way to cope with a cornerer—be vague. He has you cornered.
(*now smiling*) You're even.

F: What do I do then?

Th: I'm not sure that question is any more sincere than the previous
ones, but I'll give you the benefit of the doubt this time. (*That's how
I felt—that's what I said.*) You seem to prefer confessions of incompetence to effective behavior. Ted says he doesn't remember. Listen.
That's where he is and who he is. You want him not to use your
hamper. Tell him. If this doesn't work, do something that will, don't
waste your time badgering him for a confession. (*I then cited an
example from my home.*) My 16-year-old son kept taking tools out
of my tool box, and failed to return them. First time, I asked nicely,
second time I was emphatic with a lecture on property rights, third
time I put a lock on the box. "You're unreasonable," my son charged.
I laughed, agreed, and kept the lock on.

I concluded, expressing my doubts that this speech and example would
be effective and hoped they *both* could learn something from it that would
permit them to be better friends. I had nothing further to say. Those two
were being thoughtful and silent, when the daughter, Diane, taking some-

thing from my speech for herself, asked if I thought kids should have privacy too. "Absolutely," I replied, adding, "If you don't, I can only conclude that your parents also do not—which I suspect already from this hamper story." Mother now joins in wistfully, "None of us has any privacy, but as parents we have to check up on how they are keeping their things. Ted just throws stuff all over the floor in his closet. . . ."

I then shared with them how we do it at our home. I agreed that some surveillance was necessary but insisted that she stay out of their dresser drawers. Then the 12-year-old, who had been silent till now, asked if he could volunteer a problem. I was delighted with this family. I could live in their home easily. They had problems but they were easy problems and they all seemed responsive and responsible. I liked them. "Sure, Steve, what's the beef?"

"Mother gets mad so easily, and when she's angry with Ted we all get it. All except her friends if they call."

We went to work on this, inviting mother to participate. She first laughed, then defended herself martyredly, then became angry and finally cried, reporting her embarrassment at what she recognized as unwarranted temper tantrums. Her family was warm and sympathetic. She began to see them less as critical, contrary kids and more as loving, sometimes obstreperous teen-agers.

I suggested, "I'd like you to tell them what they can do to help you with your temper tantrums besides be perfect children."

She looked at them and fought back her tears. I urged her to tell of her need to hold back sadness from her family, and she cried painfully and loudly. Steve, interestingly enough, tried to turn her off. I comforted him, urged him to know his mother's sadness and give sadness a place in this home. Steve began to tear. Mother talked briefly of her loneliness and sense of estrangement from her family. The hour ended on that note. It was a full hour.

As they walked out father smiled at me and said, "You're a powerhouse but I like you—and know you can help us." I, too, smiled and expressed my feeling towards him, "You're no pushover either. You and your family are a great bunch and I'm delighted to be part of your family for a while."

In the next family there was a mother, father and two children, a 12-year-old daughter and a six-year-old son, Dan. This was the third session and much time had been spent attempting to mobilize the parents to become assertive with their children. Dan had a studied way of gradually increasing his volume and general intrusive behavior to the point of absurdity before it drew the attention of his parents. His parents cooperated beautifully with this, always glancing at him and making other gestures, all of which said, "You don't have to stop what you're doing, but you should try to do it a bit more gradually." On this occasion as the parents and I were engaged in some negotiation that did not involve the boy, he asked if he could go outside. His mother granted him permission with great relief, and his father, as usual, said nothing. But then he came back. He knocked on the door and when mother opened it, inviting him to come in, said, "No." She replied, "Well, all right then, don't knock on the door and just stay outside." To which he responded, "I don't want to stay outside."

Mother: What do you want?
Dan: I don't know.
M: (*To husband*) What should I do?
Father: I don't know. Are you sure he doesn't want to come in?
M: (*To son*) Why don't you come in, Dan?
D: (*With a sly smile*) No.

From my previous experience with these people I knew that talking would be of little use. I was angry. I was angry with all three of them. I walked over to the door, picked Dan up, and planted him firmly in a chair, saying, "And you will sit there without moving out of the chair for the rest of this hour."

He looked at me utterly shocked and then burst into tears. I ordered the mother to sit down and I went back to my chair. Mother kept looking alternately from me to her husband and over her shoulder to her son. Father looked a little surprised and the boy continued to cry. I told the mother to ignore him and to pay attention to what I had to say to her.

When I finished my tirade against her incompetence, I launched a similar one at the husband, tailoring it to my impressions of him. I concluded by suggesting sarcastically, among other things, that they consider placing Dan for adoption if they would not offer him any guidance. This was met at first with a stunned silence. Then, with slight encouragement, the father directed an angry response to me. Gradually a profitable exploration was begun between mother and father. I was free of any rancor at this point and was eager to help them. Dan cried for about five minutes and then sat silently in the chair for the remainder of the hour without moving.

At the conclusion of our session, for emphasis, I spelled out to the parents the connection between my behavior with Dan and his model behavior the rest of the hour. On subsequent sessions it was not necessary for me to ever become involved with Dan's discipline again. It is difficult to say which of the three had changed the most but there was little doubt that a change had occurred.

I did not wish to take over and be a parent in this family. When my verbal assistance failed my irritability rose and needed to be met. In this instance it was satisfied by action, setting an example for the parents and advising them bluntly to follow suit. I would not do this with all parents.

In the next family the wife called stating that after 12 years and two children, she could no longer stand her husband's temperamentality: his pouting, his outrages, his petulance. They had agreed to separate but as an afterthought decided to consider family therapy before following through with their separation. They had both been through several years each of individual psychotherapy. I elected to omit the children.

This was our second session. The husband again appeared like the vigorous adolescent: tennis shoes, lightweight pants and sportshirt, and an air of intense eagerness. The wife wore a black skirt, white blouse, and a haggard, worried look. She volunteered that she was most pleased with our active work in the first hour, comparing it favorably with her years of previous psychotherapy, from which all she could recall was her therapist saying to her dispassionately on rare occasions, "And what do you feel about that?" Her husband eagerly agreed and expressed gratitude for my confronting his adolescent air which characterized his total being. "It was very helpful. It is absurd for a grown man to behave like a child. I've stopped it," he said with pseudomature grimaces. He not only acted adolescent, but also thought like an adolescent.

They fell silent after concluding that the intervening week was exceptionally pleasant. "The honeymoon phase," I thought, "born more of hope than change." I was pleased with the first session and found them both quite likeable—even before they appreciated me. Several minutes passed. I spoke first, "It appears that I'm the only one with a beef today so I'll start." To her, "I don't have anything to say to you today. We aren't acquainted yet" (though I thought she must have some interlocking personality traits to have lived with this 45-year-old adolescent for 12 years). Turning to him I said, "I like you. I'm pleased with your eagerness to grow. But you still come across as the adolescent. For instance, you missed an important part of my prior message. It is adolescent to think grown men mustn't act like children, and that it can be stopped just like that (snapping my finger). It's your pretense that denies your adolescent leftovers that I object to."

I started at a content level for this is all there was. We had no affect, no behavior yet to focus on. There was only our ideological differences and my restlessness about them. He responded as in our first session. He looked profoundly thoughtful with furrowed brow, first looking at the ceiling, then at the floor as he scratched his chin. His intense, large baby blue eyes darted all around, at random, though careful to avoid mine. And he came up silent. I confronted him again with posturing matureness. Only this time, since I was ineffective last week, I caricatured him, then invited him to comment on my gesturing. He laughed and again berated himself, "Isn't that ridiculous of me. I wasn't even aware of it."

The difference between our attitudes was all I had to go on, so I offered it, "You deny your compulsion to adolescence and when aware of it, condemn it. I am aware of it and condemn your refusal to embrace it openly and richly, or at least acknowledge it."

Husband: How can I embrace such behavior? It is unacceptable to me.
Therapist: Part of adolescent thinking to me. I don't care whether you
  like it or not. It is you. Know it. To me it would be more appropriate
  to ask, "How can you not acknowledge yourself?"

I am still at content level, attempting to engage him more fully. I think of this as the intellectual road, one of many paths to reaching people's being. I am negotiating with his intellectual self-image of a capable adult and am going to press it into my service. He can be influenced with logic and the weight he lends me as an authority.

H: (*Feeling my pressure, begins to retreat, still grimacing*) I don't want
  to be a child. I'm confused. I can't embrace behavior like that.
  (*Shaking his head, looking about*) How can I?

Now I have decided to move off content. I like his honest efforts. I am going to move closer.

Th: Can you look at me when you talk to me?
H: It is hard for me to look at people.

Th: Look at me anyway. You can tell me how hard it is or anything else about it as you do it. But do it.

He now tries, but it is extremely difficult for him. His interspersed words, as I gently but firmly continue my demands, are, "It's painful." "I feel like running out." "I'm confused and don't know what to say." "It is ridiculous that I can't do a simple thing like that." I notice more than confusion which is usually a camouflage of one's self-image to avoid contacting affect. I say, "I sense some sadness." (I think he is punishing himself for not complying with my "simple" request but ignore my thoughts.)

He appears sadder, turns away and says, "Isn't that ridiculous." Rather than pick up his objection to being ridiculous, which would have felt like a sound gestalt manipulation, I chose to be a participant, as I felt. "You're being ridiculous for denying the sadness you feel. That's the ridiculous part of you." I think I am lending my weight to his adolescent who wants the right to be heard. He takes out his kerchief, turns away from me and his wife, wipes away his tears. Several minutes pass. I feel tender but am afraid to move closer for fear of scaring him off. He finally says, "I feel like running again. I feel so weak."

Th: (*Supportively*) You're strong enough to stay and say it rather than do it. (*and to work further*) Envision yourself leaving. Where would you go and what would you do? (*I'm no longer demanding he face me. We are moving towards deeper involvement and that's the crucial aspect.*)

H: (*After a thoughtful moment, through his handkerchief*) Sounds crazy but I'd go to Clare (*his wife*).

Th: And what would you do?

H: (*Crying harder*) I'd ask her to hold me like a baby. Isn't that shameful.

Th: No it is not shameful. Go to her now.

H: (*Turning farther away from both of us, still tearful*) I can't.

Th: What stops you?

H: I don't know.

Th: If you were your wife now what would you think?

I want to ferret out his objection to being accepted as the crying child. I asked him to go to her for I saw her tears and knew she could receive him now. So the obstacle was obviously within him and must refer to another time and place. This approach is to lead us there.

H: She would accept me, I know, and I can't.
Th: (*Noticing her leaning forward*) May she come to you?
H: No, no.
Th: (*Softly*) I like your tears. I'd like to come close to you but I'm afraid to scare you.
H: (*Emphatically*) My father didn't. I remember one time (*breaks down sobbing*) I remember one time I came to him in tears and he pushed me away. He was angry that I'd gotten tears on his coat. (*He was crying hard, facing the wall.*)

My fear left me. I moved over to him, sat on the ottoman in front of him and held him to me. He and his wife cried. I rocked him, not caring if my tears fell on him. As we began to settle back, I urged him to envision his father and speak to him of his sadness.

H: He wouldn't listen.
Th: Then tell him how that makes you feel.
H: No. It would be useless.

I drop this experiment. My awareness goes to his wife who has silently cried with us. I invite her comment to him.

"I feel so free with you right now," was all she could say. He responded without grimacing, "I'd like to stop now."

We did.

The "I" statement, whether a simple "I want . . ." or an angrily shouted "I hate . . ." is, as a rule, superior to any other intervention. It provides the basic frame for the fullest personal expression and at the same time offers the other person the clearest possible target for a response. Granted, on occasion it would seem stilted or inappropriate, such as when it has failed to stop an incessant tongue-wagger; a commanding "shut up" is more effective. Here the "I" statement is merely modified so that it may be heard. Successfully imparting the "I" statement is, naturally, as important as creating it.

There is only one serious hazard worthy of attention when considering the use of the "I" statement: the tendency to stop after the first "I" statement and not follow through. "I revealed accurately how I felt, but then things didn't seem to go right and I did not know what to do next" summarizes a common experience of the novice. What is done next, and next and next again is to persevere with "I" statements. For this example "I don't know what to do now" is an appropriate beginning.

Such a comment may be associated with a slight feeling of embarrassment. The intervention is better when the entire message is included: "I am uncertain as to where we should proceed and feel some embarrassment." Gradually, other feelings will emerge during this encountering and these, too, can be usefully included. It is, of course, his own critical self-image that condemns the therapist for not knowing what to do next, that causes the feeling of embarrassment. Sometimes one's self-image is so severe it even prevents the recognition of the embarrassment and substitutes instead a sensation identified as confusion or, perhaps, petulance. Whatever the feeling, the therapist's *self-image* is being tolerant of his *self* which is daring to expose a transient ignorance. It is first necessary for the therapist to become aware of the intolerance and then to acknowledge the feeling of uncertainty without criticism. Uncertainty is an accurate appraisal of what the therapist is at the moment and should be appreciated rather than denied. It is likely that there will be a kaleidoscope of feelings: the embarrassment of the self-image, the excitement of the self and the uncertainty of the beingness. All are aspects of the person at this moment of reorganization. Attempts by the self-image to restore composure should be curbed.

The complete "I" statement is the impelling force for successful encountering and therapeutic interventions. Let us consider therapist boredom. At first, this is likely to be excluded from therapy and possibly even from the therapist's awareness. Inspired by the concept of the royal "I"ness, the therapist now may include the awareness in therapy: "I am bored with you and am embarrassed admitting it to you." In time the embarrassment wears thin and the intervention is simply "I am bored." Eventually, the therapist becomes bored with this boring intervention and searches instead for something else to say that will eliminate his boredom, not merely announce it. This eliminates interventions which have been diminished by embarrassment (imposed by the self-image). When motivated purely in the interest of *being*—of being excited in one's own experiences—new provocative interventions will emerge: "I don't like what we are doing (or not doing). I suggest we . . ."

Every patient is worthy of sharing the desynthesis and reorganization of a portion of a therapist's personality.

"I dread my next appointment. They are the most boring people I have ever known," a colleague reports. "Tell them," I suggest. "Should I?" he asks with an excited grin. "You mean just tell them exactly how I feel? That sounds so novel . . . so simple . . . so obvious . . . and so appropriate." With each hesitation from "novel" to "appropriate" his brain, without his awareness, rapidly confronts and resolves objections to his becoming more thoroughly "I."

Thus what from one standpoint may have been considered an "occupational" hazard, when acknowledged and pursued, becomes a permanently available benefaction, a point of return.

> When in doubt as to how
> Flee with haste to the ever now
> And with your fear herein allow
> The refreshing tickle of I and thou

A final word of caution:

Experiential psychotherapists, beware! Beware of stringent unbending adherence to any rule no matter how sound, such as "no questions!" Such behavior by therapists will be encounter-diminishing. An atmosphere of experimentation and exploration always takes precedence. When coupled with an open expression of who you are in that moment, such atmosphere becomes the ultimate encounter-enhancing retreat for the transiently frustrated or momentarily adrift therapist. This is the basic guideline of our search for better ways of hearing and being heard, seeing and being seen. No technique "works." There is no behavior that, of itself, is therapeutic. All rules, ideas or actions must be filtered through the therapist-person to emerge tailored to the context.

The most therapeutic intervention is the total and currently pertinent "I" statement imparted so that it will be experientially heard.

SECTION II

Example of Experiential
Psychotherapy within Families

8

Interview One

This section contains verbatim exchanges (with parenthetical comments by the therapist) derived from each of three sessions that composed an entire treatment program for a family of four. Appended are comments by the family members that were part of a follow-up visit two months later.

Not all therapy with families is so brief. Nor does this imply that further therapy would not be valuable, or that in the future it will not be necessary. All things considered, among them this family's financial status, we all concurred on the duration of this particular treatment program at the outset.

The mother in this family appeared initially as a rather dour, martyred woman, articulate, complaining, and the person who promoted this, their first therapy consultation. The father, with some reluctance, agreed to come along, relying on his wife's judgment that therapy might be an aid to solving their child's problem. The youngest son, Steve, is identified as the problem. According to mother he "sets fires, lies, and steals, but is basically a good boy." Steve is 12. Steve is the spark, mother is the engine, and father is the reluctant passenger. The brother, Don, who is 14, joins us at the insistence of the therapist who requests that all available family members be present. The names of the children have been altered to obscure their identity.

Mother cautiously and courteously leads the family into the office, and there is nothing unusual about our introduction. During the initial moments of silence, the mother visually checks out each member of her family and then looks at the therapist, while father alternates between watching his wife and looking at the therapist. He finally settles visually on his wife. She begins.

Mother: (*To therapist*) Where would you like us to begin?

Therapist: You may begin with what you do not like about living in this family.

M: What I don't like is a good thing to start with. What I don't like is that I feel that . . .

Th: (*Interrupting*) I suggest you speak to specific individuals rather than to me.

M: (*Thoughtfully*) Well, I will start with Don, although I don't think the problem focuses on him.

Th: You would not like to start with the problem?

M: Oh, I thought it might be hard to start on Steve, but maybe I should start with him. He doesn't do what he can do. He is not happy or content with what he can do . . .

Th: (*Interrupting*) I would like you to talk to Steve.

M: (*Turning to Steve, she continues, softly*) I don't feel that you are doing what you can in school or with your friends, and what makes me unhappy is that you are unhappy and I cannot help you. I cannot help you find out who you are, I can't help to make you comfortable in a group so you don't have to be misbehaving all the time, and I can't make you happy at school to do what you can do instead of coming home and telling me stories. (*Turns to others*) So that is what bothers me much about the family, I think, and that we all aren't as pleasant with each other as I think we should be, (*turns to Steve*) but all these things seem to pile up on you because you are the unhappy one. And that is the end of what I have to say to you Steve. (*turning back to therapist*)

Th: (*To Steve, invitingly*) What do you make of all that Steve?

Steve: (*Smiling sheepishly*) I don't know. I don't understand.

Th: Would you like some help with it?

(*Steve nods*)

Th: (*Sensing his reluctance to speak, yet, and not wishing to burden him with a demand, I suggest*) That's what parents are for. Let's invite them to help you now. Okay?
 (*He nods again and we look from one parent to the other and wait. After a brief silence:*)
Th: (*To parents*) It seems difficult for you all to begin. I'm asking for volunteers.
M: You see, that is why I need help. We talked about this before.
Th: And then, what?
M: I come to you and I say "help." I really don't know what else to do.
Th: Then let me suggest that you talk with your husband about it. That's what spouses are for.
M: I have talked with him, but he hasn't been able to help. Things would go on over a period of time. We have talked to Steve about things he does when he was unhappy. We have had a problem with matches for a long time. There were fires started a great many places, and then he takes things that do not belong to him, and we have talked about that because we can't have that. He doesn't tell the truth much of the time. I don't want you to misunderstand. He is basically a good boy and we love him dearly.
Th: I'm wondering what is absent from your conferences that keeps them from being effective. Do either of you (*to parents*) have any ideas?

> This is a gentle attempt to redirect the focus towards the family operation and at the same time encourage an interaction, albeit at a content level.

M: We could be kinder to him, that could help, I don't know what else. Put more emphasis on what he does right and less emphasis on what he does wrong—that would help him. He is under such pressure because so much attention is paid to what he does wrong, and he does so much wrong so much of the time. I can't think of anything else specifically. (*to husband*) When you come home and when you are home you establish the climate of the home, and I have said this before, often I think the climate is one of discipline and a case is made about what everybody has done wrong, and it seems to me to be harder on Steve than on Don.

Father: I don't think it bothers Steve; I don't think he pays much attention to it.

M: (*Smiling*) You are wrong.

> *As yet I don't know how much to intensify the encounter. Mother appears sturdy and cooperative and, since she is the one who initiated the interviews, I know she is motivated.*

Th: You are smiling.

M: I always smile when I talk.

Th: No, you don't always smile when you talk.

M: I suppose I put up that smile as a defense, I always smile when I talk.

Th: No you don't always smile when you talk.

M: Yes, I do.

Th: No, you don't.

M: May I ask you a question: Why does that bother you?

> *She is quite sturdy.*

Th: Because it is fake. Because when you get emphatic as you did and start to smile like that I suspect you are irritated. That is what I see. It was not a happy smile. Smiles are for happiness. Yours was deadly.

F: (*To therapist*) You're so right.

Th: And I suspect you put up with it and never challenge it.

F: You're so right, again.

Th: I wish I had been wrong.

M: I think anger is destructive.

Th: I don't know where you learned that. I enjoy mine.

M: There is no enjoyment in it to me. I don't like the things I hear myself say. I don't feel that the total effect is a useful one, that is why.

Th: I don't believe your fake grin is useful to you either.

M: Yelling all the time is no help either.

Th: I am not recommending it, as a panacea. I say if it is there you might as well acknowledge it, have it and use it, otherwise your conversation dwindles down into nothing which would be even more destructive.

F: Not if I don't have something constructive to offer. I am as tough as everyone else. With the boys I have tried to control my temper and I've tried to compliment them on things that are done and be thankful for the things that are done properly. My temper admittedly is a problem. More things annoy me than annoy my wife.

Th: (*To Father*) I suspect you waste much energy trying to be reasonable and at the same time you are unreasonably intolerant of your anger.

F: They know the things that annoy me, especially chores not being done, such as mother having to clean up their rooms and pick up after them. But it is a helpful thing to have them do these things themselves without having to be told each time. Such as Don knows that his chores are taking out the trash everyday and Steve cleaning up the walk and patio and these are to be done no later than 5:00. When it is about 6:00 or 7:00 and nothing has been started yet and the waste baskets are overflowing and they say, "Oh, I forgot." When I come home and things are done I try to make some thankful sounds that they are done. What really annoys me is that their mother, instead of leaning on them and telling them to do something, will do it herself. And they take advantage of her. If they take advantage of her, it doesn't leave me time to take advantage of her. All through life they will have things required of them and won't always have someone around to do for them.

He ignored my provocation. I decide not to engage in a fruitless debate or an impassioned argument over his behavior. Since he was so unmotivated and tight, I didn't want to get angry yet for fear of scaring him away. Instead, I chose to remain at a content level, selecting what impressed me as a critical pattern in the family matrix.

Th: What impresses me is that you hold the children responsible for the difficulty.

F: They are old enough to be responsible.

Th: And so is your wife. She is old enough for you to expect her to assume the responsibility of extracting from the children the behavior you both require. (*after several minutes of silence*) The impression I have is that there are really no parents in this family. The children are expected to be the responsible ones. (*to mother*) You expect Steve to be something. You really don't have the expectations of your husband that you do of Steve. You don't expect him to participate as a father and husband, to come in, monitor and participate in discussions and give you something constructive. He offers very little to you at this point. Yet you claim Steve is the problem. (to father) You do the same thing when you focus on the kids not doing their share of the work, yet you don't apparently place any responsibility on your wife. (to both) You don't hold each other responsible as parents in this home, but instead come down hard on the kids. (to the boys) I want you kids to feel free to tell me whether you think I'm right or wrong.

Don: I kind of think you are right. I don't think they do enough for us.

Th: And how do you feel about that?

(Don begins to cry.)

Th: It's sad, isn't it?

(Don sobs.)

Th: Come over and sit here with me Don. (Don comes from other side of room and sits in chair pulled close to therapist, who puts his hand on Don's shoulder.) I'd like to hear some more about your sadness.

D: I don't have the impression that they know what we are like . . . Sometimes they expect too much of us.

Th: Can you think of a for instance?

D: (After thinking a moment) No.

Th: Okay. It's not necessary. If you do later it could be helpful. Let us know. Sometimes parents don't understand but they would like to. We sometimes forget what it's like to be kids.

(To parents) Do either of you want to comment to Don?

F: I find this a little startling. One of my objections is that my wife is constantly doing extra things for the boys and putting out more work than she should, and now he is saying he isn't getting enough.

Th: That you find it startling isn't enough for me. Are you saying this is a hoax? He isn't sincere?

F: No. I feel very possibly, from his viewpoint, that he is very possibly not getting enough from his parents. However, I don't know what it is he isn't getting enough of.

Th: Are you interested?

F: Sure.

Th: I don't see any inquiries of him or searching of yourself to find out what he means by all this.

F: (*To Don*) What things are you talking about Don?

D: You do enough for me but you don't do enough with me.

M: Could you tell me, because I thought I understood you pretty well. In what way?

D: You don't go places and have fun with me. I don't think you or Dad really understand me. He always expects me to do more. He doesn't know what I'm really like.

F: In what did I expect you to do more?

D: In Scouts, for instance.

F: There are things you wanted to do in Scouts and if you wanted these things I felt that you should work toward them.

D: You wanted me to do so much more than I was able to do.

F: No, I felt you were able to do these things. I'm thinking of some of the merit badges you could have earned a year or two ago when you did everything except pass the final review on them. You'd earned your hiking merit badge, your cooking merit badge and your camping merit badge and you didn't go ahead to finish them up. I think you were perfectly capable of finishing it up. The other boys who were on that camp-out and did finish them up were no more capable than you.

D: I think you should have been a little more with me instead of just telling me and urging me to do these things.

F: On the merit badges, this is something you were supposed to earn yourself and not my earning those for you. I'm not supposed to be helping you. You are capable and . . .

Th: (*Interrupting—I decided the boy was no match for the father and needed more help. I decided to speak for him.*) But Dad, you are doing the same thing again now as you did before. You are telling me what you want to do and what you expect from me instead of appreciating me for who I am, what I am, as I am. (*to Don*) Does that say it, Don?

D: (*Drying his tears*) Yes, that's pretty close.

Th: (*Continuing for Don*) If I could have done those things, I would have. The fact was I couldn't achieve it, and I wasn't appreciated for what I could do. If I had a little more friendship with you, a little more encouragement from you—appreciation—then maybe I would have more confidence in myself to do some of those things.

F: But, he could have done them.

Th: If he could have done them, he would have done them. (*emphatically*) You are doing it again.

F: I think it was just procrastination.

Th: You are criticizing him again now. He is coming to you for help. He wants some recognition of him, and all he gets is that he is not measuring up to some picture you have got in your head of who he is. Some picture in your head of what Don should look like, be like and function like.

F: Everyone has a picture of what his kids can do.

Th: Don says, "Get rid of the picture and take a look at me. I'd like you to see me, me, me. Not some picture of me."

F: And I should ignore the fact that he worked so hard for the merit badges all those months.

Th: Never mind about what he hasn't done, recognize what he has done. This is what he is asking for. That is the stuff that will give him the encouragement to go on. What he has not completed he knows very well. He doesn't need your reminders.

D: You criticize me more than you do anything else.

F: I don't criticize him more than anybody else.

Th: Not more than anyone else, more than anything else. It has nothing to do with others.

F: His constant cry is that so and so always . . .

Th: There you go again. You began this conversation inviting him to tell you what he would like and, as he tells you, instead of listening to him and seeing what you can do about it, you try to wipe out his position with criticism.

F: I'm not trying to wipe out his position.

Th: That's what you just did. Now if you are going to ask him, you have an obligation to get his answer and see what it means and not just to argue it away. That is the thing that will stop him from talking to you.

F: Do you notice the times that I am not unhappy with you?

Th: I object to your asking such questions. No questions—if you have something to say, say it.

F: If you made an effort on the things that I criticized you for, then I wouldn't criticize you on them.

Th: You missed the whole point of what I am saying. He is coming to you for help, and you give him a critical lecture. He wants to be better friends with you and you are just telling him, "Well, be the picture I want you to be and never mind who you are." He is saying to you, "I don't want to be your picture, I want to be your son, the son I am—Don." And you're saying, "You're not acceptable as Don. You have to measure up to the picture I have of you."

F: I think it is important for him to measure up to a great extent.

Th: He wants to. But he must have some recognition first. *First*— not after. Not after he becomes this cardboard mock-up picture you have of him, and then he gets the recognition and appreciation. It doesn't come that way.

F: Trouble is, I don't know how to function that way.

Th: If you would like some help with that I suggest you talk it over with your wife.

F: (*To wife*) What do you think about all this?

> *He has retreated again, this time to complete ignorance. He flows between being an unperturbed talker and an impenetrable listener who asks questions and ignores the answers. He has just shifted gears. He is not more negotiable yet.*

Th: (*To Father*) I object to your question. I suggested you talk with your wife, not question her from a position of complete ignorance.

F: If I had answers I wouldn't be here. Where do I start?

Th: That's a question.

> *After a few minutes of silence mother rescues him.*

M: (*To Don, with obvious tenderness, yet at the same time again relieving Father of responsibility*) Can you tell us something we do right so we can get a better idea of what you mean?

> *Though obviously sincere she has once again focused away from father and at the same time capitulated any responsibility to search on her own. Don is invited to become the answer man. Father remains silent. Rather than push harder for him to react to my confrontation I choose what seemed easier for me—to talk with her and keep composed. With him I would have gotten angry. I offer a map (my fantasy).*

Th: (*To Mother*) I'm going to interrupt your question. I want to spell out again what I see. Don is in a bind. He is constantly being asked by both of you for responsible adult-like behavior, such as, your question right now, which places the burden once again on him, presumably for information, but actually for solutions. Father also asks for behavior that is not Don. Yet both of you are critical of everything he does, and he feels like a failure. No matter what he does, it is not quite enough, and if he doesn't do it he gets criticized for that. First he needs encouragement and an opportunity to identify with Father as a man. He can't do this with Father constantly belittling him for not measuring up to a fantasied standard. He needs to know more about his obvious successes. His longing right now is for someone who will appreciate him and give him the encouragement that he needs. Your task is to help your husband get in touch with this, not Don. On this particular issue and perhaps others it is with your husband that you have business and I see you back off from him.

M: (*To husband*) Are you aware that you are usually too tired or cross for Don or me to talk with you? I'm trying to find a starting place to talk with you now.

F: I think that sounds like something I had known.

M: The feeling that I get when you come home or are home is that very often you wish that you were someplace else—someplace quieter maybe where there were not so many people around. I think you do not listen to me, and I think you do not listen to Don.

F: That's very possible. When I first come home I would like a little bit of peace and quiet. A home is not always quiet when you have a family, kids and record players—a home is not always quiet. You all come at me with a lot of stuff that doesn't interest me. When I get home I am not all that excited about Toby, if he has eaten a tomato or not. (*to therapist*) Toby is a rat, by the way, not one of the children. (*back to wife*) When I get home I am tired and it seems reasonable that I would like some peace and relaxation for a little while, but I open the door and I get hit with everything that has been happening and got saved up all day.

M: I can understand that. But we—Don and I and all of us—wouldn't talk to you unless it was important to us to say what we had to say. So maybe we could start by making some arrangement so that you could experience some peace and quiet for a while so that you would really listen.

F: Sounds like a fair trade.

M: (*Beginning to cry*) Because you can't have a good relationship with Don unless you listen when he talks to you. To go back to the relationship you were talking about. That's just for an opener. Do you think you could do that?

F: I can try.

Th: I object. I don't want you to try.

F: You want it done.

Th: No. I don't want you to do it at all. I don't want you to do something *for them*. What they are saying is, "You are important to us, we need you, we need your appreciation, your guidance, your interest. We need just to be heard, for if you listen to us that tells us we are worth something." And that's an eloquent plea. But you also have needs. I don't want you coming home and saying, "Oh I'll have to be something and do something for everybody here." That won't be successful. I would rather you come home and tell them something about you. Tell them about what you need. Tell them how you want a little peace and quiet. Apparently you don't know how to use a family either. Tell them about how you want a little quiet.

F: True, and very often I feel that I'm not needed in the family.

Th: That seems so strange to me in the midst of their expressed starvation for you.

F: Very often I get the feeling that they would be much happier without me around.

Th: Without your criticism, granted. But you're not just your criticism. You are much more than that to them. (*There is now a long silence in which father is obviously working.*)

F: I seem to be the problem.

> *This to me was a remarkable step for this man who initially came dutifully at the insistence of his wife to help her and their son.*

Th: (*Tempering his newfound awareness*) They seem to be a problem to you, also.

F: And I, to them.

Th: Have you ever thought you might like to get rid of the whole family?

I want to help him express and accept his heretofore denied negativity.

F: No. Running away from a problem doesn't solve it. I certainly don't want to get rid of them.

Th: Did you ever have that thought?

F: Sure, I think everyone has. (*admits it but calls in reinforcements and then quickly adds*) But it doesn't last very long.

Th: And the less you say about it, the longer it lasts.

After a silence of several minutes I drop in another fantasy, or map, to sweeten the pot, so to speak.

Th: I see you on the outside of your family wanting to get in, they are on the inside wanting you in, and between you all is an invisible barrier.

F: (*Thoughtful, less impervious, not questioning*) I may be expecting too much from them and I'm not sure what they expect from me or how to give them what they expect from me. (*Pause*)

This is a good place to end the session as he begins to become introspective. I hadn't hoped for this much as he appeared so remote and walled off initially. She was so much more articulate and psychologically minded I expected her to make more progress than he.

(*Don, who is still sitting beside me, comes into my awareness.*)

Th: Don, you're not crying but you look like you still have a lot of sadness left.

D: Yes.

I want to hug him but realize it isn't me he wants.

Th: (*To Father*) I think you should be here, not me.

F: You may not like this, but I'd rather Don came here.

Th: Never mind being so damn considerate about what I'd like. Tell him what you want.

F: (*To Don, tenderly*) Come here, Don. (*Don moves slowly over to a chair alongside of Father. Father puts his arm around him. This is not the solution but it's a beginning. After a considerable silence Father finally says to Don)* We've both got some work to do. I think we can do it, don't you? *(Don nods weakly.)*

I chose not to pick up on the father's use of the question or the doubt in Don's affirmation. Instead I chose to answer with hope.

Th: *(To Don)* We've made a start and I'd like you to come back so we can work some more, Don. Would you?

D: *(Still sad)* Yes, I would.

Th: *(To Mother)* I'd like a word from you, Mother. I know you want to come back *(seeing her sad expression)* but I'm curious: Do you feel any more hopeful than when you arrived, or were you not aware of how hopeless you felt? You, too, are entitled to cry.

M: I didn't think my sadness shows.

Th: What shows is your "noble" struggle to hide your sadness.

M: *(Tearfully)* I knew all this before, so I don't feel any more hopeful. I have a tendency to want to add to the conversation, "yes I do" but really, I don't.

Th: You have made some progress. You are more honest. You aren't smiling. *(pushing for the commitment I know is there)* Maybe I am wrong. If you don't feel more hopeful, then what's the use of coming back?

M: I had some hope when we came. That is still there. I haven't lost that, but the walls are still up.

Th: I agree that the walls are not down. I feel more hopeful about Father than when I first saw him. I don't think your old martyred and sad tactics will work with him though. He and I are probably going to have one hell of a fight before we are through. Sometimes I don't know how else to break down walls except by fighting—and I'm talking about verbal fighting—vigorous negotiating—I don't want to get bruised.

M: And what do you do when that doesn't work?

Th: Well, I'll have to see when I get there. As I've said, it's no panacea. It is part of the work. It works better than wailing. I don't think the walls are exactly the same as when you came in. Father has some awareness that he didn't have before. That is an important step. He is aware of some walls that he wasn't aware of before. Don's sadness is an important awareness today. This is all part of starting on the wall. Just getting angry is no great thing, but that may be part of what we need to do. All I'm saying is that I'm less afraid to be angry than you. Anger is a part of our birthright, to be used as part of our communicating. I say all this as I see each of you wasting a lot of energy avoiding the anger that this frustrating situation must create —rather than dissipating it by being angry and freeing yourselves to go on with further negotiations.

My mental meanderings have led me (Diagnosis: Aggressive-aggressive personality) to conclude that if Father (Diagnosis: Passive-aggressive personality) can be brought back into this family and Mother's tearful wall of bitterness (Diagnosis: Reactive depression) can be overcome, then their encountering will be enhanced. His diagnosis is sustained by single-mindedness, questioning, feigned reasonableness and distorted selflessness; hers by a martyred sadness and turning to the children for support. Her sadness increases his sense of failure (aggravating his passive-aggressive qualities) which, in turn, increases her sadness. I was pleased with the interview.

From the historic blank screen of this family-in-trouble we have ferreted out the significant obstacles in their family encounters: Mother's blinding wall of tears and Father's wall of aloofness, born of unrewarding selflessness. I touched both of their walls and put a crack in Father's. I proved to him that I was a reasonable man. Also, I warned him that his behavior angered me and that I would be less hesitant to express myself more fully in the future, since I felt this is where we must eventually go. Don and I are friends and Steve is, I am sure, relieved to learn that he is not "the problem."

I finish all my business with them and feel good towards all of them.

9

Interview Two

The second session opens with Steve taking Don to task for his part in the loss of a pet frog. They bicker for about ten minutes when Don says with exasperation, "Let's drop it. I can't see what all this arguing has to do with our family problems."

Father: That's part of the family problem.
Therapist: The problem that I see is that Don, once again, is the assigned parent who stops all this nonsense while you parents just sit.
F: I wanted to see where it would go this time. (*silence*) This sort of thing has its variables and, unfortunately, the way it works out, I think more often, is either Steve versus Don or Steve versus someone and, as always, Steve ends up on the short end of these things, whether he wants to be or not.
Steve: It isn't always my fault. Like, in the night his rat gave me quite a few little problems. Like, during the night he was making little noises and I couldn't sleep. Don laughed at me and teased me and wouldn't stop. And you always blamed me.
F: There were quite a few nights and you never made any mention of this to me, at least I don't think . . .

245

S: (*Interrupting*) I told you that in the morning. You just don't mind. You don't care about my problems (*starting to cry*).

F: That's not quite right. What did you tell me in the morning?

S: You said, "You're just trying to be mean . . . so forget it!"

Mother: Does that frequently happen? Do you ask us when you need help, and we just don't listen?

S: When I ask Dad, he just doesn't care, he just says forget it.

F: Well, yes, that's a very good point there. I often do not care. That's because many hours after something has happened, and it's all been figured out, and everyone is calm and quiet again, you . . .

S: I'm not going to tromp in and wake you at 3:00 in the morning, just to tell you about that. Then you would really get angry.

F: Some things happen during the day, also, but when you're telling something to me, I think it's fine if you're trying to get a solution to it. But when I feel that you're just trying to get someone else in trouble, I'm not happy about hearing it at all (*silence*).

S: Well, Dad, I wasn't trying to get Don in trouble. I was just trying to get him to move his dumb rat out of the way 'cause it was also interfering with everything. I couldn't (*pauses to cry a little*) sleep comfortably because of the way I had to put my legs so the rat wouldn't chew 'em. That little rat was just everywhere.

There is a long silence. Father looks both perplexed and somewhat exasperated.

Th: (*To Father*) What are you aware of right now about yourself?

F: (*Logically but not psychologically*) I'm not sure. I wasn't thinking of being aware of myself or of something of myself; I was thinking about this particular thing, (*short pause*) this hassle with the rat and what I had supposedly thought I had set up beforehand to take care of that whole thing. I thought the preplanning of it would take care of that. This problem I hadn't heard about—the rat causing trouble and keeping Steve from sleeping by bothering with his blanket.

S: (*To Don*) I knew that you are just trying to get me in trouble, so just forget it.

Don: Well actually, Steve, that rat wasn't making any noise and you didn't have any trouble keeping asleep. Yet, you kept waking me up because you kept making noises in your sleep.

S: Listen, you said I was making them when I wasn't making any sound, you said I was making noises but I don't think . . .
D: (*Interrupting*) How can you know, when you are sound asleep?
S: No, you woke me up.
F: It seems we've lost the whole idea.
S: The minute I tried to prove it to him, he knows that I probably get a . . .

I interrupt. The boys have taken over again with their bickering. Father allows it. My first thrust was futile.

Th: What would you like to say now? What would you like to do? (*no response*) I have a suggestion. Try on the sentence to both of them: "Both of you shut up right now because I'd like a little peace and quiet."
F: (*Pause*) I'm not in a peace-and-quiet mood right now.
Th: Well what is it you want? You're here but you're not here.
F: Yeah. My thought is just, good grief, why bring all of it up now? When something is happening—try to get it taken care of then.

He's getting close but he's gossiping to therapist.

Th: So what do you want to say to *them* now?
F: (*Turning to children*) Next time let somebody know what's going on beforehand. If you're going to say something about what happened the night before, Steve, don't come out sounding like you're just trying to get someone in trouble. You start out with a lovely whiney-type voice.
Th: (*More emphatically*) Well, what do you want right now?
F: Right now, I say just leave it all alone for it's all done and past.
Th: Then you are saying what I said: Be quiet, I'd like a little peace and quiet right now.
F: Be quiet on that subject.
Th: Finally! But you don't say it promptly, loudly and clearly, instead you become bewildered and uncertain and quite ineffectual. Again, this is one of the things that you want for yourself, yet you don't take for yourself. You're certainly entitled to say, "Be quiet, I don't want to hear any more of this. Stop it now."

F: I tell them this from time to time.

Th: You didn't tell them now. Their bickering was dragging on, and Don even objected before you did.

S: (*Inspired, I suspect, from the previous session and wanting his day in court*) You let Don tell on me, but you don't let me tell on him. Like you let Don . . . he picks on me, so when I lose my temper, I pick back on him and I get in trouble. When I tell on Don, I just . . .

F: We get this from both of you, so it's not you in particular. Each boy feels he is picked on and thinks the other boy doesn't get punished. And this is not so. It doesn't work out that way.

S: (*Starting to cry again*) But Don, I don't know why, but Don seems to actually hate me.

F: Yet you do things together and enjoy each other together. Part of the trouble, I think, is the fact that you are boys and you are growing up. I can remember that short period I lived with my cousin, and we had trouble with each other. We certainly didn't want to be denied the right to play with each other. We had a classic case of walking to Sunday school, and my couisn being older had the dandy game as we went by the gas station of knocking over the tire display, which he thought was pretty hilarious. And I was scared stiff that the man was going to come out and beat us up or put us in jail or something, so I finally complained to my parents about this, and they gave me a very simple solution: We'd each walk different routes, that way if my cousin got in trouble, I wouldn't be around, and if he didn't get in trouble, I still wouldn't be bothered by all this. But I certainly didn't want to do that and neither did he. We didn't want to go different routes; we wanted to go together. So we continued to do the same thing. So we had this problem of these things we didn't like to do with each other and things we did like to do with each other. And you boys have things you do together that you like and things you don't like; it's just part of the problem of being boys growing up.

S: I try to be nice with him, but he just doesn't let me.

Th: (*Impatient with father's feebleness, I become a principal and say to father*) Wait a minute, that lecture just didn't send me at all and apparently had little effect on Steve either. (*to Steve*) Steve, don't you sometimes hate Don?

S: Yes, sometimes.

Th: Oh, wonderful. Wonderful. And sometimes he hates you, too.

Then, for economy, since Steve can listen in, I continue to father with my lecture, delivered in anger.

Th: You're giving us another lecture now instead of saying, "Be quiet." You give him a lecture instead of saying, "Don hates you, why shouldn't he hate you sometimes? All brothers hate brothers occasionally. I want you to hate him too. Enjoy hating him once in a while and be quiet about it now." You don't tell him what you want. Instead you pick at him. You bicker, lecture and criticize in your attempt to be reasonable and selfless. You all have a way of condemning. All of you do this. What you are doing is knocking him now. (*To wife*) That's what you do when you try to help father. I notice it comes out like it's a criticism of him instead of trying to tell him what you want. You've done this consistently here. You tell him what you don't want. You tell him what you don't like. But you don't ask for what you want. You don't say, "I want . . ." This is the other side of the same coin that bothers me so much. You don't talk about what you want. (*back to father*) I want you to want things *from* these people and I want you to go after what you want from them. I want you to tell them to shut up when you want them to shut up; I want you to tell them to take a walk with you, if you want them to take a walk with you.

I am both saying it and doing it.

F: (*Answering concretely after a brief silence*) I don't care if they take a walk with me or not.

Th: Ask for what you want. You pay attention to my words and not to what I mean.

S: I . . . I don't understand even how we got to this. Before we were talking about . . .

Th: (*Determined to make contact with father*) Wait a minute, Steve. (*to Father*) I want you to want what you want.

F: I don't feel I should necessarily have what I want all the time because . . .

Th: Try! You can't get it all the time, but try. Try for it.

M: Why not? Why do you always have to be the one who picks? (*silence*)

F: Picks what? Or picks at?

Th: (*To Mother*) Don't ask him a question. Tell him what you want.

M: All right.

Th: You see, "Why do you always have to pick" comes out as a criticism again.

M: (*To Father, after a thoughtful pause, she starts hesitantly and gains momentum*) If you want something, ask for it. What you do is you . . . you decide when you're going to do something for somebody and how . . . but you don't ask them what they want. You decide when you're going to sacrifice yourself for somebody else or make an inconvenience for yourself for somebody else that may not even be what they want. And if you came right out and said, "I want to do this. I want to do that," then we wouldn't have to be so careful of your feelings, and we could say, "No, we don't want to do that." And that would really be better, as a working arrangement than what we have worked ourselves into now.

> *She has come much closer to an "I" statement and I chose not to interrupt. Her remarks were a good start for now.*

F: A basic thought that you mentioned seemed to be that the family is so very considerate of me and what I want to do or when I want to do something and that's not the feeling I get. I still have this catch-as-catch-can feeling from my part in the family.

M: But that's because you're so busy being put upon and being considerate and not doing what you want to do and doing what you don't want to do. But you don't ask. You don't say, "Should I make this noble sacrifice for you or shall I not?" (*silence*)

> *Though mother is gaining momentum and is on the right track with me, I push ahead as a principal. My anger must be discharged and I also know I can lean on him much harder than she can.*

Th: (*Loudly, slamming the desk*) Or better still, "No I won't make this sacrifice for you." I wish to hell you'd learn to stand up to your family. Tell them what you want. Tell them what you don't want, loud and clear.

F: You think that would be better than . . .

Th: A hell of a lot better than what you're doing now. Now all you do is pretend. (*exaggeratedly mocking his whimpering ineffectuality*) "Well I don't know, I want to help. What is it you want? What is it you want?" (*then sharply*) You give nobody nothing. (*smiling*) Or is it anything?

F: Nothing I must admit. Nothing.

Th: That's right. That's right. (*pause*) Least of all, yourself. You get nothing from them. Because you won't stand up. (*pause*) What will they all do, walk out on you? Desert you? What? What's the worst thing that could happen?

F: Well, they wouldn't walk out.

Th: Then what's the worst that could happen?

F: Just general unhappiness in the family, more arguing and more . . .

Th: You have general unhappiness. You've got unhappiness. You've got arguing. Believe me, more you wouldn't get.

F: (*Silence*) Sort of an intriguing idea.

Th: (*With obvious exasperation*) It's still just an idea. Maybe that's the way you learn. But that's not enough for me. I want you to take the chance of being whoever you want to be with this bunch.

F: And that may be part of the problem. Just what do I want to be with this bunch and I may not . . .

Th: With or without them.

F: I'm just not that sure . . . I don't believe . . .

Th: Can you do it as an experiment this week?

F: Yes.

Th: You try. Don't come home if you don't want to come home. Don't come home till you *want* to come home. Till you *want* to see these kids. Don't do a thing for them unless you want to. Not because it's good for them. Never mind, let's put that in ancient history now. You just do what you want for them because you want to do it for them.

F: Not because it's the right thing to do, but because it's the thing I want to do.

Th: That's right. That's right. Their tears notwithstanding.

> *Eureka! for the first time his stony facial posture softens and there is a touch of sadness in his look.*

F: I just have this deep feeling that . . . for so many years of being concerned with everything all around with this family . . . what I do . . . I have to consider or be thoughtful of the rest of the family.

Th: And that's why you're here.

M: But you're not considerate!

Th: This is the monstrous situation you've created with that attitude.

F: (*To wife*) But, I'm not considerate, you say?

M: You're not! You're considerate of a make-believe family that you have built, and you're considerate of who you think we are and what you think the situation is.

F: My thought is "Good grief, how much worse it would be if I wasn't even that much."

M: I don't see how it could possibly be any worse. I certainly would be willing to take the chance. Because if you paid attention to what *you* need and what *you* want, then the rest of us can be who *we* are.

> *My needs have been met. I'm no longer angry. Mother is inspired and has picked up the cudgel. I encourage her to be more effective at the same time I goad him.*

Th: Nice speech, but I don't think he listened to you.

M: He doesn't understand, and I don't know how to make him understand what I mean.

Th: (*Silence*) He's too busy being selfless.

M: (*Emphatically, to husband*) That's why it's not going to work, because you're going to go back and do exactly the same thing for a week that you've been doing all the way along. And you're just going to call it something else. And it isn't going to make the slightest difference.

F: But we won't know until we try, will we?

M: I know.

> *Mother's cloud of hopelessness is beginning to descend. She has dropped the cudgel. I focus away from this talk of the future in favor of attention to our nowness.*
>
> *I gossip to her purposely. I know he is listening and expect my gossiping to be more irritating to him than speaking directly to to him.*

Th: (*To Mother*) You needn't wait till next week to find out. He's not going back to anything, for he has never left it. We pick at him now, tell him we have no confidence in him and he fakes rather than telling us all to go to hell.

F: I don't want to tell you all to go to hell right now because I find a lot in what you all are saying. I like listening to what's going on.

Th: (*Driving more directly*) Then, you are no different than you have ever been.

His posture has changed. He is responding. He is leaning back in his chair, his hands clasped behind his head, his armpits soaking.

F: (*Still on content*) Yes, but there's a lot I haven't heard before. Steve's interpretation of what I've been saying, for instance. I hadn't realized he was interpreting my behavior in that manner.

I have attempted to intensify the encounter by changing the content from what might happen next week (future) to what is happening now. Father deflects this by retreating to past—to material earlier in this session. Before I can point this up Steve responds.

S: All vacation that's what you were doing—taking advantage of us all.

F: I sincerely doubt that.

S: You were.

F: But I figure that from your age level, you might very well have been thinking that.

I crassly demand a return to the here and now.

Th: I am more interested in what your armpits have to say. They are pouring. I want to know the words that would come from them, rather than the words that have been coming from your head.

F: I don't think he knows what he's talking about.

Th: Then tell him! Or are you going to start that next week?

F: Why be impolite all the time? You can still say what you want without being impolite.

Th: (*Furiously*) No, you can't say what you want. You haven't said or done what you want for years. If you can learn how to do and say what you want *and* be polite, fine! I haven't learned how, obviously, or I wouldn't be sitting here shouting at you. And you haven't learned how, because you're not saying what you want.

M: (*To father, obviously agitated*) There's nothing polite about sitting and seething at somebody and not saying anything and just not listening to them.

F: As a result of our last session, I tried diligently to listen to the boys all week . . .

I have become aware of how he must cling to others through words. He adheres to content like it is a lifeline to others. I choose not to confront this but rather to climb on it to reach him. I merely interrupt his retreat to the past.

Th: Listen to me. I'll give you a new clue this week. Listen to your armpits. Let them speak. I liked what they had to say. Listen to the kids, also. But that doesn't mean that you don't answer them with what you have to say. You do both. You listen to them and you listen to yourself, too.

Now he is working.

F: I'm not ready for what I want. Peace and quiet. I'm not sure what the peace-and-quiet stuff is all about. I have always thought that what I wanted would really be peace and quiet. Now I wonder if this is an idealistic phrase that I like . . . I don't know . . . what I want and expect of me, I'm not even sure anymore.

I'm delighted with his introspection.

M: You're not going to find out, if you're afraid to try. It's not fair to put us between you and what it is you want.

Th: (*To Mother*) I'm wondering if I sound like you? As I listen to you, I always feel like you're picking at him. Am I picking at him?

M: Yeah, I think we both are.

Th: (*To Father*) Do you feel that we are picking on you?

F: You sound more reasonable about it. That may be because . . .

Th: I'm more reasonable about it?

F: Uh. Maybe because you're a newer one.

Th: Oh?

M: I even sound to myself as if I were picking on him. But, I don't know, I don't know how else to sound.

F: That goes back to what we said before about my always picking on the kids. I don't get that feeling unless someone points it out that way. I don't think that I am picking at them.

Th: What comes to mind is something my family tells me. Sometimes instead of getting angry, like I was with you awhile ago and just saying it as I feel it, I complain or whine or pick, like you sound to me. And they have told me time and time again, that they can't stand that picking. They can't stand the whine, and they can't stand the complaining. But when I really shout, when I think I'm being most unreasonable, that's when they're most receptive. (*pause*) And you just tell me the same thing. You tell me, I sound more reasonable, while I'm sitting here shouting at you and she sits there calmly picking away at you.

F: What it sounded like is that I'd be better off at the times when I think I'm worse off. When I think I am being more kind and considerate towards the family, I'm probably working just the opposite way. When I blow up and get real mad, things work out more easily.

Th: (*Silence*) I'd like you better.

M: (*Silence*) You hardly ever do that.

F: Because I don't feel it's the right thing to do.

Th: How come you say it's all right for me to do it? You didn't seem to find my anger objectionable.

F: I think you're better trained, so you know more about family relationships. Otherwise we wouldn't be coming to you.

Th: It doesn't have to do with family relationships, it has to do with my right to have my anger, if that's what I have. You see, right now, I feel much better towards you than I did before.

F: You said last week you figured the way things are going, you'd have to get angry with me sometime.

Back to the past.

Th: Yes, I felt it coming on. How do you feel right now?

F: I'm rather interested in the whole idea.

Th: That's what you're thinking right now. Do you have any kind of feeling right now? Do you know what I mean by that? Feeling good, feeling bad, feeling intense, feeling edgy?

F: Restrained.

Th: Okay, I would like you to get in touch with your restraint. Could you better feel your restraint now? Feel how you're holding in. Try to increase your restraint. Feel it?

F: Well, I'm not trying to increase the restraint.

Th: Well, become aware of it. Pay more attention to it.

F: (*Silence*) I feel restrained or cautious.

Th: Okay, now I'd like you to see if you could try on being your restraint. With the words, "I am going to be restrained with you and cautious with you," let's become better acquainted with your restraint.

F: I don't know what to say . . . I just feel tight.

Th: (*Silence*) I want you to get in touch with that. To me, that's the important part of you right now.

F: (*Silence*) How do you mean—get in touch with the tightness?

Th: Describe it. Where is it.

F: I'm holding my breath part of the time . . .

Th: Go on.

F: (*After a brief silence*) I don't really understand what you're aiming at.

Th: Can you ignore that for the moment and just attend to your own body sensations.

F: (*Obviously trying*) Doesn't seem that I can.

Th: (*Silence*) All right, let's experiment with something else. Could you close your eyes, and let your imagination go—like looking at a movie. See if you can observe what might happen here if you abandoned your restraint.

F: (*Silence*) It would have to be in relation to something else happening, not just sitting here quietly myself. The restraint has to be in relationship to something, to an activity or conversation or something going on.

All experiments fail. He obviously cannot identify with, or as, his restraint although he is sincerely trying.

The attempted experiments revealed his need to cling to words in a most literal fashion in preference to exploring the more subtle substance of their meaning or becoming involved with his own person. He wants to cooperate with me but cannot let go of me long enough to succeed. He is like a man being urged to jump from a burning building—knowing that the fireman is correct yet unable to just let go.

I feel he is allowing himself to become vulnerable now and I feel protective and find myself speaking softly.

Th: I have the feeling that you are so tied to me and to being here right now that you can't withdraw from us and allow yourself a little fantasy or to know your own body sensations.

F: I feel all very close in with this thing right here, trying. . . .

Th: I'm also aware of your restraint, and I'd like to help you with it.

F: But I cannot at this moment separate myself with a dream-like thing of myself and go off and look at the whole thing and see what will happen.

Th: All right. Stop trying so hard. If you can't leave me, is there something you can tell me that you would like from me? I want to help you to diminish your restraint. (*he looks thoughtful and says nothing*) Is there anything that you can ask me for, or of any one member of your family, is there any one of us here that could help you with your restraint? Or help you to get rid of it? It seems to be like you're in chains.

F: I don't see how because it seems important to me to use restraint and self-control.

Th: Are you saying that you don't want to give it up? Do you want me to leave you alone so you can keep your restraint? You don't want me to keep working at it, is that what you are saying?

F: No. I want you to keep working at it, although I'm not sure how you can get where you're aiming at with me because I don't seem to be giving you much help at the moment.

Th: (*Ignoring his apology, I hear his wish to continue*) You seem to cling to your restraint like it was a life jacket.

F: You know that's exactly it. A long time ago, I worked up this sort of protective feeling, that by not showing too much of my emotion with self-control, then I'm not going to be expected to hurt that much. And so that is a very integral part of me and of my make-up.

Th: So really, what you are saying is that you must be restrained with all of us because you are afraid that we might hurt you.

F: Not specifically this group. I think it is a habit or a protective color. It is part of me, from back in junior college days.

Th: Is there some scene that comes to mind?

Deciding to permit distance from nowness.

F: Yeah! It goes back to early romance, getting jilted by somebody, and then after that deciding that (*pause*) not showing emotion or having more self-control over my own emotions, I would be less likely to be hurt than I would otherwise. Throughout the years I've kept that and used it, or misused it sometimes.

Th: So you didn't cry then either?

F: Yeah. That's the type of thing, yes. At least not when someone else was around. I might in my own privacy. If I were hurt I would know, but other people wouldn't know it. At least they would not have the additional joy of being able to hurt. (after long silence) That's the way I feel about it. There is the physical part, the physical feeling of sitting sort of hunched in; and there is the emotional part. I think they are tied in together.

Th: You are suddenly quite eloquent. Yes, they are tied together. And what I am also aware of is the sadness that lies on the other side of your restraint. In other words, what I hear you saying is that you are restraining yourself from sharing your sadness, your vulnerability.

F: I think vulnerability is a very good word.

Now he is finally "negotiable." So I want to turn him towards his wife.

Th: Have you ever talked with your wife about that?

F: No.

Th: Could you now? Tell her how important it is that you protect yourself, that you not be vulnerable to the possibilities. . . .

F: (Arms down, leaning forward on chair) That would make me more vulnerable right there. If I share this feeling with somebody else, I feel then they are going to know that much more about me so they would have an advantage shall we say.

Th: An advantage? What's the advantage that you give?

F: If somebody else knows that actually I can be hurt, whereas before they thought I couldn't be hurt, then that would be their advantage, that they would know that it is possible to hurt.

Th: I wonder if we don't really all know that, already.

F: (Laughingly) Kind of discouraging after all these years of shell building sort of.

Th: You want to ask her?

F: (Testing for reassurance) She is frowning.

M: (Reassuringly) It was just a listening frown.

F: Did you know about this protective shell thing?

M: Yes, sure.

F: (*To himself with a wistful smile*) Well, so much for all that work all these years.

M: You didn't surely think that you could build up a shell like that, and I wouldn't be aware of it? I don't know how to get through it, but I certainly know it's there.

F: I never really thought about it in that respect. . . . I don't self-consciously use that shell as much as initially. Initially it was something I was very conscious of trying to do, and since then it has just been a built-in part of me. (*looking tentatively at his wife*) I see something is going on in that head over there. What?

M: You . . . you use it all the time. That's why it's so hard to talk to you, and the reason I was making faces was that I was not going to say anything unless you asked me.

Th: (*Feeling extremely protective of him at this time*) You're picking at him. What is it you would like to say about yourself in relation to him? What can you say to that pretend wall of invulnerability of his?

M: It baffles me, and I think the reason I have nothing to say to it is that I don't feel I am talking to the person inside, I don't . . . No! I don't . . . (*to therapist*) You'll have to help me.

Th: Okay, let me lay out a little map . . . my fantasy . . . I'll share it with you but you don't have to buy it. What I see is that he is now saying to you something from behind that wall of invulnerability. Usually you talk to him, but you aren't really talking to him. You're talking to his wall of invulnerability that he's built up through the years. So the answers you get back really just bounce off the wall. And you've been frustrated bumping against that wall, thinking you were really talking to that man behind the wall. In effect, today he says to you, "I have a wall of vulnerability that I keep in front of me for fear of being hurt." Now he is saying something, not as the wall, but rather dares to speak as the fearful man behind the wall. He has now shared something of his vulnerable person with you. There are now two things out there that you are looking at: the man and his wall. They are no longer fused when you say, "*It* baffles me," you talk to the wall.

M: Well, but it's a package, he . . .

Th: (*Interrupting*) It's been a package.

M: But it is still. I knew that it was there, I know that it is something he needs and does on purpose.

Th: I'm disappointed that you didn't see what I saw today: a crack in his wall and a glimpse of the man behind it. That he is able to say to you, in effect, "I'm afraid to be vulnerable," is, to me, quite an achievement. Tell me, do you feel any differently towards him now than you did at the beginning of the session?

M: No.

Th: You feel pretty much the same?

M: Yes, yes I really do, I really do.

Th: Well, I needed that knowledge but I don't know what to do with it at the moment. I feel so differently towards him now.

M: I hear a lot of words, while you hear something else.

Th: Have you heard those words before: that he has felt vulnerable?

M: Yes.

Th: Yet he says . . .

M: No, he's said that before.

F: I didn't think so.

Th: Perhaps he's never felt it when he's said it before.

M: Maybe. Maybe, the difference is in him. I've heard those words from him.

Th: (*Noticing her bafflement changing to sadness*) How do you feel right now? (*after a few moments of silence*) You look like you're fighting sadness, am I wrong?

M: (*Starting to cry*) No, no, you are not wrong. I don't feel (*sobs*) I don't feel that *I* am getting anywhere (*pause*) and I hear nothing (*crying*) that gives me the feeling that, that there is going to be a different . . . (*pause*) I am pessimistic about the next week. I, I just don't have, for *me*, the feeling of hope.

F: (*Tenderly*) What difference do you want as such? It concerns me. The things that make you sad and unhappy bother me.

Th: (*To her*) You are holding back your sadness. There's more to all this.

M: I don't know.

Th: (*To him*) Stop asking her so much what she wants and you decide what you want from her.

(*to her*) At this moment I see you more in love with your sadness than with anyone else in your family. I see your sadness as what blinds you from seeing changes, and possibilities for change in your family. I don't hear you asking "Now, what am I going to do to help impinge? What did I learn today that I am going to use to be more effective next week? Is there any difference at all?" None of this. You just decide there is no difference. You said that to me last time, and I was rankled because it was so obviously untrue to me.

M: I know that.

Th: For instance, what Don was able to say to his father was different. They both acknowledged that it was different, yet to you there was no difference. Something blinds you from seeing differences, and I think it's your veil of tears, that you seem to delight in.

M: I'm not sure that that's so, although it's possible, there is something in the way. Maybe that's what it is, I'm really not sure. I'm really not sure. But what I see is (pause) . . . is flashes of something that might go somewhere like what Don was able to say last time. But (pause) if, if they can have that, and then if we can go back to a week of making all the same mistakes we did before (bursts into tears) and I can't do anything about it . . . That's one of the things that I think bothers me. Certainly it's one of the things that makes me sad when I think about it.

F: Well, I don't think we went back to making all the same mistakes.

Th: (Dismissing his reassurance—to her) What makes you say sad?

M: That I can't do anything, I can't help them, I can't make it any different.

Th: Tell them how much you want to, right now! Tell each of them. Start with your husband.

M: What could I say that I haven't already said?

Th: What you just said. What you just said to me.

M: (After very long silence, to husband) I want you really to try to do something different. It isn't a question of whether it's right or wrong, I just want you to try to do something different. It is not enough for me that you say . . .

Th: (Interrupting with astonishment) But that wasn't what you told me. You were telling me how you wanted to be different. How you wish that you could help more. That's what I understood you saying to me.

M: Yes, I want to help them, I want to do something for them.

Th: But that isn't what you are saying to him. You are saying something quite different to him. You are picking at him instead of talking to him like you were talking to me. Quite a different message.

M: (To husband) Yes, it is. But I do want to help you.

F: I personally feel that I have such a low priority. The kids' priority is better than mine, but not that much compared to so many other outside activities that seem to be so much more important than the family. Much more important to do things for the other groups, more often than for us.

M: You say that but, but that doesn't help me to help.

F: If it were possible . . .

M: What can I do?

F: Look now, the basics: dishes, ironing, things like that.

M: That doesn't help.

F: Yes, it does, because it is very discouraging for me and for the family—at least I know Don sometimes feels that way—to come home and find that, since you had been out for one of the activities you are working on, doing so much more for them, that the house is not a welcome place to come home to physically. Yet knowing . . .

Th: (Interrupting) Do you speak for yourself? In terms of the first person, like, "I don't feel welcome."

F: It's not a case of not feeling welcome. It's a case of coming home and Mother is trying to do too much. I always have the feeling that if something is not going to get done, it's going to be something for the family or the household, rather than the nurseries or Cub Scouts or things like that. I feel that you are trying to do so much more than you have time for, that they have a higher priority. You are going to be doing something for them because you feel nobody else will do it for them, and we can more or less take care of ourselves. And we can survive with the conditions at home, whereas no one else is going to help out these other people and do it for them. I get the strong feeling that they are more important.

Th: (To husband) When you started to talk all the good feeling that I was beginning to generate just disappeared. (to wife) I don't know if you experienced that. I noticed you stopped crying.

M: Yes, yes.

Th: (To husband) You didn't experience anything like I experienced? You couldn't tell by her wiping up her tears and sitting back that you were really turning her off?

F: I'm not sure I was reaching her, sort of . . .

Th: I want to share with you what was going on within me. I felt that she was beginning to get close to saying something to you about her wish to be helpful to you. It was coupled with a feeling of failure; that she has really failed you as a wife; that she hasn't been that person that she would like to be in the family. Again, I'm introducing my fantasies now. It doesn't mean it is true, and ... (*to her*) you listen and check it out, Mother. (*back to him*) That's where I saw it going. She was beginning to really talk with you in a vulnerable area of hers, as you had come close to earlier. But somehow you didn't hear that part and what you did was, sort of, came in and started to criticize her, which is what I would see as having turned off the feeling. (*to her*) Does that make any sense at all to you, or am I way out?

M: Yeah, Yeah. That makes sense. That's right.

Th: (*To her*) I would like you to know that this fear that you have of talking so intimately with him is the same kind of fear that he was talking about earlier when he was speaking of his vulnerability. And in a sense I don't blame either one of you for being a little cautious with the other one, because each of you has a wall that not only keeps other people from seeing in but that keeps each of you from seeing out. Walls work both ways, and it's not just his wall that gets in your way, but it's also your own fear of being vulnerable. It's very difficult for you to talk with him. It's much easier for you to tell me how you wanted to help and be more to your family. But your wall was there and you weren't able to say that to him.

I don't want to go any farther today, and I don't want either of you to take any homework assignments either. You all needn't try to think about all this and work on anything.

F: You can't help but think about ...

Th: Fine, just let whatever happens, happen. What I am saying is don't force it. You all might want to spend some time together just sitting around and exploring some of what we talked about today, each of you becoming more familiar with your own wall. It is voluntary. We've all worked hard today.

This was the crucial working session. Father was confronted and became negotiable, only to find his wife not ready yet to emerge from behind her martyred wall of tears. She too was then confronted.

10

Interview Three

Most of our work was done during the second interview. This session, though extremely valuable, was largely a rounding out, an integrating, a gratifying closure.

Mother: I really have been thinking, and I want to say something to you, because I was really stupid last time and I owe you an apology for being so dense. You gave me a lot of help and a lot of useful things. It was two hours after we left you that I realized that I had been sitting here waiting for the others to change, to change for me, and that I really wasn't listening to what I could do, or to what you were saying to help me. So I have been doing a lot of thinking. I really didn't want to hear about different ways I could do things. I only wanted to hear about different ways they could be for me.

Therapist: It sounds like you owe yourself a word of appreciation for your recognition rather than an apology to me.

M: You asked me for something, and you had done something to help me, and I didn't even listen to what was going on.

Th: Well, if you appreciate it, the appreciation I want is not an apology but effective behavior.

264

M: Well, I think you have got that.

Th: I'll see. Do you feel that you are functioning differently?

M: (*Smiling*) Uh huh.

Th: Do you people feel that way?

Father: It is very obvious she is making an effort.

Don: Well, I think she is doing more with the family instead of giving herself out to everybody.

Th: (*To mother*) I see. Do you like your family better? Do you feel that? I don't want to put words in your mouth.

M: That isn't quite right, but I can't think of better words. I feel more comfortable with them, it is better, yes.

> *Following this, Steve, originally the identified patient, tackles Father's temper tantrums, admitting that by contrast he, Steve, gets "mad inside" and walks away. This is a critical topic and pertinent to Steve's frustration behavior that precipitated the consultation.*

Th: (*To Steve*) I like arguing better than walking out. I like talking about what I am mad about.

Steve: I do, too. But I can't.

M: (*To therapist*) Even when everybody is tired and angry, you think it is better to stand around and yell at each other if necessary?

Th: I believe it can help to get it out. I like to stand and rave. Then I don't *have* to walk out. If I want to I *can*. It is then optional.

M: Don't you say things that later you regret?

Th: Oh, absolutely. It's no fun otherwise. Of course I say things I don't mean, that is the whole object of it. We have a rule at our house: What you say in anger doesn't count.

F: That's easy to say, but still someone is going to remember it.

Th: Only if they have not gotten angry back and didn't finish their business: Then they strike back later by remembering.

M: And that really works that way?

Th: It does for me.

F: Let's talk about last night, 'cause that's what this conversation is all about. When I came home, my wife wasn't there. She had left a message with the boys that she'd be late because of traffic at the airport. The message seemed vague to me and, as time passed, I became increasingly upset. I tried not to get upset, since she had a good reason for being late. Is it your theory that I should have blown up anyway?

Th: Yes. Wonderful. Get it out of your system. Feelings don't know about reasonableness. Since you are deterred by reasonableness, there is no place for your open anger in this family. So you will store them up and blow up later at Steve, for instance, over something trivial.

F: That's exactly what happens.

Th: It's inevitable. Your wife has a different trick. She follows that house rule that says, "You can't get angry if a good excuse is provided" and then becomes depressed and pouts.

M: That's also true.

F: (*To therapist*) But when I do blow up then I feel guilty afterwards.

Th: All that tells me is that you aren't quite finished with your anger. Your reasonableness takes over and you don't know what to do with the remaining anger, so your clever mind whips it around and turns it on you. That's all guilty feelings are. When you really get finished there is nothing to feel badly about. You are still not quite finished, if you feel guilty. Go back for some more.

F: I don't know . . . It goes against the grain. I try to be considerate.

Th: (*Obviously irritated*) How about being considerate of your own feelings?

F: That is what we were working about last week.

Th: Yes, it is the same thing.

F: I haven't thought much along that line. It's very difficult to separate what I really want for myself and what I think I want for myself based on other people's feelings. It is not easy to separate.

Th: (*Angrily*) Feelings are irrational. It is ridiculous to try to make them rational. They aren't. Even right now, as I get irritated with you, I know it isn't rational. What basis do I have to be irritated with you?

F: 'Cause I irritate you.

Th: So what? You're not doing anything to me. What you are doing, you are really doing to yourself. Yet I become irritated, and I refuse to store it up. What do you think would happen if you really got mad and really blew up and just dumped the whole thing on her.

F: A multiple choice. I guess she would have got mad and just blown up back or she would have started weeping and wandered off to the kitchen.

M: (*To therapist*) You said I was putting my sadness between us and you were really right. I thought about the things that made me cry.

I cried quite a lot while I was doing this, but learned something and I don't do it as much anymore. I don't think anybody has noticed. (*to husband*) I don't believe I would have pouted last night. I felt good about what I did, I knew I had to make a choice and I knew you'd be unhappy, but I had a reason for what I did—a reason that I felt was important. I felt all right about it. I wouldn't have minded if anybody yelled at me. I would have told you why I did what I did.

F: But, would I have listened at that stage? I don't think so.

Th: There is nothing to listen to. The object is just to discharge your anger and get rid of it. Whether she gives you a reasonable explanation or not. I am delighted that she said that she wouldn't have been bothered particularly by your anger. But apparently she would have been bothered enough to offer you an explanation back. I would even object to that. I would like you to get to the point where you could have your explosion and have her just sit and laugh at you and not offer you any explanations. After you have cooled down you might want to sit down and have a talk.

M: That is going to take a long time because that bothers me when he or when anybody gets angry.

Th: And you try to turn him off with your tears. That is a very clever device, and a popular one with women.

F: One of the things I don't like is when Mother cries, because that is evidence that she is hurt and I don't like to see her hurt.

They are doing much better. They spontaneously talk to each other more now. Yet there is a bunch of rules by which they live in this family that hampers them. One by one I am attacking them, using the power with which they have ordained me.

Th: (*Sarcastically*) Aw! You are such a nice guy.

F: It is not by conscious choice. It's just the way I feel.

He is saying, "See, I'm not responsible." I ignore that in favor of mapping out mental processes for him (and her also).

Th: I don't think you help her a bit when you behave that way. She really doesn't even cry. She whimpers at you. If she really cries, that would be fine. I would be delighted to let her have her tears. But not to use them to turn other people off. Not to use them. Her tears are for herself. To finish her own sadness.

M: That's right. That's something else I figured out this week. I am entitled to my sadness.

Th: That's right. You are entitled to have your sadness, not to manipulate with it.

M: (*With obvious pride*) I really did figure that out all by myself.

Th: (*Smiling*) You have been working.

M: (*Cheerfully*) Oh, I have. I have indeed.

Th: (*To husband*) So, what else are you a sucker for? You are a sucker for her tears. What else turns you off?

F: I'm so dense that I don't realize a great deal of it.

Th: You are not dense—just overcivilized. Also, you have learned to ignore some of the fine points about human behavior, much as I have learned just the opposite. I don't like to see you criticize yourself for this plight. It was obviously unavoidable while you were growing up. This is no longer true, and I see you struggling diligently to change.

F: (*Thoughtfully*) It sounds like you are saying, anger can be used as a tool for escape, an escape valve. If I don't blow up I get worse and if I just got mad—really mad—once in a while and got rid of it, I'd be better off.

Th: Not once in a while.

F: Whenever necessary.

Th: That is right, whenever you have it. I have a little saying, "Anger is its own reward." Something that I have discovered for myself is that if I get angry about something and can continue to be angry about it and just to try to *maintain* that anger, instead of trying to *curb* it, to persevere with that anger and verbalize it and tell the other person, I eventually find myself in tears. And if I can continue with my anger and sadness, I eventually find myself laughing at myself and . . . Wow! When that happens to me—it is not too often that I can go that far —but when I do, I feel marvelous. I feel so unburdened. That is the kind of atmosphere I want to create in my home.

At this point Father stretches and exclaims, "Aheeee!" I read it as, "This is hard work but I'm trying." Before I have an opportunity to check this out and, if true, urge him not to try so hard, Steve speaks.

S: Dad . . .

F: What? . . . Wait a minute . . . (*to therapist*) I was thinking of the child's right to talk to a parent when he chooses. He has rights, too.

Th: But they aren't the same.

F: I seem to have gone over backwards worrying more about his than about mine.

> *He told Steve to "wait a minute." This is the first time I have witnessed Father's placing his own action above one of the children's. I say nothing about this but observe with delight.*

Th: Exactly.

S: (*Wisely*) Like last night when you were reading the paper. When you finally told me, I stopped. Before that I didn't know I was bothering you that much.

F: Exactly. I could have said that earlier, but was afraid of hurting your feelings, so I tried to listen to what you had to say each time you interrupted my reading.

S: You wouldn't have hurt my feelings, if you just told me.

Th: Good for you, Steve. (*to father*) You don't hurt your children's feelings when you stand up for your rights. You set a good example for them. You teach them self-respect by your example. That's another rule in this family that I can't stand. Hurt feelings can take away anyone's rights. You frequently permit your wife's hurt feelings to take away your rights to your feelings. Don't do it.

F: Another rule we have around our house is that if someone is irritable he should warn us and we'll try to stay out of his way. This is what Steve was referring to. He was just saying I should have warned him.

Th: (*Chuckling*) He's hoisting you by your own petard . . . You people sure have lots of difficult rules about anger in your house. I like you all but I doubt that I could survive for 24 hours in that rule-ridden atmosphere—all geared to depriving me of my spontaneously delightful and irrational anger. Is there anything you want to say to Steve now?

F: Yes. Steve, that rule no longer exists. Beware.

Eureka! Father is taking his rightful place in the family and I am satisfied. His confident "Beware" signaled the end of therapy. Our key goal had been achieved. Many important, though less central aspects, such as Mother's depression and Steve's getting "mad inside," were also changing. A bonus was the rapprochement between Don and Father and Father's developing awareness of psychological matters. But still, best of all, was Father's ringing "Beware" delivered clearly, firmly, lovingly. With this, he became the father in his own home. I was confident that he would "rule" kindly. From the pleased facial expressions of the others when he said it, I knew they agreed.

The remaining few minutes of our session were spent finishing our business with each other. The business consisted largely of appreciative recognition of one another, expressions of the wistful relief and satisfaction we were experiencing from a job well done.

The path unwinding up from despair was first to open the door to admit their previously unacceptable backlog of blinding anger, borne of frustration, manifested by Father as aloofness and temper tantrums directed especially at the children, by Mother as sadness and martyrdom, by the children in what likely and appropriately would be labeled sibling rivalry. Then we proceeded to treat the sources of their frustrations, such as the father's idea that doing for others always takes precedence over asking for what one wants, and their shared premise that concurrence is always better than appreciation of individual differences.

11

Interview Four

By prior agreement we met again three months later.

Father, obviously in command, ushered in his family and, after brief friendly greetings, initiated the discussion with the announcement, "I'm feeling a lot better about myself and my family." He continued his report, "I've noticed a difference in my work too. On occasion I've dared challenge customers and I've been pleasantly surprised at how well things have worked out. I've stopped agreeing with everyone, whether I wanted to or not. My mother, who has meddled in our family for years, is even catching some of my ire. She has been quite unreasonable for years. I can't understand how I put up with her intrusiveness for so long. My wife has been saying this for years and I never knew what she was talking about.

Father: (*To wife*) Mother's holding up pretty well, don't you think?
Mother: (*Smiling*) That's a question.
F: (*Assertively*) I still want your opinion on things.
M: (*Still smiling*) You are so different, it's a pleasure. You're so much happier these days. Even the neighbors commented on it. You're really a lot nicer to be around, and you're right, I could be a lot nicer about some of your questions. Things are much better with

your mother, and I think she's happier, too, now that she's over the initial shock.

F: Yes, I'm grateful that she's done so well.

M: I'm grateful you've done so well.

Therapist: (*To wife*) Enough hearts and flowers. Where are you in all this?

M: I feel much better. I don't know if it shows.

Th: Your smile looks more sincere to me.

M: It is. I feel much better about all of them too (*waving her hand around the room*).

Th: Good. How about you kids? Steve?

Steve: Things are better. I'm more responsible now.

Don: Things have improved 100%.

Th: Like what?

D: Mother and Father get into it now. They've had some big fights, but it all seems to blow over fast. They used to just not talk for days. Now they get over it right away.

Th: I'm delighted to hear that. That's the kind of capable reporting I don't often have the opportunity to get from families.

F: One of the things that's happened to me is that I've begun talking to people about family problems, and they have them, too. It's opened up a whole new world for me. I don't feel so alone like I did before our meetings.

Th: Good.

F: Yesterday, driving with the whole family I remembered your asking me if I ever felt like chucking the whole family (*everyone chuckles*).

Th: Remembering or wishing?

F: We were coming back home from a weekend in the mountains. I was resentful that I had all the responsibility of driving; the traffic was heavy; there was a little trouble with the brakes; it was hot with five people all crowded in the car. I had to get them home safely. No one else was doing a thing. They were all enjoying themselves.

D: I wasn't enjoying myself. I was hot, too.

F: I was aware that I was resentful of responsibility, not of the family.

Th: What did you do with that feeling?

F: I decided to hell with it all.

Th: Did you tell them?

F: No. Everyone was quiet and I didn't want to stir things up.

M: I wish you'd shared those feelings with us. We could have handled them. We couldn't help you with the heat and the traffic, but we maybe could help you with your irritation.

F: I never thought of it that way. (*thoughtfully*) I still have a way to go. (*Pause—then to therapist*) I have moved though. I resigned from a couple of organizations in protest since we've seen you.

> *The next few minutes are spent with the parents successfully discussing father's desire to be nonresponsible and still feeling burdened occasionally. Mother, without guilt or criticism, invites him to acknowledge this more openly as he is doing now. He is speaking about it seriously but without the sense of oppression previously felt.*
>
> *They finish and after a brief silence Steve smiles at Father and says provocatively, "Tell him about the big fight."*

F: (*To therapist*) Everything fell apart. I said everything that was on my mind and went to bed. Next morning I went to work and didn't know if I'd have a family when I got home. I was glad to see them when I got home—and relieved.

M: I really hated you with a passion that night, but it never occurred to me to leave you.

F: I realized all that. (*then after a thoughtful moment*) It's as though I'm still in the process of realizing that.

D: But it was all over so fast. In the past you (*to Father*) would go off half mad and wouldn't talk for days, and you (*to Mother*) would be sad for a long time.

Th: I'm delighted with the bunch of you. But I'm wondering if there is any work to do today.

M: Yes, there is. I still am afraid to let go completely, so instead I go off and build up this big thing about how noble I have been and how great I am until I choose to forgive them. I make them pay for it. I don't mean to do it but I can't seem to help myself.

Th: You poor innocent victim (*everyone laughs*).

M: All right. I'm glad when I do it and I really want to make you all pay, but I still wish I could be different.

F: Now that we're wise to you, I'm sure it won't work as well for you—I won't pay like I used to.

Everyone is quiet, and the subject seems ended. Then Don tells Father, "I don't always get an answer from you" (referring to his wish for explanations when father says, "No"). Father explains in a friendly yet firm fashion, "I don't have to always give you an explanation. I will when I feel it's necessary or advisable."

As the hour concluded we all knew further scheduled visits were unnecessary. It was said amidst warm sounds of departure, possibly never to see one another again. Some weeks later I received a clipping from a magazine from Father which told of Indian tribal customs in Guatemala where families are brought together to solve problems of wayward members. He thought it would be of interest to me.

The atmosphere in this family has changed. These people are now enjoying each other more, are less fearful of one another and much more ready to reveal themselves and negotiate. They have successfully weathered a serious crisis; Father has kept and expanded his position as father; both Mother and Father are admitting and accepting their foibles and both are changing; the children speak up better and also like the family better; Mother's attitude towards Father is dramatically altered. Where she acted martyred before and turned to the children, she now realizes and shares her martyrishness lovingly with her husband.

And just as the sun shines forth in redoubled beauty after the rain, or as a forest grows more freshly green from charred ruins after a fire, so the new era appears all the more glorious by contrast with the misery of the old.

—THE I CHING